Mind Without Fear

Mind Without Fear

Rajat Gupta

JUGGERNAUT BOOKS
C-I-128, First Floor, Sangam Vihar, Near Holi Chowk,
New Delhi 110080, India

First published in hardback by Juggernaut Books 2019
Published in paperback 2022

10 9 8 7 6 5 4 3 2 1

The views and opinions expressed in this book are the author's own. The facts contained herein were reported to be true as on the date of publication by the author to the publishers of the book, and the publishers are not in any way liable for their accuracy or veracity.

P-ISBN: 9789391165871
E-ISBN: 9789393986115

Typeset in Adobe Caslon Pro by R. Ajith Kumar, Noida

Printed at Thomson Press India Ltd

This book is dedicated to three generations of amazing women in my life:

Anita, who has been a true friend and partner for more than fifty years.

Sonu, Megha, Aditi, and Kushy, who add meaning to my life, keep me humble, and make me proud.

Meera and Nisa, who are a constant source of joy and who visited me in prison every week.

Lekha and Riya, whose births have been the happiest events since my release.

Where the mind is without fear and the head is held high;
Where knowledge is free;
Where the world has not been broken up into fragments
by narrow domestic walls;
Where words come out from the depth of truth;
Where tireless striving stretches its arms towards perfection;
Where the clear stream of reason has not lost its way
into the dreary desert sand of dead habit;
Where the mind is led forward by thee
into ever-widening thought and action—
Into that heaven of freedom, my Father, let my country awake.

—Rabindranath Tagore, *Gitanjali*

Contents

Preface

Westport, Connecticut, January 2019

I am an orphan. Immigrant. Businessman. Leader. Philanthropist. Role model. Convicted felon. If you read the business press you might have followed my story, which captured the public's attention during 2011 and 2012. Here is the version most people heard, summed up in three headlines:

> "A Stunning Fall from Grace for a Star Executive."
> —*The New York Times*, October 26, 2011
>
> "Rajat Gupta Guilty of Insider Trading."
> —*The Washington Post*, June 15, 2012
>
> "McKinsey, Goldman, jail."
> —*The Economist*, October 25, 2012

Hundreds of articles have been written about my case, as well as two books, detailing how I was charged and found guilty of insider trading in June of 2012. But my side of the story has never been told. I never spoke to the press or gave interviews to those writing books. Most critically, to my great regret, I chose not to testify at my own trial. Consequently, the jury, the press, and the public saw only, as my lawyer put it, a "cropped picture." The judge went out of his way to block any reference to my character and to the aspects of my work that mattered most to me. The prosecutors were skillful in manipulating the press. And I missed that opportunity to tell my own story, and to let the jury, and the public, see who I am directly. For that, I take full responsibility.

This book is that story. It's a much bigger story than the courtroom drama that unfolded in the summer of 2012 and the tumultuous years leading up to it. I am in the eighth decade of my life, and my primary intent is to share the lessons I have learned from the interesting and in many ways extraordinary journey I have taken. From Kolkata to Delhi to Harvard to New York to Scandinavia and to every corner of the world. From humble beginnings to global influence. From consultant to leader to business statesman and humanitarian. From respect and authority to suspicion and disgrace. From freedom to incarceration to freedom again. Like any life, mine has had its ups and downs, its struggles and triumphs, its dark nights and its bright mornings. And some of the most precious lessons of my life were found in the unlikeliest of places—like the jail cell where I began writing this book.

My intent, in these pages, is not to protest my innocence or seek redemption. The justice system found me guilty of a crime and I have served my time and paid my dues. I can never reclaim the greatest costs of this episode: the years of my life it took away, the friendships lost, the reputation destroyed, and the important work put aside. I know that I did not commit the crime, but I also know that I would not be the man I am today had I not gone through this painful series of events. It perhaps would have been easy to say "why me?" and indulge in self-pity and victimization, but I prefer to accept what has happened and strive to become a better person as a result of those experiences. All of it has brought into sharper focus the trajectory of my entire life, illuminating the philosophy and values that have guided it.

Like anyone who has lived a full life, I have some regrets. The one that haunts me most is my choice not to take the stand. Could I have persuaded the jury that the charges against me were false? I honestly don't know. It's hard to prove a negative. And in those years following the financial crisis, when so many hard-working people were suffering its devastating consequences, it was all too easy to ascribe guilt to anyone connected to the financial industry. Had I testified, perhaps I could at least have filled in many of the blanks and added all-important explanations for events which, taken out of context, seemed much more damning than they were. Perhaps I could have demonstrated that the crimes with which I was charged made no sense in the context of my life, my motives, and my values. Perhaps I could have convinced the men and women of the jury that I was a human being guilty of nothing more than an all-too-human misjudgment of character, and not the caricature of Wall Street greed that was being drawn by the prosecution. But I will never know. In the end, the prosecutor told a good story—not a true story, but a believable one, given the climate of the time. And in my silence, I did not offer a better story.

Not too long ago, I took my twin granddaughters to the US Open tennis tournament. We were strolling between the courts when two strangers approached me—both Indians in their twenties. "It's so good to see you here," one of them said. "You've been a role model for us. I hope you are doing well." We chatted for a couple of minutes, and they took some pictures with me, before we went our separate ways. If I think about who I would most like to read this book, it's people like them. People who encountered my story or my work, who were inspired by my values or my success and confused or disheartened by my downfall. People who have been wondering: Why did this happen? And how is he doing? Perhaps they will see parts of their own life story reflected in mine. Perhaps they will learn a lesson or two about what to do and what not to do.

This book is also for my granddaughters, who asked me, "Nana, who were those people? Why did they want to take pictures with you?" They were too young to understand the drama that erupted in the heart of their family during the first few years of their lives, or to realize where they were when they visited me, week after week, in prison. But as they get older, I would like them to have the full story, even when I am no longer here to tell it.

I've been out of jail now for three years, reorienting myself to a new phase of my life, coming to terms with my losses and appreciating my many blessings more deeply than ever before. With my sentence behind me and my legal appeals done, it feels like the time has finally come to speak out. Many doors are now closed to me, but many others have opened. I feel the possibility of doing something completely new—something I might never have experienced had I continued on the path I was on. I have made peace with my past and look to my future with a "mind without fear and a head held high," to quote one of my favorite poets, Rabindranath Tagore. I consider this book my testimony, and this time I have no hesitation about taking the stand.

Part I

Crisis

O Krishna, drive my chariot between the two armies.
I want to see those who desire to fight with me.
With whom will this battle be fought?

—Bhagavad Gita, 1:21–22

1

Solitary

Let me not beg for the stilling of my pain,
but for the heart to conquer it. . . .
Let me not crave in anxious fear to be saved,
but hope for the patience to win my freedom.

—Rabindranath Tagore, *Fruit-Gathering*, 79

FMC Devens correctional facility, Massachusetts, October 2014

Four concrete walls and a cold concrete floor. One small window but not enough light to read. A steel door with a grimy plastic window and a small slot in the center, locked shut. A narrow metal bunk with sharp edges, fixed to the wall, and a metal toilet with no seat or curtain for privacy. This was to be my home for the foreseeable future, which wasn't really foreseeable at all. I had no idea how long they would keep me in the "special housing unit" or SHU—a prison euphemism for solitary confinement.

It was a shoelace, of all things, that landed me here. I bent down to tie it, right as the Corrections Officer (CO) came by for the "stand-up count." A few seconds earlier or later and I'd have been fine, standing to attention outside my bunk in the prison camp, as I did every morning at precisely ten, every afternoon at four, and every night at ten. The rotating blue light on the ceiling flashed to alert us that the guard was about to begin his walk through the dormitory, counting each inmate. The rules specify you must be standing straight, and not move or speak during the count. While technically I wasn't upright, there was no way that my improper stance had impeded his ability to count me.

But it didn't really matter. If it hadn't been this it would have been something else. As I've learned the hard way, if someone in a position of unchecked power wants to lock you up, they can come up with an excuse to do so. It doesn't take much at all. A moment of carelessness. A misjudgment. Bad timing.

I was jailed on June 17, 2014, for the crime of securities fraud, generally known as insider trading. In my case, specifically, I had been charged with being part of a conspiracy to pass privileged "nonpublic" information about Goldman Sachs and Procter & Gamble (P&G), two organizations on whose boards I sat, to Galleon hedge fund manager Raj Rajaratnam, who then bought or sold stock in those companies and made a profit, based on his "inside" knowledge.

There was no such conspiracy. Although I did not know it at the time, Rajaratnam had indeed cultivated an extensive network of insiders, each of whom he compensated well for providing him with tips. But I was never one of them. I did no trading in either of those stocks, I received no payments, and made no money. Raj was a business colleague (a poor choice, on my part, but not a criminal one) and my calls to him during 2008 and 2009 were all made in that context.

To prove insider trading, as it is legally defined, the government needed to prove three things: one, that I passed nonpublic information to Rajaratnam; two, that I did so as part of an explicit quid pro quo agreement in which I knew he would trade on it; and, three, that I received some benefit in return. They had evidence of none of these—no wiretap recordings of information being passed, no emails, no money trail, and no direct witnesses. Rajaratnam himself was never formally charged with illegally trading either Goldman or P&G, although in 2011 he was charged with and found guilty of insider trading in numerous other stocks, including Google, Polycom, Hilton, and Intel. The logic of charging me with these violations when they did not have evidence enough to charge the man who allegedly profited from them baffles me to this day. Moreover, no one could come up with a reasonable explanation for why I, a trusted advisor to countless corporations who had held sensitive insider information for decades, would suddenly decide to betray my fiduciary duties, and for no personal benefit. And yet I was found guilty, fined heavily, and sentenced by the judge to twenty-four-months' imprisonment. The basis of my conviction was a handful of circumstantial interactions and hearsay statements that an overly zealous prosecutor spun into a conspiratorial narrative—one that was all too easy for a jury to believe in the wake of the financial crisis.

How did I end up labeled "the recognizable public face of the financial industry's greed," as one television anchor put it on the day of my arrest?[1] I am an immigrant, born in Kolkata, one of the first wave of Indians to make their way to the US after the Civil Rights Act paved the way for landmark immigration law reform in the mid-1960s. When I arrived, in 1971, to attend Harvard Business School, I was one of only four Indians in my class. With few role models, I rose to the top of my field, becoming a consultant at the storied firm McKinsey & Company and working there for decades, eventually being elected the first non-American-born head of the firm. At the time of the charges, I'd already served my maximum term of nine years as McKinsey's leader, and was still consulting part-time, while pursuing new opportunities in private equity and spending more than half of my time on global philanthropic causes. I also served on several prominent corporate boards, including Goldman Sachs and P&G.

In the eyes of the prosecutor, the Justice Department, and the general public, I was a big fish—a high-profile businessman with connections to the titans of industry and government. The Occupy Wall Street protesters who cheered my arrest didn't care that I'd had nothing to do with the sub-prime mortgage meltdown that had triggered the financial crisis. Almost no one directly responsible for the crisis had been charged, and, meanwhile, ordinary Americans were losing their homes and their jobs. Now, finally, there was someone in the dock who was associated with major brands and household names. I was an easy target at a time when the public was desperate for someone—anyone—to be held accountable.

Bad Guy

"You don't really like it here, do you?"

The Corrections Officer, a dour, heavyset man with a florid complexion, sat behind his desk, typing something on his computer. Following the shoelace incident, I had immediately made my way to speak to him, hoping to apologize and explain myself. Through the glass wall behind him, I could see into the TV room, which doubles as a visitors' room on weekends. Just that afternoon, I had passed several hours there with Aditi, the third of my four daughters, catching up with her life. I'd listened empathetically to her stories, advised her on her career, and done my best to play a father's role despite my circumstances. I treasured this kind of one-on-one time with my girls, even if it took place in a glass-walled room under fluorescent lights, amid a hubbub of conversations and vending machines. Now, with the visitors gone, the TV was turned back on, though the inmates seemed much more interested in peering through the window at my visit with the CO than in watching whatever inane show was playing on the screen.

The CO's question struck me as odd. *Like it here?* I wasn't aware we were supposed to like being in jail. And no, I didn't exactly like it. But I suspected that the CO's frustration with me actually stemmed from the fact that I was more content than most. Yes, I had many dark days, revisiting every detail of the events that landed me here, second-guessing my choices, agonizing over my mistakes. Yet in a curious way,

I was quite happy, day-to-day, at the prison camp. I'd found a kind of equanimity in my daily routine. I walked for miles each morning on the track, enjoying the mild fall weather and the beauty of the surrounding foliage. I had friends. I played card games and Scrabble. I'd started a book club and a bridge club. There was a group of over-sixty guys with whom I'd eat breakfast and try to solve the world's problems. Every weekend I had visitors—there were a hundred names on my list, which I knew irked my counselor. I followed the rules, as best I could, but I didn't walk around like a repentant criminal. I felt more like a political prisoner.

So I knew full well that this reprimand wasn't about my ill-timed shoe tying—it was an attempt to break my spirit. The guards took my intact dignity as a personal affront. They weren't bad people, but they were keenly attuned to the dynamics of power and they expected inmates to be subservient. This particular guard was actually one of the more benign characters—he'd been there forever and rarely left his desk. There was only one thing he cared about: the count. "If you mess with the count, you disrespect him," my fellow inmates had told me. "Don't mess with the count and you'll be okay."

I apologized to the CO for my mistake and assured him it would not happen again, but he shook his head. "I warned you," he said. "I warned you." This was true—I had been a few seconds late for the count once before, lost in thought over a tricky move on a Scrabble board, and I had gotten off with a warning. Clearly, there would be no leniency this time around. He was writing up an incident report, he informed me, and I would be called in due course. Dismissed, I made my way to dinner. I knew I should eat, because if I was to be taken to the SHU there was no knowing when my next half-decent meal would be, but I felt sick to my stomach and could barely manage a few bites.

My mind was occupied with my upcoming visits—my wife, Anita, was due to come the next day with my other three daughters, Geetanjali (known as Sonu), Megha, and Deepali (known as Kushy). Two friends were flying in from Germany and India the following week. Would I be allowed to see them? And would my family worry about me even more when they heard? I knew I could cope; I was not sure I could convince them that I could cope. When the announcement blared out telling me to report to the CO's office, I left my largely untouched dinner and set out to learn my fate.

The CO handed me the incident report he had written up, and asked me if it was accurate. It stated, correctly, that I had been tying my shoelace, but also that I had been listening to music, which I had not. Trying to adopt a deferential tone, but determined not to play his game, I told him that essentially it was accurate, but some details were wrong.

"So you're disagreeing with me?"

"No," I said carefully, "some of the details are incorrect, but I guess it does not matter. It is true that I was not standing for the count." His expression made it clear that I had failed his test—I was not supposed to challenge his version of events.

"The disciplinary unit will decide on your punishment," he told me, "but if I were you, I would get ready to go to the SHU." Turning back to his computer, he left no doubt that our conversation was over.

Back at my bunk, I was inundated with advice from long-time inmates, many of them veterans of the SHU.

"Take a shower, while you can."

"Put away your valuables."

"Call your wife."

"Give your wife's number to a friend so he can call her."

"Eat."

I sat, frozen, the information coming at me too fast to process. The small cubicle, with its two bunks, two closets, two footlockers, and two chairs, suddenly felt like a home of sorts, compared to what awaited me at the SHU. I felt a strange pang at the thought of leaving it. Quickly, I gathered my few important possessions—my spare eyeglasses and my music player—and gave them to a friend for safekeeping. Before I had time to call Anita, I was summoned to the guards' office.

Here, I was handcuffed. When I asked to use a restroom, the guards said no. After some time, one of the guards appeared with three plastic bags containing all my belongings, which he threw down carelessly on one side of the office. I wondered if I would see them again, and was grateful my friend had the things that mattered to me.

Eventually, four guards marched me to my new accommodations. I was put in a holding cell, strip-searched, and given an orange SHU uniform to wear. The entire process seemed unnecessarily rough and dehumanizing. I was not referred to by name; rather, they called me "the bad guy." Still handcuffed, I was taken to my cell, where they locked me in and then instructed me to stick my hands through a small slot in the door so they could remove the cuffs. I asked if I could make a phone call to Anita and let her know not to come, but I was told "maybe next week." Next week? My family were coming tomorrow, driving several hours to see me. The guard just shrugged. "So?" he asked as he walked away. I was left alone, sitting on the small steel stool, to adjust to my new surroundings and wrestle with the sense of injustice that once again threatened to overwhelm me.

Involuntary Simplicity

The cell was in fact not unfamiliar, since this was not the first time I'd been in the SHU. Four months earlier, on my arrival at FMC Devens, I'd spent my first few nights in an identical cell, before being transferred to the "camp" as the minimum security facility was known. I had hoped I would never be back here. Every inmate knows, however, that you can end up in the SHU at any time, for any reason. Friends would suddenly disappear for days, sometimes weeks, returning with a gaunt, haunted look and a heightened subservience to the guards. Now, it was my turn. Frustrated, I lay back on the lumpy, plastic-covered mattress, squashed to less than an inch thick by the weight of previous occupants, and closed my eyes.

As they often had during my imprisonment, my thoughts turned to my father. He too had spent many months confined to a cell. Although the context was completely different, I drew strength from his memory. More than seventy years earlier, Ashwini Gupta had been a freedom fighter on the front lines of India's struggle for independence. He was jailed repeatedly by the British and suffered greatly at their hands. As a child, I remember staring at the knotted scar running the length of his back. When I was old enough to understand, he told me he had been beaten in jail until the flesh split open. The poor medical care he received left him with one leg shorter than the other, by almost two inches, and a permanent limp. Another scar commemorated the surgery that removed one of his lungs after a severe case of tuberculosis almost killed him. His British overlords had deliberately locked him up with a TB patient so that he too would become infected with the disease, fully intending that, like so many others, he would die in prison, suffering and alone.

He never said much about that episode—indeed, it was only much later in life that I learned the full story from other family members, including the fact that his infection had not been accidental. He only survived because, by a stroke of fate, one of the jailers in the prison where he lay racked by fever turned out to be an old friend and classmate, now working for the British. Seeing my father close to death, he arranged for an ambulance to take him to hospital, and also contacted his sister, my aunt, who came to care for him. If it had not been for that man, my father would have died in that cell.

Born in Kolkata in 1908, my father was a proud Bengali who exemplified the intellectual prowess and fiery, independent spirit of his people. His own health, safety, and happiness were never a primary concern in the fight for independence. Although he met my mother, Pran Kumari, in his early thirties, they were only wed in early 1947, when independence was visible on the horizon. My sister Rajashree (who I call Didi, meaning older sister) was born before the year was out, and I followed on December 2, 1948, with my second sister, Jayashree (known as Kumkum), arriving two years later. My younger brother, Kanchan (known as Anjan), completed the family six years later, after we moved to New Delhi. My father became a celebrated journalist and confidant to the country's leaders, and we lived in an apartment provided by the newspaper where he worked.

One of my most vivid memories of my father is that he always wore a *dhoti* (a traditional garment made from homespun cotton cloth, which is wrapped around the waist and looped between the legs) and a traditional shirt on top. He explained to me that this simple choice of clothing was a symbol of his values—it represented a rejection of imported foreign goods and an embrace of Indian tradition, and it also reflected his Gandhian commitment to simplicity. He owned only three such outfits, and each day he would wash one by hand while he took his morning shower and then wear the second, saving the third for travel.

My father's character haunted my thoughts as I lay in my own prison cell. The ideals that shaped his life were freedom, learning, high thinking, and simple living. Generosity to those in need, forgiveness to those who did him wrong. Never once did I hear him express a hint of bitterness or resentment toward the British, who had inflicted such suffering upon him.

In many ways our situations could not have been more different—he was jailed for a noble cause and a high-minded ideal; I was jailed for alleged personal gain, for a fabricated white-collar crime, and, at most, a careless mistake. Yet one of the lessons he taught me was that while we cannot always control what happens to us, we can control our own attitude in response. In this sense, I was determined to strive to be like him: to be free of bitterness and anger, to not think ill of my captors, and to bear my situation with grace and dignity. Thinking of him also reminded me that many people suffer much more harshly in incarceration than I did. While not pleasant, especially in the SHU, the conditions of my own confinement were certainly better than those he had endured and those many endure in the US prison system today.

My father moved through the world with detachment, never holding on too tightly to his accomplishments, his possessions, or his feelings. When it came to our family, often it was up to my mother to temper his generosity toward others in order to ensure our well-being. She would secretly save money so he could not give it away. From a certain perspective, I had lived an opposite life to his, blessed with wealth and comforts, enjoying my influence and access, always busy and on the move. But in deeper ways my life had been shaped by his values—helping others, improving society, serving my country. I'd always striven to be a "servant leader"—in my family, my school, my college, and the many institutions in which I've worked.

Now that my worldly goods had been stripped away, some part of me felt that the enforced austerity of prison existence might offer an opportunity to return to my core values. Was this a message from God telling me I needed to change my way of life? Had I been too driven, too busy, too focused on making a bigger impact? If this had not happened, would I have just continued the same way for another decade or more? Was it time to simplify—to focus on the inner life, to spend more time with my family, to slow down?

From the moment I'd surrendered to the prison camp, I had decided to approach my incarceration as if I were entering a monastery. I would live in the present moment, make it a learning experience, and try to help others who were less fortunate. With my father's example to guide me, I was determined to emerge a better and stronger person—physically, mentally, and spiritually. My prison uniform would become my *dhoti*, and I would wear it with pride.

Counting Days

When I awoke in the SHU, after an uncomfortable night, I had no idea what time it was. It was light outside, but the tiny window did not allow me to see the height of the sun. Had I missed breakfast? The guard could have come by while I was sleeping. I was hungry, and the thought of waiting till lunch was unpleasant. Thankfully, breakfast came, thrust abruptly through the slot in the door. A bread roll, some dry cereal, a small carton of milk, and a Styrofoam cup containing powdered coffee. I pressed the button by the sink for hot water, but the best I could get was lukewarm. I forced myself to eat the tasteless fare, knowing that it was all I'd be getting for a while.

I wondered how long I would be held in solitary. The guards did not seem to feel any obligation to inform me of their intentions. I was at their mercy, and any inquiry or complaint was likely to simply extend my confinement. The walls of every SHU cell bear witness to this cruel practice of indefinite punishment: Rows of scratches marking days and weeks, faded lists of dates that chart the fading morale of past occupants. A United Nations Special Rapporteur on Torture found that holding someone in solitary confinement for more than fifteen days is equivalent to torture and can lead to trauma.[2] One set of markings on the wall of my cell recorded fifty-one days.

On my second day, I heard a knock on my door. I looked up at the small window and saw a pair of eyes, and a hand beckoning me to come. At a brief glance, I saw empathy in those eyes, and so I was surprised, when I got closer, to discover that they belonged to the CO who had sent me here. He seemed uncomfortable, and I wondered if he felt bad about his actions.

"Are you doing all right?" he asked me.

What does he want now? I wondered. Hasn't he done enough damage already? Wary of walking into another of his traps, but wanting to believe that what I saw in his eyes was concern, I nodded.

"I've locked away all of your things in a safe place for your return," he said. "You will be back in the camp next Tuesday. You should be fine. Just don't disrespect the count again." His tone was conciliatory. After a couple of minutes he wished me goodnight and turned to leave. I was still standing at the door, trying to process this strange visitation, when he turned back.

"Is there anything I can do for you?" he asked.

Hesitantly, I said, "I have nothing to read or to occupy my mind. Could I get some books?"

"I'll see what I can do," he replied.

An hour later, a small library cart arrived and I was allowed to look through the window in my door and choose a couple of books. The selection was poor, and many books were clearly missing pages or whole sections, so I picked two that looked most intact. One was a biography of Winston Churchill by Roy Jenkins; the other was a book called *The Iceman,* about a mafia hitman who dispatched of his victims with an ice pick. As these precious volumes were passed through the slot in my door, I silently sent my thanks to the CO for showing some humanity. Perhaps, in his own way, he was asking my forgiveness for his harsh treatment of me.

I started out with the ice pick killer, but quickly realized this gruesome tale was not the best prison reading. I turned instead to the Churchill biography, which was over a thousand pages long. I am a slow and sporadic reader—the butt of many jokes among my family of avid book lovers. Would I be able to finish it, if I really was going back to the camp on Tuesday, as the CO had promised? I could almost hear my wife and daughters laughing in my head, and I told them firmly that I could and would read it.

The book was a godsend, immersing me for hour upon hour in the life and passions of one of the twentieth century's most controversial characters. However, for all its exhaustive detail, it didn't touch on the story about Churchill I had been told as a child: the man who fiercely opposed Indian independence and blocked food shipments during the Bengal famine of 1943, in which millions of people died of starvation. It got me thinking about how history gets written—what is remembered and what is forgotten.

I lay in my narrow bunk with its lumpy mattress, night after night, reading and trying to shut out the noise. One might imagine that solitary confinement would be eerily silent, but in fact the SHU made the Kolkata train station seem peaceful. Day and night, prisoners would bang on the steel doors with their fists and yell, trying to get the attention of a guard. Every transaction was conducted by shouting.

Each cell's lights were controlled by a switch outside the locked door, so some people shouted for the lights to go on, while others shouted for the lights to go off. Some demanded information, phone access, legal counsel, or medical attention. Some tried to conduct conversations with friends in other cells. Some just yelled torrents of abuse and rage, often in incoherent Spanish, that reverberated off the steel doors and concrete walls. The guards ignored most of it. I tried to tune it out. When it started to get to me, I looked at the scratches on the cell wall and told myself that maybe the crazy guys had been here fifty days or more. If they kept me in the SHU that long, who's to say I too would not be howling curses into the night?

The thought of being in the SHU for weeks on end struck fear into me, for all my attempts at equanimity. I hoped the CO was as good as his word, and I would only need to endure a few days. Lying sleepless on my metal bed, staring at the ceiling, I felt the walls closing in. But I was determined not to give the guards the satisfaction of hearing me yell or complain or beg for information. I'd make the best of it. There wasn't much room, but at least it was only me. There was no storage, but then again, I didn't have anything to store. Think of it as prison with room service, I told myself. Rise above it, as my father would have done.

2

Uncertain Winds

If you shut your door to all errors truth will be shut out.

—Rabindranath Tagore, *Stray Birds,* 130

December 2009

"There's a lawyer from Goldman Sachs on the line and he says he needs to speak with you right away."

I was hurrying through Detroit Metro Airport, on my way to Boston to see my new twin granddaughters, and I was late for my flight. Ahead of me was a long line for security.

"Can I call him back later?" I asked my assistant Renee, explaining where I was.

"He says it's urgent," she replied, so I told her to put the call through.

Having served on the Goldman Sachs board since 2006, I knew Greg Palm, their internal legal counsel, quite well, and we were on friendly terms. So I could tell that something was up the moment he got on the phone and informed me in an uncharacteristically formal tone that one of his colleagues was also on the line to listen to the conversation. He skipped any pleasantries and got straight to the point.

"I need to talk to you about Raj Rajaratnam. Did you ever disclose any sensitive information related to board discussions to him?"

"Of course not," I told him, taken aback. "What is this about?" The security line shuffled forward, and I checked my watch, reluctant to give up my place when my flight was leaving in less than an hour.

"Your name has come up in relation to the Rajaratnam case," he replied.

"Come up?" That could have meant anything. "In what sense?"

"We learned from some other lawyers that reference had been made to phone calls between you and Rajaratnam."

"What kind of phone calls?" I demanded.

"They think you may have provided him with inside information about the bank, specifically relating to Warren Buffett's $5 billion investment in September 2008. They have Rajaratnam on tape telling a colleague that he got information from someone that something good might happen to Goldman."

I'd reached the front of the line and the TSA agents were indicating that I needed to get off the phone. "This is ridiculous," I told him. "I've done nothing of the sort. Look, I have to go through security. Can I call you back in a few minutes?"

"Sure," he said. "But you should know that your interests and our interests may diverge, and I represent Goldman. I would advise you to get a lawyer." His tone was ominous.

As I went through the mindless ritual of removing shoes and belt, taking out my laptop, and pushing my briefcase through the scanner, my mind was racing. What could possibly have happened? How had I gotten pulled into this mess? Surely it was all a mistake. But nevertheless, it was worrying. For the thousandth time, I wished I had never crossed paths with Raj Rajaratnam.

An Ill-Advised Relationship

I met Rajaratnam in the late 1990s, when I was working on creating the Indian School of Business (ISB), a world-class business school in

India. Of course, I knew him by reputation before then. Among the South Asian community in the US in the late 1990s, Rajaratnam was something of a legend. A Sri Lankan native, he'd worked as an analyst at the investment bank Needham & Co. before striking out on his own in 1997 and forming Galleon Group, a New York hedge fund that would grow to manage around $5 billion in assets. By focusing on the tech sector, his area of expertise, just as the bubble was beginning to inflate, Rajaratnam became one of Wall Street's rising stars, with Galleon's main fund rising 93 percent in 1999 and its founder joining the ranks of the billionaires.

Our lives might never have intersected had it not been for the small world that is the South Asian immigrant community and ISB, a project that was close to my heart. We didn't move in the same circles—Rajaratnam liked the company of hard-partying trader types while I favored a much quieter lifestyle. But he stayed connected to several of his fellow South Asians from Wharton Business School, one of whom was a guy named Anil Kumar, who worked with me at McKinsey.

Kumar was based in the firm's Silicon Valley office. A young Indian who, like me, had attended the Indian Institute of Technology (IIT), he had naturally seen me as a role model and sought my advice and mentorship. When I began trying to raise funds to start the business school project, Anil eagerly offered his help, and his connections. Soon, he excitedly announced that he had convinced his wealthiest classmate to make a million-dollar donation. Thus, I made the acquaintance of Raj Rajaratnam, and when we were both invited to a dinner at the house of another mutual friend, Ravi Trehan, I was glad to have the opportunity to thank him in person. A million dollars was a large sum for an individual to contribute to the school, especially when the individual in question was not even Indian.

My first impression of Rajaratnam was of a larger-than-life figure, both in body and in personality. He was charming and engaging, with a booming laugh and an infectious sense of humor. His wife, Asha, was

Punjabi, like my mother, and he captivated guests with tales of their unconventional courtship. He was a great storyteller who came across as disarmingly honest. He seemed well acquainted with my life and career and expressed great enthusiasm for the business school project. I enjoyed his company that evening, but left with no expectation that I'd ever see him again. As it turned out, however, Ravi, our host, had other ideas. He had been trying to get into business with the billionaire for a while, and he hoped to get me involved.

Ravi was a family friend and neighbor who lived next door to us on weekends, renting a house we owned. Our children grew up together and we shared holidays and vacations. Ravi worked in investments, first at Goldman Sachs, and then at Japanese and European banks. He'd already made a couple of unsuccessful attempts to get into business with Rajaratnam, but in 2005 he had an idea he thought was a winner. He proposed to create a highly leveraged structured fund, for which Rajaratnam would put up $40 million, and Ravi and I would each contribute $5 million (with an option to put in another $5 million at a later point). Rajaratnam was intrigued by the structured nature of the investment vehicle, and Ravi was eager to build his own investment record. They would manage half each.

I gave Ravi's proposal serious consideration and concluded it was a good investment opportunity. I would be an entirely passive investor. We named the fund Voyager, and it was initially very successful; in our first six months it was up more than 50 percent.

People ask me all the time, why did you go into business with a guy like Rajaratnam? In hindsight, it seems like a more than fair question. It's easy to look back and say I should have seen the trouble coming. He did have a certain arrogance, an above-the-rules air that should have been a red flag. However, it's also easy to forget that at the time he was being celebrated as one of the most talented traders on Wall Street. His record was incredible and his work ethic was legendary. His flamboyant confidence looked like brilliance to a lot of very smart people. In fact, one of those people was Hank Paulson, then CEO of

Goldman Sachs and a very good friend who I'd known and worked with for more than a decade. I knew that Rajaratnam's Galleon hedge fund was a Goldman client—one of their most important "Tier 1" clients, in fact—so when I was considering the Voyager idea, I asked both Hank and Goldman president Gary Cohn their opinion of him, and they both gave their enthusiastic endorsement. To this day, there are few people I would trust more than Hank, so when he made a point of affirming Rajaratnam's generosity, that meant a lot. I also trusted Ravi deeply, so if Rajaratnam was okay in his eyes, I was inclined to trust him too.

As I got to know Raj myself, I thought I'd got the measure of him. I felt a certain respect for a fellow immigrant who had fought hard to get to the top of an industry that had never made it easy for him. It quickly became clear that he had a penchant for exaggeration, name-dropping, and self-aggrandizement, but I judged it to be more bluster than dishonesty. Our relationship was strictly business—I was never invited to the lavish parties he threw, like the infamous birthday when he flew seventy friends to Kenya for a safari. This was fine by me—his social scene didn't appeal to me. Anita was also hesitant about me getting too involved with the financial industry in general. "These aren't our people," she would say. "You're too trusting, and you think everyone will be nice to you. Financial people are different than consultants!" It was one of many moments when I wish I'd trusted her instincts. But Rajaratnam was always respectful to me, and I concluded, perhaps naively, that it would be interesting to work with him.

I'd always had an unusual ability to get along with all kinds of characters—even those whose rough edges or more obvious egos were off-putting to others. I tried to treat everyone well and not be too quick to judge, and I had been rewarded many times with surprising generosity and goodwill. People would do things for me that they wouldn't do for others. In fact, this approach was central to my leadership capacity: Expect the best from people, and they often live up to that expectation. Treat people as if they are worthy of trust and respect, and they will prove themselves to be so. I wasn't always right, but I'd been right so many times that it had become a point of pride—perhaps more so than I realized.

Looking back, I can see that in a strange way I became convinced that my own goodwill could override less wholesome motives, and that my very lack of defenses was a protection against betrayal. It wasn't that I thought I'd never get hurt; rather, I thought that the hurt couldn't ever be that bad, and the rewards of all the times I was right outweighed the risk of being wrong occasionally. So I overrode my wife's misgivings and entrusted a substantial amount of my money to Raj Rajaratnam, without even requiring signature authority.

Not long into the life of Voyager, Ravi and Raj began to quarrel over who was in charge of the fund. I tried to mediate, but with little success, and in 2006 Ravi decided to exit. I was pleased with the fund's performance, however, so I kept my money in. In fact, at the end of 2006 I decided to exercise my option to put in another $5 million before it expired in the new year. I was taken aback when Rajaratnam balked, insisting that I could only put the money in at the current valuation, not at the original rate, as we'd agreed.

Frustrated, I consulted with my eldest daughter, Sonu, a fund manager herself. She, too, had misgivings. "It's a risky, highly leveraged investment anyway, Baba," she advised. "Why would you put more money in? It's better to diversify." The deadline passed, and I let it go, though not without some annoyance. I had turned my attention elsewhere, caught up in the ongoing busyness of my life, when Rajaratnam abruptly changed his mind a month later and told me I could put in my extra $5 million at the original valuation. It never occurred to me to question why he'd changed his mind; I just felt glad he was honoring our agreement.

In the spring of 2008, I got a call from Ravi. His accountant, who also did the Voyager books, had mentioned something about a large withdrawal from the fund by Rajaratnam more than a year earlier. "Did you receive a distribution?" Ravi asked. I told him I knew nothing about any withdrawals, and if any had been made, I had not received my percentage.

“How much did he take out?”

“About $23 million,” Ravi replied, “plus $25 million in fees and commissions.” I was shocked—if Raj had withdrawn that much money, I should have received several million. Plus, we’d never agreed that he would be paid fees or commissions. Surely Ravi was mistaken—or just trying to stir up discord between me and Raj to get me on his side. When he insisted it was true, I asked him to get me a statement from the accountants so I could see for myself.

All of this was taking place during one of the busiest times of my life. I was transitioning out of McKinsey, where I’d worked since I was twenty-four years old. I was involved in numerous humanitarian causes, including a major global initiative to reduce malaria deaths that was launching later that year. And I was planning my eldest daughter’s wedding, for several hundred guests. Nothing moved quickly, because I simply didn’t have the time to follow it up. However, I finally got the audited statements in June or July, and there it was, hidden in the fine print. Raj had indeed taken almost $50 million out of the fund without my knowledge. Not only that—he’d done it right before telling me I could put in my extra $5 million. I felt betrayed by his actions, and his continued evasiveness when I tried to clarify the matter with him. I kept hoping there was some simple explanation, but I could not get a straight answer.

This dispute defined my relationship with Rajaratnam during the second half of 2008 and was reaching a crisis point right around the period that Palm had mentioned in his call: late September 2008. Of course, that personal crisis was overshadowed by the much greater crisis that was gripping the financial markets during that period. On September 15, 2008, Lehman Brothers had announced its bankruptcy, sending the markets into a tailspin. As a Goldman Sachs board member, I had a front row seat to the panic that gripped Wall Street. Who would be next? On September 23, at 3:15 p.m., Goldman’s CEO

Lloyd Blankfein called an emergency board meeting to announce some surprisingly good news in the midst of all the doom and gloom: Warren Buffett's Berkshire Hathaway had agreed to make a $5 billion investment in the bank. The board approved the deal, and by the time the evening's papers went to press, it was official—a huge win for Goldman in the midst of the surrounding turmoil, and one that gave the stock price a boost the following day.

This was the event that Palm was referring to in his call—the "something good" that Rajaratnam claimed to have heard about from someone at Goldman before the news broke. And he seemed to be suggesting that that someone was me. I was shocked that anyone who knew me might think that I was capable of that kind of crime. And the nature of my relationship with Rajaratnam at the time only confirmed how implausible the idea was. Why would I be doing any favors for a man who was proving to be untrustworthy and duplicitous? If I had called Rajaratnam during September 2008—and I had done, repeatedly—I wasn't calling him to give him tips, I was calling him to try to figure out what had happened to the Voyager money.

Arrest

Rajaratnam might not have played fair in his dealings with me, but I had no idea that he was at the center of a criminal conspiracy until news of his arrest broke in October 2009. I was in Santiago, Chile, where I'd been invited to speak to the South America conference of the International Chamber of Commerce (ICC). I'd gotten up early to prepare for my speech when the call came from Jean Molino, McKinsey's legal counsel.

"Rajat, have you heard? Anil Kumar and Raj Rajaratnam have been arrested and charged with insider trading."

I was stunned. I'd had nothing to do with Rajaratnam for almost a year at that point. The Voyager drama had escalated in the midst of the 2008 financial crisis. Not only had Raj lied to me but his withdrawals had left the fund without a cushion in the turbulent markets, and eventually the banks shut it down. My entire stake looked like it was gone. Rajaratnam, meanwhile, had not suffered much of a loss, having taken out almost as much as he had put in, between the redemptions and the fees. He continued to be evasive, telling me that he was working with the banks to try to recoup the equity, but by early 2009 it was clear that all such attempts had come to nothing. I was forced to accept that the money was gone, and that was the last I heard of Rajaratnam until the news of his arrest.

Given what Raj had done to me, I cannot say I was entirely surprised to learn that his corruption ran much deeper. Anil Kumar was another matter, however. I knew him much better than I knew Raj, and his involvement in the affair shocked me.

Anil was a McKinsey man, and as such I had expected him to act honorably. The firm's culture was built on principle, integrity, and discretion, and Anil was someone I'd personally mentored, helping him out countless times. I had trusted his integrity and his sense of loyalty. He was effective at serving clients, although not popular among his colleagues. People didn't like working for him, and his reputation was that he was good at "managing upwards"—impressing his superiors—but not at managing downwards. As head of the firm, perhaps I only got to see his best side, but I liked Anil well enough. He always seemed honest in his dealings with me, although he had a habit of using my name more often than was really appropriate to advance his own career.

Holding confidential information is second nature to every McKinsey partner—it's something we do every day. It was hard to fathom that Anil would have deliberately betrayed his clients and his partners. Perhaps he had let something slip by accident in his eagerness to make a good impression on his powerful friend, I reasoned. Raj had a way of fishing for information—he'd throw out something he'd heard, casually looking for confirmation or further details while implying that he already knew the facts. I considered myself adept at dodging these hooks, but maybe Anil had not been careful.

Anil was always trying to impress Raj. For a while, he was hoping to land Galleon as a McKinsey client, which would have been good for an ambitious partner. Later, he became dissatisfied with his McKinsey career, feeling like he wasn't getting the recognition he deserved, and he was eager for his far more successful classmate to hire him to work for Galleon. He kept boasting that Raj had promised him a job, although it was unclear how true this was. Either of these motives might have led him to be less discreet than he should have been, I told myself, but surely he hadn't deliberately conspired to commit a crime.

Anil called me a few days after the arrest, clearly in shock and full of denials and justifications. He insisted he was innocent, and was panicking about what this all meant for his family's future. In particular, he was worried about his son Aman—a bright boy who suffered from severe physical disabilities as a result of being born prematurely. I did not yet know the details or the extent of Anil's involvement with Rajaratnam—that would become clear in the weeks and months ahead. But I knew that no matter what the outcome, Anil's career at McKinsey was over, and there was nothing I or anyone else could do to change that. There was one matter on which I felt some sympathy for him, however: he was about to lose the firm's health coverage, which was critical for Aman getting the care he needed. McKinsey had a policy that if a partner's age and duration at the firm added up to seventy-five or more, that partner could keep the firm's insurance for life, no matter what. Anil fell just a year short of qualifying for this policy, and the loss of coverage could be devastating for his family. He begged me to intercede on his behalf and ask the firm to make an exception, which I reluctantly agreed to do. I felt a certain loyalty—if not to Anil, to Aman, for whom I'd become something of an honorary uncle.

"Why on earth are you trying to help this guy?" was the only response I got. As the details came out over the next few months, I was forced to realize the degree to which I'd been blind to the duplicity of both Anil and Raj. Their conversations, captured on the government's wiretaps, were far from accidental slips; they were part of a carefully orchestrated conspiracy. Not only was Anil getting paid for his tips to the tune of several million dollars, he had set up a convoluted system to hide the payments offshore in a Swiss bank account in the name of his Indian maid. It was a harsh and humbling lesson for me, one that left me disoriented and questioning my own judgment of character.

Gathering Shadows

Just a few weeks later, this sorry tale had taken a turn for the worse. As soon as I got through security that day at the Detroit airport, I called Palm back, anxious to learn more about the vague allegations against me and to set the record straight. The Goldman lawyer repeated what he'd said about representing the firm, not me—clearly he wanted me to know that I was not protected by attorney–client privilege during our conversation. I recounted briefly the key facts about my relationship with Rajaratnam, and explained the Voyager debacle. "Why would I be giving information to the guy who cheated me out of millions of dollars? It simply makes no sense." I tried to get him to tell me more details about the specific allegations, but he was frustratingly vague. I assured him that I'd be happy to provide as much information as he needed, but my flight was boarding, so we arranged to speak the next day.

I tried not to let the matter weigh too heavily on my mind as I took my seat and settled in for the short flight. Whatever they thought, they were wrong, and I'd be able to set matters straight once I knew all the facts. It was a grave accusation, but nothing was official yet. Surely it was just a mix-up. I'd never been involved in Rajaratnam's web of informants, so I had nothing to be concerned about. It was hard to take it too seriously. Lawyers are trained to look for problems, I reasoned, and they were just doing their job in giving me the heads-up. We'd get it all straightened out tomorrow.

I would later learn that Goldman almost didn't warn me at all. It was my old friend John Bryan—former CEO of Sara Lee Corporation and fellow Goldman board member—who had urged Palm to call me immediately and give me a heads-up about what they'd heard. John and I had known each other for decades; he'd been my client during my time at McKinsey. He didn't believe for a moment that there was any basis to the idea that I'd been involved in this conspiracy, and his main concern was that my reputation not be damaged and I be given the chance to be proactive and protect it. I was grateful for John's friendship, but Goldman's inclination toward reticence was disturbing.

When I arrived in Boston, after cuddles with my granddaughters, I sat down with Sonu and told her about the call. She looked worried. "Baba, you should do what they say and get a lawyer."

"For what?" I asked. "I don't even know what I'm being accused of!"

"Of course we know there's nothing to it," she agreed, "but you need to protect yourself, just in case. You're too trusting."

On that count, I knew she was right. Maybe it was time to start protecting my own interests—although what they needed protecting from was unclear to me. How was I supposed to stand up and fight, when my adversary was merely a shadow? How could I defend myself, when the threat was still hidden from view?

3

Reluctant Resignation

I have had my invitation to the world's festival,
and thus my life has been blessed.
My eyes have seen and my ears have heard.
It was my part at this feast to play upon my instrument,
and I have done all I could.

—Rabindranath Tagore, *Gitanjali,* 16

December 2009

"Don't you worry about it; let us worry about it."

This seemed to be the catchphrase of my new lawyer, Gary Naftalis—a white-collar defense specialist with a track record of successful cases who had been recommended to me by Greg Palm at Goldman. Indeed, I lost count of how many times I heard those words as 2009 dragged to a close. Gary was a folksy character, whose somewhat disheveled appearance belied his brilliant legal mind. He radiated confidence and kept assuring me that my concern was unnecessary and this situation would all work itself out. I did not find it easy, however, to just hand the matter over to the professionals, let them worry for me, and go on with my life.

The most frustrating part was feeling utterly in the dark. There was nothing official I could respond to—just rumors that one lawyer had heard from another who heard them from another, none of whom were really supposed to be discussing the case. No one else knew about any of it besides the Goldman leadership and my family—a state of secrecy that was critical for my reputation but difficult for my psychological well-being. It was as if I was living in two parallel worlds—one in which I continued to fulfill my various commitments as a respected elder in the business community and another in which I was slowly but surely being framed as a criminal.

On January 7, 2010, Anil Kumar took a plea bargain. Clearly the government had convinced him to testify against Rajaratnam in return for a more lenient sentence. Soon after, a superseding indictment was filed, adding two more charges and extending the list of companies in which Rajaratnam was accused of illegally trading. Goldman Sachs, however, was mentioned nowhere in the new indictment, and it shed no more light on the shadowy accusations against me. Whatever the Justice Department thought they had found, it was not enough to warrant a charge. That seemed like a good sign. Perhaps this would all die down once Rajaratnam's trial was over and I could go back to focusing on the things that mattered.

Meanwhile, Goldman began conducting its own internal investigation of the matter. My lawyers met with their lawyers and reiterated the story I'd told Palm. I kept inquiring as to the outcome of this investigation, but heard nothing. Frustrated, I went about my business, feeling hamstrung. Why would no one give me any information? I'd heard nothing from the Goldman legal team, from Goldman CEO Lloyd Blankfein, or even from John Bryan. In early March, I was in Florida on a short vacation with my family, when I got a call from my lawyers. The annual Goldman board elections were approaching, and apparently the bank's lawyers had told my lawyers to inform me that if I was going to run for re-election, they would have to disclose to the board what they knew about the allegations regarding my role in the Rajaratnam case.

"What about Goldman's investigation?" I demanded. "Have they come to any conclusions? Does this mean they think I'm guilty?" My lawyers had no answer.

I was due to return to New York that night to attend a Goldman board meeting the next day. Couldn't they have given me a little more time to consider this decision? I was reluctant to let the entire Goldman board know what was happening. If word got out that my name had in any way been connected to the case, it would be catastrophic for my reputation, and the more people knew, the riskier it became. My only other option was to withdraw my name and not stand for re-election. Either path felt like a capitulation to an unjust narrative.

I hated the thought of bowing out, when I hadn't done anything wrong. Why should I be forced to act like I was guilty, when I'd been charged with no crime? When I met John Bryan for a drink that night, I asked him, "What should I do? Either way, people are going to assume the worst."

"Withdraw your name," he advised. "You can't afford the reputational damage that will be inevitable if news of the investigation becomes public. Besides, why would you want to serve a company that doesn't trust you?" He told me that Goldman would like to offer me a consulting contract instead, but it felt like a bribe, so I refused. In hindsight, I should have taken it, and negotiated an exit package. I didn't even think to cash in the stock options I'd been awarded for my service to the board. (It never occurred to me that the bank would take these away, but they did, relying on some fine print in the contract.) I still saw myself as part of the Goldman team. I hated being pushed around like this, but in the end I just couldn't see the sense in fighting, particularly when Blankfein had made it so clear he didn't want me there.

My relationship with the Goldman chief had never been particularly close. It was his predecessor, Hank Paulson, who had encouraged me to join the board, but in the interim between the invitation and my acceptance, Hank was made treasury secretary and Blankfein took over at Goldman.

The Goldman board meeting on March 5, 2010 was my last. Before we went in, Blankfein assured me that the reason for my withdrawal would be kept confidential. I announced my decision to the assembled directors, trying to frame it as simply a matter of timing. "It seems like now is as good a time as any for me to go," I told them, adopting what I hoped was a philosophical tone. The whole thing felt like a charade. The other board members looked surprised. Blankfein somewhat awkwardly thanked me for my service, and that was the end of my tenure on the Goldman board.

Later, I would learn that, as soon as I exited the room, he told the assembled directors the real reason for my departure, breaking his promise to keep it confidential. I might as well have stood firm and let him carry out his threat to disclose the allegations against me to the board—the result would have been the same. The other board members were my friends and I wish I had simply trusted them and leveled with them myself. At the time, however, I thought I'd done what was necessary to protect my reputation.

I should have known this was a fallacy. Such short-term expedient moves are invariably wrong moves, and it went against my commitment to honesty and transparency. The story was going to come out sooner or later, and when it did, the board members would probably think worse of me as I'd kept it from them.

Trial by Media

As the plane slowly made its final descent, I looked out the window at the familiar smoky skyline and bustling chaos of Mumbai. I could almost hear the cacophony of car horns, bicycle bells, and human voices. And I could imagine that somewhere down there, on a protected rooftop above the city streets, a handful of young boys were gleefully flying kites, as my childhood friends and I had loved to do. After the drama with the Goldman board a month earlier and the ongoing tension of the past few months, I was happy to be back in my homeland and far away from it all.

It was early April 2010, and I had come to India for a couple of days of fieldwork with fellow P&G board members before their annual board meeting in Singapore the following week. Maybe the distance would help me to finally put the worrying rumors behind me, I thought to myself as the wheels touched down. And then I switched on my phone.

"We're running a story tomorrow about the fact that you are under investigation for allegedly providing tips to Raj Rajaratnam about Goldman Sachs." The voicemail was from a reporter at the *Wall Street Journal.* She had left a number, and asked me to call before a certain time if I had any comments, but by the time I got the message it was already too late. The story had gone to print.

"Goldman Director In Probe," declared the headline.[1] My inbox and voicemail were full of concerned messages from friends and colleagues who had read the story on the front page of the morning paper. The article repeated the same vague allegations I'd already heard, with no more detail on the specifics. Of course, the reporter didn't name the "people close to the situation" who had provided the information, and I'll never know for sure where the leak came from. But if the Securities and Exchange Commission (SEC) or the Justice Department* wanted to plant seeds of suspicion in the public mind—and in the minds of future jurors—they couldn't have chosen a better way to do so. With the wounds of the financial crisis still raw—beloved homes foreclosed, jobs lost, families struggling, futures uncertain—it wasn't difficult to convince people to think the worst of anyone connected to the financial

* For those not familiar with the US system, the SEC is the civil agency charged with regulating the securities industry and enforcing federal securities laws. SEC violations are punishable by fines but not imprisonment. The Justice Department prosecutes criminal cases.

industry. In fact, one survey on community attitudes conducted in 2009 found that 74 percent of jury-eligible New Yorkers blamed "senior-level corporate executives" acting with "greed and carelessness" for the economic crisis, and almost half the respondents believed that if the US government accused a senior-level corporate executive of committing financial fraud, he or she probably did it.[2]

Despite this climate of suspicion, I was determined not to start acting like a guilty man. I wanted to maintain a semblance of normalcy in my professional life. I flew on to Singapore for the board meeting, accompanied by former American Express CEO Ken Chenault, who was also a P&G director. He was extremely supportive, offering to help in any way he could. The other P&G board members were also understanding, but I knew that not everyone would react this way. There were plenty who would be quick to judge. As Jim McNerney, a fellow P&G director and former McKinsey guy, said to me at the time, "Now you'll find out who your real friends are."

Many people assumed that following the article, I would resign from all of my board seats, but I resisted this pressure. P&G, Genpact, Harman International, and AMR Corporation (the parent company of American Airlines) were all aware of the situation and had made it clear they considered me innocent and wanted me to continue to serve as a director. P&G CEO A.G. Lafley and Genpact CEO Pramod Bhasin even spoke out publicly in my defense. Every one of the nonprofits I served felt similarly—from the Gates Foundation to ICC.

McKinsey had begun conducting an internal inquiry, and I spent many long hours meeting with their team and sharing everything I knew about Kumar and Rajaratnam, as well as my own story. My lawyers, meanwhile, were trying to get more information on what, if anything, the SEC or the Justice Department thought they had on me. Through some legal back channels, they were able to learn a little about the contents of the wiretaps.

It appeared that there were two tapes in which Rajaratnam mentioned Goldman, one being the September 2008 recording of him telling one of his traders that he'd heard "something good" might happen to the bank, and another, from about a month later, in which he told one of his lieutenants that he'd been tipped off about a shortfall in Goldman's earnings. In neither of these tapes was I named as the source, but some people clearly wanted to believe that I was. My lawyers, however, were quick to assure me these tapes had no legal merit. Not only were they vague, they were hearsay, which was not allowed by the rules of evidence.

"What about calls between Rajaratnam and me?" I inquired. "If they've been tapping his phones all this time, surely there would be recordings that show the kind of things we actually discussed?"

It turned out that there were seven recordings that featured my voice, of which six were simply voicemail messages requesting a call back. That was no surprise—in my attempts to recover my Voyager investment, I'd left dozens of such messages for Rajaratnam, and he rarely returned my calls. There was one longer recorded conversation from July 2008, the lawyers told me, but it contained nothing to do with insider trading. I did not particularly like the idea that someone had been secretly recording our call, but I knew I'd never given Rajaratnam any tips. What could the tape possibly contain that would incriminate me?

Lastly, we learned that they had call records showing that I'd placed calls to Rajaratnam on the days in question—calls that had not been recorded but which they were imagining contained tips. I knew, of course, that this wasn't the case—there was only one reason I was calling Rajaratnam in the fall of 2008, and that was the Voyager investment.

My lawyers continued to seem upbeat. If this was all the government had, they told me, it wasn't enough to make a case. A couple of conversations that were clearly hearsay and never mentioned my name, plus a couple of phone records, does not amount to anything close to proof. This seemed reasonable enough to me. I also knew, as I reminded my lawyers, that Raj had plenty of other connections at Goldman—he was one of their best clients, and had hired numerous former Goldman people to work at Galleon. Any number of people inside the bank could have been the actual tipper.

The spring and summer of 2010 was a strange and disconcerting time. I felt like I should be defending myself, yet I'd still not been charged with any crime. My lawyers repeatedly reached out to the SEC, asking them to let us know if I was under investigation so I could cooperate. But we heard nothing. Then, in August, we abruptly received SEC subpoenas for information about my investments and my contacts. After some negotiation, we agreed to hand over relevant parts. Things went quiet again, but I was under no illusion that this was a good sign. "Don't you worry," Gary told me. "Let us worry for you." I worried anyway—but not as much as I should have.

In November, the SEC informed my lawyers they wanted me to come in and testify. I was relieved—finally I could tell my side of the story and straighten out this misunderstanding. My lawyers, however, were not happy about the timing. Rajaratnam's trial was scheduled for January, and they were concerned that if I testified to the SEC, I'd end up getting dragged on to the stand as a defense witness. The trial had all the makings of a media spectacle, and the last thing I needed was to play a starring role. So we told the SEC I'd be happy to testify, but requested that it be postponed until after the Rajaratnam trial was over.

They refused. They also refused to give us any assurance that my testimony would be kept sealed. A date was set for December.

"Same Answer"

"I'll just tell them the truth," I told Gary. It was early December 2010, and we were meeting to prepare for my SEC testimony. "If they insist on bringing me in, I'll just explain what those calls to Rajaratnam were actually about."

But Gary was concerned this approach was too risky. We had not yet seen all the evidence, so we had no idea what they might bring up, he explained.

"What could they possibly have?" I demanded. "There is no evidence because there was no crime! And if I tell the truth, I don't have anything to fear." Their argument simply didn't make sense to me, but Gary was adamant. The best strategy, he advised me, was to exercise my constitutional right against self-incrimination; in other words, to take the Fifth.

"That will just make everyone even more convinced I'm guilty!" I objected. I couldn't see how this would be any better for my reputation than telling the truth. I could just picture the headlines: "Gupta Takes the Fifth: What Is He Hiding?"

Gary offered me an alternate way to say it: "Upon the advice of counsel, I respectfully decline to answer the question at this time based on my right under the United States Constitution not to be compelled to be a witness against myself."

I looked at him skeptically. "I'm going to need to write that down." So I did, and when the day of the testimony came, I took the piece of paper with me. We were shown to a small, nondescript, rather shabby room, and sat down. Soon, three SEC agents entered, and introduced themselves as Sanjay Wadhwa, Jason Friedman, and John Henderson. I knew that Wadhwa, a fellow immigrant, was a Punjabi, like my mother. Under different circumstances, I would have liked to ask him about his family and his history. Instead, I took a seat, with the piece of paper in my pocket for reference if needed, and waited for the questions to begin.

I don't recall the opening question, but my answer was already prepared. I used the same phrase for each of the first few questions, feeling rather foolish, until Henderson suggested that for the sake of expediency I could simply abbreviate it to "I take the Fifth."

Gary shook his head. "I don't like that formulation." So they agreed I could simply say "same answer," which I did to every one of their fifty or so questions. It seemed a pointless and ridiculous exercise, and it felt terrible. Never in my life had I refused to answer when someone asked me a direct question, no matter what the consequences. I conceded to my lawyers' insistence that this was the best course of action, but it made no sense to me. In hindsight, I think I made a mistake. I should have told my story. At least then they would have known the facts from my perspective.

That Christmas was a somber one in our home. Although we are not Christians, my family had always enthusiastically embraced the holidays of our adopted country, and Christmas was traditionally a rowdy affair with a house full of family and friends. As 2010 drew to a close, however, no one really felt like celebrating. I was exhausted by the long-drawn-out game of cat and mouse with the SEC, and still frustrated by the ongoing lack of information. I was moving through my days in a kind of trance, feeling strangely disconnected from the events unfolding in my life. Try as I might, my usual strategic thinking abilities eluded me. It was hard to devise any kind of rational response to such an elusive and unpredictable adversary. I felt as if I were playing a chess game in which I couldn't see my opponent's pieces, and in which the rules were apt to change at any moment.

Another small piece came into view toward the end of January, when Rajaratnam's co-defendant Danielle Chiesi, a teen beauty-queen-turned-analyst who extracted tips from her married lover and passed them on to her hedge fund boss, pleaded guilty. In the wake of her plea, yet another superseding indictment was filed, and this time, hidden in a sub-paragraph describing "overt acts" of one of several alleged conspiracies, was a reference to Rajaratnam passing a tip about Goldman to an associate. My lawyers seemed encouraged by this, explaining that it confirmed that the government didn't have enough evidence to add a charge for the Goldman trades. If this was all they had on Raj, then surely whatever they thought they had on me was even more insubstantial.

The end of January brought what should have been a highlight of my year: the annual World Economic Forum (WEF) conference in Davos, Switzerland. I'd become a friend and advisor to WEF founder Klaus Schwab during my McKinsey days, and had joined their board. The

Davos gathering was always a welcome opportunity to reconnect with old friends, but this time I could see the unasked questions in too many eyes, and it was hard not to imagine that people were talking about me and speculating about the case. It was a relief when those who knew me better just came out and asked me about it. One of these friends was Mukesh Ambani, the prominent Indian businessman, who sat down with me for more than an hour, ignoring the constant demands for his attention, and asked how I was doing and how he could help. I was touched by his concern, and likewise by that of my friend Sunil Mittal, a very successful Indian business leader who traveled home with me and spent the whole trip expressing his support.

On January 28, we received what's known as a Wells Notice—a letter from the SEC informing me of their intent to charge me with violations of securities law. This was far from welcome, but at least it afforded us, for the first time, some information about the specifics of my supposed crimes and the "evidence," such as it was. I'm not a lawyer, but even I could see that they didn't have much to go on. In fact, there was little here that we hadn't already heard about.

In addition to the allegation that I'd tipped Rajaratnam about the Berkshire Hathaway deal on September 23, 2008, there were three other incidents mentioned. First, they alleged that in June 2008 I had disclosed Goldman's better-than-expected second-quarter financial results, allowing Rajaratnam to buy stock before the shares went up and sell at a profit. Second, they alleged that I had disclosed Goldman's financial results for the fourth quarter of 2008, which reported a loss, allowing Rajaratnam to sell Galleon's holdings and avoid losses. And third, they alleged that I disclosed P&G's financial results for the last quarter of 2008. All they had, as far as evidence went, were call records showing I'd called Rajaratnam following Goldman and P&G board meetings, and the two wiretaps we already knew about, in which Rajaratnam mentioned—but did not name—a source at Goldman.

We had thirty days to prepare a response to the Wells Notice and provide satisfactory reasons why the SEC should not charge me. "Don't worry," Gary said, an admonishment that was falling flatter every day. We began preparing a lengthy document telling my side of the story. Why couldn't I have just done this at my testimony in December? I wondered, yet again. It would have saved us all this trouble. The lawyers insisted this was different—now we had the evidence in front of us and could tailor our statement accordingly. But I knew my story would not have been any different two months earlier: the truth was the truth and all this legal maneuvering was frustrating.

I put the final touches on our response on Friday, February 25, 2011, working via telephone from a hotel room in Japan, where I had business meetings that day. My lawyers delivered it to the SEC that night, and the next morning I flew to India. After a meeting with Kamal Nath, minister of urban development, about an urbanization initiative we were working on, I would travel south to Bengaluru, where Anita and I would spend a couple of days with our friend and ISB board member Kiran Mazumdar-Shaw, and then we would travel to Delhi to celebrate my sister's sixtieth birthday.

Charged

"It's not looking good," Gary told me by phone on Sunday. Rumors were growing that a charge was coming. Anita and I were at an India–England cricket game, but everything seemed surreal to me. Could this really be happening? Was I actually going to be charged with a violation? What had once seemed unthinkable suddenly seemed imminent, and there was nothing I could do to prevent it. Had all the lawyers' admonitions not to worry been foolish, their optimism dramatically misguided? Adding to the strangeness of that day was the outcome of the match: a tie, almost unheard of in the sport of cricket.

The next day, our fears were confirmed. I received word that the SEC had authorized a suit against me and charges would be filed within days. I was shocked by the speed at which this happened. We'd only submitted the document on Friday night! Surely they had not even had time to review my response, much less consider it. Had they been reading it all weekend? It seemed unlikely, and there was no record of any meeting of the five SEC commissioners on those dates. The moment the mandatory thirty-day period was up, they pounced. Had the Wells Notice just been a meaningless exercise? Were the charges always a foregone conclusion?

Arriving in Delhi, we headed straight for my brother-in-law Avinash's house. He and his wife, Madhuri, were with us throughout those difficult days—the first of many times they would be by our sides as we reeled from bad news. The charges weren't public yet, but it was just a matter of time. All I could do was damage control. A lot of people needed to hear this from me rather than from the press.

The first person I called, with a heavy heart, was Dominic Barton, the current managing director* of McKinsey. At that point, I was still working with the firm as a consultant, and I maintained an office and a secretary at the Stamford office, a privilege that was offered to all former managing directors for life. The firm's good opinion of me meant almost more than anyone's—it had nurtured me and I had been honored to represent it on the world stage. I hated to think that any of my partners might believe the allegations for even a moment, but I didn't want McKinsey to get caught up in this. After explaining the situation to Barton, I offered my resignation.

I'd been acquainted with Barton since he joined the firm, and we'd known each other quite well since he became partner. He was a charismatic, client-oriented guy and very popular. As I had hoped, he was immediately supportive, insisting that I just take a paid leave of absence until it all blew over. I thanked him, and assured him once again that I'd do everything within my power to resolve this matter quickly and with minimal damage.

By the time the SEC charges were officially filed, on March 1, 2011, I had resigned from all my corporate board seats. I had also

* Sometimes referred to as "managing partner," this was equivalent to the CEO role.

written an email to all my friends and colleagues telling them that I would fight the charges and assuring them that the evidence was merely circumstantial and wouldn't stand up in court.

When the media learned of the charges, it sent shock waves through the corporate world. Walking through a hotel lobby in Delhi the next day, I was so busy trying not to be noticed that I almost missed a familiar face. "Rajat!" I looked up to see my old friend Marcus Wallenberg, grandson of the legendary Swedish industrialist Marcus Wallenberg, Sr., who had invited me to chair the ICC board. Accompanying him was Josef Ackermann, CEO of Deutsche Bank and a fellow WEF board member. They were in town for a conference. It was such a surprise and relief to see some friendly faces, and they promptly sat me down and tried to cheer me up for the next hour.

The respite was brief, however. It didn't matter that I'd not been found guilty—the damage to my reputation was now irreparable. And it was not just me—all the institutions I'd built and stewarded would now be forced into the spotlight for negative reasons. Some of these I'd founded and raised like my children—the Indian School of Business, the Public Health Foundation of India (PHFI), the American India Foundation. Others were globally significant philanthropic giants in which I'd played a key role—the Global Fund to Fight AIDS, Tuberculosis and Malaria (GFATM), the Gates Foundation, the United Nations, ICC, the Rockefeller Foundation, and many more. I'd poured my time, energy, and creativity into each, and now I was faced with the painful reality that to protect them I must resign. I tendered my resignation from every nonprofit board seat in the spring of 2011. It was one of the hardest weeks of my life.

Many of these institutions protested my resignation, but there was one that flat out refused to accept it: the Gates Foundation. Bill Gates and I had become acquainted in the 1990s, after we met at one of his CEO conferences. I'd begun advising the foundation soon after its inception. "You're innocent until proven guilty," Bill told me, in a message via his executive director, Sylvia Mathews Burwell. "Don't resign." I appreciated his solidarity when so many people seemed to be assuming the worst. Sylvia added her own words of support—she and I had known each other for many years, first at McKinsey and later at the foundation. Soon afterwards, however, Gates took a trip to India, and was mobbed by reporters asking him why I was still on his board. I couldn't sit by and watch while my troubles detracted from the important mission of the foundation, so I insisted that he accept my resignation, which he reluctantly did.

There was one resignation I decided to tender in person: my chairmanship of the ICC board. A meeting was scheduled in Paris the coming week, so I flew there directly after returning from India. It was a sad event, made more poignant by the lengths to which my colleagues went to give the proceedings some dignity. Marcus Wallenberg even flew in for the occasion. I'd deeply valued the opportunity to serve such a unique global institution and was sorry to be leaving before my term was up.

The meeting was held in the ICC offices, overlooking the Eiffel Tower. As I took in the spectacular view, I thought back to how the organization had ended up in this space. When I'd taken over as chairman, I soon realized that the ICC was on a precarious financial footing. What it did have was a prime piece of real estate, on the banks of the Seine, that was unsuited to its needs. It occurred to me that if the organization could find another home and sell the building, it would solve several problems at once. I asked my colleagues, is the French government doing anything to support us? The response was no. "All they do is tax us." This didn't seem right to me, given the organization's prestige. Perhaps we should move somewhere else. I went to Geneva and told local officials that ICC was considering a relocation and they offered us an impressive package of incentives. Returning to France, Marcus Wallenberg and I requested a meeting with the finance minister, Christine Lagarde. "This is the oldest global business organization in the world, and its home is Paris, but we can't afford to stay." We asked her if she might consider giving ICC one of the many vacant government buildings, allowing us to achieve financial stability. She did just that, which was why I was now looking out over the iconic Parisian landmark as I reluctantly prepared to resign from the board.

I hated to walk away with my work only half done. But I felt I had no choice. Back in New York, Raj Rajaratnam's trial was beginning. My shadowy opponent was lining up the pieces on the chessboard, but I had no idea what the next move would be.

4

Elephant

The real with its meaning read wrong and emphasis misplaced is the unreal.

—Rabindranath Tagore, *Stray Birds,* 254

April 24, 2011, New York City

"Throughout Raj Rajaratnam's trial . . . there has been an elephant in the courtroom: Rajat K. Gupta."

I was reading the papers over breakfast in our New York apartment on a chilly spring morning, as I had done every day during Rajaratnam's trial, which had begun six weeks earlier. On this particular morning, the *New York Times* was on top of the pile, and my name was in the headline. The article continued, "Mr. Gupta, once one of the world's most respected businessmen, is not being tried here nor has he been charged criminally. Yet hardly a day has passed when the jury in Mr. Rajaratnam's trial—the government's biggest insider trading case in a generation—has not heard about Mr. Gupta . . ."[1]

"At least I'm not imagining it!" I said to Anita. The *Times* had just perfectly described the feeling I'd had for the past few weeks. I'd not set foot in the courtroom during the Rajaratnam trial, but I'd felt as if

I were the one in the defendant's seat. It was as if I were being tried in abstentia for a crime I'd not even been charged with, unable to defend myself as my name echoed through the courtroom again and again. The amount of time dedicated to me at his trial seemed disproportionate, to say the least—a fact that only confirmed my growing sense that I was being set up.

The wiretap conversations were played daily. The jury heard Raj talking with his sources—the colorful Danielle Chiesi, the dour Roomy Khan, and of course the smooth-talking Kumar. They heard Raj relaying information and instructions to his traders, whose attitudes and vocabulary only served to reinforce the worst stereotypes of Wall Street stocksters. They heard him boasting to his lieutenants about tips he'd received, including the two that related to Goldman. And they heard my name. Repeatedly.

The prosecution kept bringing up Goldman, and trotting out the allegations against me, despite the fact that there was no substantive charge related to the bank and I was named nowhere in the indictment against Rajaratnam. I was referred to in the courtroom as an "unindicted co-conspirator." Strangely, underscoring both my centrality and my absence, I heard that a large sketch of me hung in the courtroom—the only one of its kind.

By far the worst moment in this particular episode of the drama had come on the morning of March 15. My lawyers called to tell me they had received word that the tape of the one conversation between Rajaratnam and myself that was caught on the wiretaps was going to be played in the courtroom that day. I could not fathom why—the conversation did not contain any tips and was not connected to any trades. I'd been assured it contained nothing incriminating, which was true. Yet it turned out to be devastating to my already battered reputation.

The recorded telephone call was made on July 29, 2008. This was early in the Voyager saga, and although Rajaratnam was being evasive about providing information, our relationship had not yet deteriorated to the point that he avoided my calls. In fact, he had called me, eager to talk because he was getting ready to meet with Goldman president Gary Cohn and wanted to be prepared. He asked me casually about a rumor he'd heard that Goldman was considering buying a commercial bank, such as AIG or Wachovia. I confirmed the rumor—which was public knowledge—but made the terrible mistake of saying that there had been a discussion about it at the recent board meeting. I cringed to think about this being played in the courtroom. The information itself was hardly private—the press had been discussing the possible acquisition for weeks at that point—but I should never have mentioned the board meeting. Raj was always gathering information, throwing out things he'd learned from analysts or research firms and looking for confirmation. In this instance, I should have been more careful. I hoped people wouldn't infer from this slip that I made a habit of such disclosures, which I did not.

I certainly did not intend to provide Rajaratnam with any inside information. Far from it. This was 2008, just a few months after the collapse of Bear Stearns and not long before Lehman. During those tumultuous months, Rajaratnam often grilled me on Goldman's stability, sometimes threatening to take his business elsewhere. In that particular call, I was trying to reassure him—a significant Goldman client—that the bank was not about to fold. I explained that Goldman's interest in a possible acquisition had nothing to do with being in a crisis or a lack of funds. They were opportunistic, I said, so if they saw a good deal, they'd likely go for it. Perhaps I said more than was strictly appropriate for my role as a board member, but my motives were to support, not betray, the bank. Would anyone in the courtroom realize this though, when I was given no opportunity to explain myself?

As it turned out, this indiscretion was far from the most damning part of the call. There was another part to the recorded conversation, of which I'd been unaware until it was played that day in the courtroom. I listened, aghast, as I heard it played back to me later that day at my lawyers' offices.

As the discussion with Rajaratnam was winding down, I mentioned our mutual friend and colleague Anil Kumar. He had seemed rather unsettled to me in recent weeks, I observed. I'm sure I immediately regretted bringing him up, as Raj launched into a lengthy complaint about Anil, as he often did. Indeed, it seemed like all those two guys did was complain about each other—Anil frustrated that Raj wouldn't commit to hiring him, and Raj irritated that Anil was always on the make and angling for a job. I could never keep up with the ins and outs of it all, a situation that was exacerbated by Raj's tendency to exaggerate everything and Anil's inflated sense of his own importance. It had gotten to the point where I just tuned it out, not wanting to be constantly in the middle of their bickering. I think that was probably what happened on that particular call, which is why it didn't raise a red flag for me when Raj uttered the statement, "I'm giving him a million dollars a year for doing literally nothing."

By the time the tape was played in the courtroom, of course, everyone knew that that payment was for providing insider tips. So naturally, hearing the tape, they assumed I'd known about, and condoned, this illegal arrangement. My response to Raj must have confirmed this: "I know, you're being . . . I think you're very generous."

When I listened back to the tape, I could hear in my voice that I wasn't fully taking in what Raj had said, or taking it literally. Quite frankly, I was tired of their complaining about each other. Besides, Rajaratnam was a generous man, so it would not have been out of character for him to simply gift large sums to a friend nor to exaggerate the size of those sums to make a point about that friend's ingratitude. In fact, Raj had been generous with Anil in many ways, giving Anil's disabled son, Aman, a job and a place to stay. He also could have been paying Anil quite legitimately for advice: McKinsey had no explicit rule against partners advising friends or family unless there was a conflict of interest that would take away work that the firm might otherwise do. Whatever the case, I just didn't want to get into this with Raj—it was their business, not mine. Never for a moment did it occur to me that he was paying Anil for illegal information.

Of course, no one else listening to that tape would have known these things, and to this day, people find it hard to believe that I could have heard his words and not reported it to the firm. Based on that one conversation—taken completely out of context and now colored by what they knew about the insider trading scheme—perhaps it was understandable that people assumed the worst: that I turned a blind eye to Raj's secret arrangement with Anil. Nothing could have been further from the truth.

Excommunicated

McKinsey. My first thought when I heard this section of the tape was how terrible this would look to the firm, and how betrayed they would feel. I'd assured them I'd known nothing of Anil's arrangement, which was true, but this tape made it seem otherwise. And I'd given them no warning that this public spectacle with their name all over it was about to get worse, because I hadn't known about it myself. That was the hardest part for me to bear—that it was too late for me to soften the blow.

Had I been given any heads-up about this part of the tape, I'd have called up Dominic Barton and explained. The firm would not have been happy, but at least they would have been prepared. Instead, they heard about it on the news. They were completely surprised, and I looked like a liar. In a cruel stroke of fate, the day the tape was played happened to be in the middle of the annual partners' conference—an event I'd proudly presided over for many years. Everyone heard it, all at once. I was tormented with visions of my friends and former colleagues listening to that recording, discussing it, and assuming I had condoned Rajaratnam's illegal financial arrangement with Kumar and had blatantly lied to them all.

Infuriatingly, all the lawyers seemed to have missed the potential consequences of that part of the tape. They'd been focused on what seemed like the more problematic part of the conversation—the discussion related to the Goldman board meeting—but neglected to even tell me about the part that was much more damaging for me personally. They didn't seem to realize that it would have made an enormous difference for me had I been able to warn McKinsey.

Naturally, the leaders of the firm were outraged. I was sitting in the waiting room at my doctor's office shortly thereafter when I got a call from Ian Davis, a long-time colleague who had succeeded me as head of the firm. I was glad he was the one who had called—we went back a long way, and I had stood by him during difficult times in his own career, eventually making him head of my governance task force, a success that set him up to be chosen as the firm's leader.

I apologized that I had only a few minutes before my appointment. "Don't worry," Ian said, "Vik and I will call you back." Vik Malhotra was head of the New York office. Ian also said that the professional standards committee would be conducting an investigation and I'd get a chance to speak about it all to them and to the shareholders' committee. But neither of those calls ever came. I never had a chance to tell my side of the story.

Instead, with very little warning, I was asked to vacate my office. My secretary Renee, my support system, and the role I'd valued so deeply were all taken away. I was asked to stop using my McKinsey email address—a small thing, but symbolic nonetheless. It was the only email address I'd ever had, because in my entire career, I'd never worked anywhere else. It was disorienting and deeply painful, but felt there was nothing I could really do, besides request that the firm ensure Renee was taken care of. She'd been invaluable to me and I hated to think my troubles would cause her hardship.

The firm I'd served for thirty-seven years turned its back on me and I was essentially excommunicated. At this point, I had only been accused, and on the flimsiest of circumstantial evidence. They never gave me a fair hearing. This shocked me—it was so uncharacteristic of the principled firm I'd always so deeply respected and antithetical to the partnership values that were supposed to be the firm's bedrock. I felt enormous gratitude toward McKinsey for having nurtured my career, but I also felt the firm to which I'd given my whole professional life owed me, at the very least, respect and due process. In their eyes, more than anyone's, I should have been innocent until proven guilty.

At home, Anita was sympathetic, but I could tell she was not as shocked as I was at the behavior of my former partners. She'd always told me I tended to romanticize the firm, and perhaps she was right. I genuinely believed in the values of the partnership, the fairness of the firm and its loyalty to its people. I understood their outrage, and I'd have been the first to encourage the leaders to appropriately distance themselves from the case. They could have made clear to their clients and the general public that no McKinsey companies were involved in the charges and that I was taking a leave of absence until the legal process was complete. That would have been enough to protect the firm. It was not necessary to erase me entirely, to kick me when I was down and in need of support. Later, I would discover that my name had even been removed from the alumni directory. How could I cease to be an alumnus after spending thirty-seven years there and leading the firm for nine?

The painful injustice of all this was only amplified by the fact that, as my lawyers reminded me, the tape had no direct relevance to the case being tried. The conversation contained no actual "material nonpublic information" and led to no trades. My comments were inappropriate, but not illegal. Why was it given so much attention, when the government had so many other much more incriminating recordings of Rajaratnam—recordings in which he gave and received actual tips? If they wanted to prove a conspiracy, they already had damning evidence in the testimony of former Galleon trader Adam Smith, who offered detailed descriptions of obtaining and passing on to his boss information about several companies. As the judge himself pointed out, "A reasonable jury could have found Rajaratnam guilty as to Count One [conspiracy] on the basis of Smith's testimony alone."[2] I can only conclude that highlighting the tape served a larger story that the Justice Department wanted to construct about me.

The focus on Goldman and on myself did not stop with the playing of the tape. The prosecutor's focus then turned to the Berkshire Hathaway deal, highlighting the fact that I'd called Rajaratnam shortly after the board meeting in which the deal was announced, and playing the wiretapped conversation between Raj and one of his traders from the following day, in which he mentioned receiving a call just before the markets closed and hearing that "something good might happen to Goldman." By the time the *Times* pointed out my central role in the trial, six weeks in, it had indeed grown to elephantine proportions.

I didn't know what to think at this point. I was starting to second-guess every decision I'd made and all the advice I'd been given. Should I have made a deal with the SEC the moment we'd first heard about the investigation? Perhaps I could have settled for a small fine while not agreeing to any wrongdoing. But I knew that even if my lawyers had suggested this, I would probably not have agreed—to me, any deal would have amounted to an admission of guilt. Had it been a mistake to take the Fifth? Should I have spoken to the SEC at the hearing? I still believed that if I just had the chance to tell my side of the story, it would become clear that I'd done nothing wrong. Looking back, I was naive, to say the least.

Tried In Abstentia

I don't believe it was an accident that I took center stage at Rajaratnam's trial. In fact, the series of events leading up to it left me fairly certain that it was part of a deliberate campaign on the part of the Justice Department to try me and find me guilty in the court of public opinion. Preet Bharara, the ambitious US Attorney for the Southern District of New York, was itching to charge me—I could feel it. I wasn't a banker, but I was of sufficient stature that maybe the public wouldn't notice the mismatch. However, with only the thinnest circumstantial case against me, he needed to ensure that the jury pool was primed to judge me harshly.

One question to which I—and many others—have given a great deal of thought is this: Why did the SEC scramble to file charges against me just days before the Rajaratnam trial, allowing no time to review my detailed response to the Wells Notice? I've reflected on this question at great length, as did the press and anyone else observing the case. Writing in the *New York Times,* the financial journalist Andrew Ross Sorkin commented, "there is something curious about the accusations against Mr. Gupta, which came just days before Mr. Rajaratnam's criminal trial . . . . Given the seriousness of the claims—insider trading by an executive who had reached the upper echelons of corporate America—why not bring criminal charges against Mr. Gupta?" However, he noted that the evidence, such as it was, seemed barely enough to warrant even the civil charges, with the SEC only claiming that it was "very likely" I had spoken to Raj on the days in question. "Since when has 'very likely' been considered enough to make a civil allegation?"[3]

Personally, I felt that this smacked of a collaboration of sorts between the Justice Department and the SEC. Surely, Bharara knew he didn't have enough evidence to press criminal charges, but the SEC charge was an "administrative" one, which carried a much lower standard of evidence than the federal court. Perhaps getting the SEC to charge me was another step in the PR campaign to set the stage for him to do so when the time was right. These charges would solidify the image of my guilt that had been planted in the public mind by the leaked article, and give the US Attorney's Office (USAO) more time to build a case.

I'll likely never know if my theory is true, but it seems consistent with Bharara's playbook. An ambitious Indian immigrant who had moved to the US with his parents at the age of two, Bharara took office in 2009. I had personally never met him, but as I struggled to come to grips with the invisible chess game, I quickly realized that this was someone I needed to understand. When I began to read up on his tenure as US Attorney and the tactics he employed to succeed, much of my own experience began to make more sense.

Bharara's appointment had initially inspired high hopes that he would aggressively pursue charges against the banking executives responsible for the financial crisis. No such charges were forthcoming, however, and soon he became the target of pointed criticisms in the press. The public was angry, and rightly so. The bankers seemed impervious to prosecution, the banks were getting government bailouts, and ordinary, hard-working people were losing their homes. Bharara must have needed a new story. If going after the big banking executives was too difficult, he needed another way to appease the public's desire for convictions. Hedge funds were an ideal target—the "next best crooks," as *New York* magazine put it.[4] They carried the aura of Wall Street greed and excess, but were not enmeshed in the global financial markets or in politics the way the big banks were. They also lacked the political muscle to defend themselves. It was a shrewd strategy: by cracking down on insider trading and aggressively prosecuting hedge fund managers and their informants, Bharara could appear to be taking a hard line on corruption without actually pursuing the tough cases and endangering his perfect record of convictions (a strategy that led former FBI director James Comey to dub Bharara and his colleagues "the chickenshit club"[5]).

To ensure the success of his strategy, Bharara seems to have done what any good politician does: he hired PR people, lots of them. Press conferences, press releases, dramatic predawn arrests, perp walks for the cameras, well-publicized speeches, and TV appearances became the norm. Bharara was a natural performer, shifting between self-deprecating humor and rather pompous moralizing. Following each arrest, he invited the cameras in and fed reporters carefully prepared soundbites ("Greed, sometimes, is not good," he told the press after

Rajaratnam's arrest, declaring that the case should be "a wake up call for Wall Street."[6]).

Bharara also became known for his habit of writing lengthy complaints against his targets, exhaustively detailing the allegations against each defendant. Reputations were destroyed long before cases reached the courtroom, and indeed many never got there. Feeling powerless to fight the government's narrative, which the press eagerly picked up and disseminated, most defendants of the era chose to settle out of court and pay hefty fines.[7] Much later, in 2015, a district judge would strongly rebuke Bharara for these tactics, noting that "criminal cases should be tried in the courtroom and not in the press." She criticized the government's "brinksmanship relative to the Defendant's fair trial rights," the USAO's orchestrated "media blitz," the questionable timing of some of his arrests, and his tendency to "bundle together unproven allegations regarding the defendant with broader commentary on corruption" in his public statements.[8] All these were tactics he had practiced in previous cases, and many of them showed up in mine.

In 2009 Bharara's playbook had not drawn much scrutiny, and the moment my name came up in the Rajaratnam investigation, he must have seen an opportunity. A high-profile global businessman with close ties to the titans of industry and politics—that would look very good on his résumé. That I, like many of those he targeted, was a fellow Indian only served to burnish his tough-guy aura. There was just one problem in my case: he had little if any evidence to go on. I imagine this irritated him—he once described to an interviewer the frustration when "you have a belief that somebody has committed a crime and you just can't get the evidence because no one has flipped or because there are no recordings . . ."[9] He kept digging, but he also began his parallel offensive, setting out to ensure that by the time I was actually tried everyone would already believe I'd committed the crime.

On May 11, 2011, Rajaratnam was found guilty on all five counts of conspiracy to commit securities fraud and nine counts of securities fraud. Even in his closing argument against the defendant, prosecutor Reed Brodsky still seemed to be making a case against me. "You don't get on the board of Goldman Sachs without having accomplished a lot in your life and having a great reputation," he declared. "Having a great reputation doesn't give you a free pass to violate the law. Nobody is above the law, no matter how good their reputation is."[10]

As I read the press coverage of the verdict, I could not shake the growing sense that I too had already been found guilty, although I had been neither charged nor tried. Even my usually sanguine legal team was somber. No one was telling me not to worry any more, not even Gary. Instead, he told me, "We need to prepare to defend a criminal case."

5

Guilty Until Proven Innocent

Thou hast led me through my crowded travels of the day
to my evening's loneliness.
I wait for its meaning through the stillness of the night.

—Rabindranath Tagore, *Stray Birds*, 241

May 2011

My calendar was empty. I refreshed the window, but it was no error: blank. I could not remember the last time I'd had a day like that. I was accustomed to every hour being scheduled—back-to-back appointments, every meal a meeting, and every break a list of phone calls to be returned. Now, the empty pages in my calendar reflected the strange sense of blankness that had settled over me since the Rajaratnam trial. It all felt surreal. Could this really be happening? Every morning, I still got up and put on a suit—a lifetime's habit was hard to break. But the reality was that I no longer had an office to go to, and the only meetings scheduled were with my lawyers.

There are few things more painful than watching friends and colleagues turn their backs and walk away, in my case often without even giving me the opportunity to tell my side of the story. McKinsey was particularly hard. Partners with whom I'd worked for years, if not decades, suddenly stopped returning my calls or spoke harshly about me behind my back. Many were people I'd helped and mentored, like Adil Zainulbhai, head of the India office, who went out of his way to call many high-profile clients and government officials in India to tell them that I had nothing to do with McKinsey any more. I learned this because many of those people immediately called me themselves—our relationships went back much farther than their relationships with Adil. I don't believe it was a personal attack on me, but I wished Adil had called me first about what he was going to do. Many others, however, did reach out to offer their support, including former McKinsey managing director Ian Davis, my European colleague Herb Henzler, my secretary Elizabeth Heno, Peter Walker from the New York office, and Ajit Jain, now working for Warren Buffett at Berkshire Hathaway. Even partners I had not been in touch with for decades suddenly got in touch, like my friend Alistair Hanna from my early days with the firm. Most of my colleagues in the not-for-profit world stood by me. I did indeed learn who my real friends were.

When it came to real friends, there were none more loyal and supportive than the Indian entrepreneur P.C. Chatterjee, whom I'd known since we hired him at McKinsey in the 1970s. I also relied on the group of friends I liked to call my "breakfast club"—my childhood friend Anjan Chatterjee, Rakesh Kaul from IIT, former McKinsey partner Atul Kanagat, and businessmen Sreedhar Menon and Anil Bhandari. Along with PC, this group of incredibly busy people would make time to come together regularly and offer their moral support. I don't know how I would have gotten through those difficult weeks and months without them. I was also grateful to my IIT friend Raji Pawar, who was especially supportive, and my friend Shiv Nadar, one of India's most prominent businessmen, who made a point of inviting me to his birthday celebration in Istanbul, sending a clear message to many of our mutual acquaintances that he and his wife, Kiran, were not allowing the charges to change their friendship with Anita and me.

During this time, I drew on my spiritual strength and remembered what my father had taught me. I practiced letting go of attachment to people, titles, and institutions. I reminded myself that the essence of who I am is not defined by these things, but by caring for others, doing the right thing, and being true to my values. I cared deeply for the institutions I'd built and stewarded, and it was hard to let go. Sometimes the regret and frustration were overwhelming. But I drew comfort from knowing that I had not built these institutions and relationships for my own glory, but for the good they might bring to the world. If detaching myself from them now would help them to remain untarnished by my troubles, I would do it gladly and with grace.

Turning the Tables

My legal case crawled forward. The SEC charge against me was an "administrative" one—a civil charge. It was the first insider trading case to be charged in this way, thanks to the recent Dodd-Frank act, which extended the SEC's power to try insider trading cases against non-regulated persons such as myself* in its administrative court, rather than the Federal District Court, the usual venue for such cases. That meant that the SEC would essentially be prosecutor, judge, and jury—and they obviously came with a built-in bias. This seemed unfair to me—what hope did I have of clearing my name in what was little better than a kangaroo court, especially considering that the SEC had already ignored my Wells submission? As many people have commentated, the administrative court gives the SEC a significant "home court advantage."[1] Every other one of the twenty-eight Galleon-related cases had been tried in federal court. Why was I being singled out for disparate treatment?

Gary was furious at this situation when we first met to discuss the

* People not associated with investment advisors, brokerage firms, or other registered entities.

charges, back in March. He was determined to find us a legal response. I remember the moment when the idea struck him: we should sue the SEC. The way they were treating me was unconstitutional. They were taking away my right to equal protection under the law by denying me a jury trial.

There was a stunned silence in the room. Sue the SEC? It was an audacious suggestion, but the more we entertained it, the more appropriate it seemed. Plus, it just felt good to finally be taking action and going on the offensive. Maybe we could turn the tables on the people who seemed so intent on destroying everything I'd built. Gary thought we had a fighting chance, particularly if we could get the case in front of Judge Jed Rakoff, who had presided over many of the Galleon cases. He might be one of the few judges who had the guts to take on the SEC if they were overreaching.

Others I consulted were surprised by the idea—it was highly unusual for anyone to sue the SEC, and unheard of for anyone to win. "Negotiate a settlement," they advised, "before it's too late. Plenty of people pay SEC fines and continue their careers without too much damage."

But I was frustrated by the ongoing presumption of guilt that I felt had been set in motion by the press and was being reinforced daily by the prosecutor at Rajaratnam's trial. I didn't want to take a defensive stance, make a deal, pay a fine, and get a slap on the wrist for something I hadn't done. I wanted a chance to set the record straight. My legal team seemed energized by the novelty and boldness of the idea. I agreed to sue. Our complaint argued that in addition to depriving me of my constitutional right to equal protection, the SEC was attempting to apply Dodd-Frank retroactively, since the incidents in question occurred before the law was passed. After laying out our case, we concluded, "the only plausible inference is that the Commission is proceeding how and where it is against Mr. Gupta for the bad faith purpose of shoring up a meritless case by disarming its adversary."[2]

For a brief moment, our unorthodox strategy seemed to be working.

We got Rakoff as judge. The SEC moved to dismiss our charges, but at the July hearing on their motion to dismiss, the tide seemed to turn in our favor.

"A funny thing happened on the way to this forum," Judge Rakoff began, outlining the unusual sequence of events that had led to this day, and seeming to acknowledge and perhaps even appreciate the audacity and logic of our "well-pleaded" case, as he described it. He seemed to take some satisfaction in thwarting the SEC's attempt to avoid bringing my case in his court, which he described as an "exercise in forum shopping." After carefully refuting each of the SEC's arguments for dismissal as being without merit, he concluded that in this unusual case, "there is already a well-developed public record of Gupta being treated substantially disparately from twenty-eight essentially identical defendants, with not even a hint from the SEC . . . as to why this should be so."[3]

With that, he ruled that our suit could continue. Now, we could proceed to discovery, and perhaps find further evidence that the SEC and the Justice Department were trying to construct a case against me without sufficient evidence to warrant it. The SEC threatened to appeal and tie us up in a long-drawn-out battle. Then, in August, they abruptly dropped the charges against me (although reserving the right to charge me again), and we, in turn, withdrew our suit. My lawyers were elated—their gutsy move had worked and they felt they had made legal history. I couldn't let myself feel relieved, however. It just didn't seem plausible that the nightmare was over. And sure enough, the reprieve did not last. Rumors that the government intended to press criminal charges grew more persistent.

My lawyers began directly petitioning the USAO, attempting to lay out a convincing argument for why, in Gary's words, there was "no basis for a rush to the courthouse." By this point, I'd also retained the services of Mary Jo White, a former US Attorney herself, who had hired Bharara and knew the Justice Department intimately. She joined the team as an advisor and was present for a series of meetings at the

USAO, culminating in a face-to-face meeting with Bharara himself. I was not present for this meeting, but the lawyers seemed encouraged. He listened carefully to their arguments, they reported.

Meanwhile, there was another troubling twist to the story. From the beginning, I'd told my lawyers that Ravi Trehan was going to be an essential witness. He was the one person who knew the whole Voyager saga, and could testify to the slow disintegration of my relationship with Rajaratnam beginning in the spring of 2008 and coming to a head well before the alleged tipping. In early conversations with my lawyers, he confirmed the timeline I'd laid out. However, in the summer of 2011, as we prepared for our meetings with the USAO, Ravi proved difficult for my lawyers to contact. Eventually, I called him myself, and he assured me that he was willing to testify. He also told me that the government had not interviewed him.

My lawyers persisted in their efforts to get a meeting with him, but soon learned some worrying news: Ravi was now represented by a former USAO lawyer, and had been in contact with the government for some time, despite his protestations to me. He continued to avoid meeting with my lawyers or speaking with me, but indirectly he seemed to be sending a clear message: he did not want to testify, and if forced to do so, it would not be favorable to me. He claimed to no longer remember the dates of the sequence of events in 2008 that was so critical to my defense. I reached out to our supportive mutual friend Rana Talwar to ask him to speak to Ravi and prevail upon him to simply tell the truth, but his attempts came to nothing. This was a devastating blow. Without Ravi to testify as to the timing of the Voyager affair, the jury would have only my testimony to go on, perhaps supported by my financial advisor Greg Orman, the only other party to the events in question.

I've never learned what they found against Ravi to use as leverage and convince him not to stand up for me, but I've no doubt they had something. Why else would one of my oldest friends desert me at such a critical moment? I still wonder, if left alone, what he would have done, and I believe he would have stood by me. I also realized, too late, that we had made a strategic error in agreeing to the meeting between my lawyers and Preet Bharara. They'd presented the case we had, of which Ravi was an essential part. We'd told Bharara exactly how to undermine our defense.

On October 13, Rajaratnam was due to be sentenced. The press had been speculating ever since the trial ended: Would the judge make an example of Raj and give him the twenty-four years the prosecutors were seeking? Or would they listen to his lawyers' pleas for leniency given his ill health and the nonviolent nature of his crimes? Raj suffered from severe diabetes, and his lawyers' claim that an extended stay in prison would amount to a death sentence was not entirely exaggerated. At fifty-four, he must have known it was possible he would live out his life in jail. Before a packed courthouse with hordes of press waiting outside, Judge Holwell sentenced Rajaratnam to eleven years—the longest sentence ever handed down to a convicted insider trader, though less severe than the prosecutors had hoped.

When I heard the news, I didn't know what to feel. Raj deserved a serious punishment, but this was clearly disproportionate. Plus, there was no doubt that this sentence would embolden the prosecutors. And it was all too clear by this point that I was their next target.

Diwali

For Hindus, the month of Kartik marks the end of the summer harvest and the beginning of the dry season. It's a holy month in my homeland, and on the night of the new moon—known as *amavasya*, the darkest night of the Hindu lunisolar calendar—millions of Indians celebrate Diwali, the festival of lights. In 2011 Diwali fell on October 26. And it was on this day—traditionally signifying the victory of light over darkness, hope over despair—that Bharara, a fellow Indian, chose to indict me on charges of insider trading. Although he later denied it in interviews, claiming to have been unaware of the significance of the date, I doubt the timing was an accident. It was like arresting a Christian on Christmas Day, or a Jew on Rosh Hashanah.

The day before, I'd had a premonition of impending doom. Anita tried to cheer me up, suggesting that we take a scenic drive with Avinash and Madhuri. I didn't think even the brilliance of the New England fall could lift my spirits, but I didn't have the energy to argue. We had barely reached the freeway when my phone rang. Pulling over, I took the call and Gary informed me that I was to surrender to the FBI the following morning and be indicted on criminal charges of insider trading.

One by one, I called the rest of the family and told them the bad news. My daughters each dropped whatever they were doing and drove out to our family home in Connecticut. My younger brother Anjan, a doctor, was living and working in Manhattan, and he and his wife, Mala, also came to join us. The phone rang all evening, as word got around to my extended family and friends. In the midst of it all, I felt strangely calm, reassuring everyone that I would be fine. I had known this day would come. It had seemed inevitable for some time. There was no reason to be shocked or overly emotional. I moved through the evening in a trance-like state, as if distanced from the emotional tumult that everyone else was experiencing.

One small mercy was that I was spared the 5 a.m. perp walk for the television cameras. There were no FBI agents banging on my door, no handcuffs, and no press, aside from a lone photographer who leapt into my driveway as we pulled out before dawn, almost causing me to hit him. Anita, her brother Arvind, and brother-in-law Ajay accompanied me to the city, but I insisted they stay at the apartment. I didn't want them to endure the media frenzy that I was sure awaited me at the FBI offices downtown.

My lawyers arrived to pick me up a little before seven. We were silent as the car crawled slowly through the city streets, already thronged with people on their way to work. As I looked at the sea of strangers, clutching coffees and briefcases, for a brief moment, I let myself imagine that I was one of them, on my way to the office, dressed in suit and tie, ready to spend a full and productive day serving clients and mentoring colleagues. But I knew that I'd never have a "normal" life like that again. Reality quickly reasserted itself as the car passed McKinsey's Park Avenue offices and carried me downtown.

Since we arrived very early at the FBI offices, thankfully there was no press. My tie and belt were taken away as a safety precaution, and I was presented with my first pair of handcuffs. The cold steel against my wrists evoked a surge of rage and shame, breaking through the strange calm that had stayed with me throughout the night. I asked my lawyers to take the first photograph of me in handcuffs. Then I was fingerprinted and taken through some other procedures before being marched back to the car, still cuffed, and driven to the courthouse. Now the press was out in force, and we entered through the basement to avoid the cameras.

I was put in a large holding cell with a collection of rather intimidating guys, mostly in on drug charges. They all seemed to know each other, and I wondered if they were members of a gang. Eventually, I was moved to an individual cell, and then, after an hour or more of waiting, I was taken to the magistrate to enter my plea of "Not Guilty." There had never been any question that this would be my stance. I would vigorously defend my innocence.

After my arraignment I was released on a $10 million bail, secured by my home. My passport was confiscated and I was told that I was barred from leaving the country until further notice. I also learned from my lawyers that the SEC were exercising their right to charge me again and had filed a new set of charges that day, echoing the criminal indictment. I was not in the least bit surprised: I'd challenged them to take my case to the federal court, and now they would get the chance to do so. Wearily, I made my way back uptown to our apartment.

My family was all there, waiting for my return. I didn't say much, and they didn't ask. Together, we drove back to Connecticut, mostly in silence. At home, Madhuri had cooked a festive meal and we sat down together for a family dinner. We lit candles for the holiday, but they couldn't dispel the darkness that I was feeling. Evoking the rituals of India only served to highlight my sudden disconnection from the culture around me. America had been good to me—welcoming a young immigrant into its finest educational and business institutions, entrusting me with positions of influence, providing freedom and opportunity to my family. But now it felt as if the country we'd all called home for so long had turned against us. Somehow, my name had become synonymous with the worst kind of greed and privilege in the public eye.

It didn't matter that I was hardly involved in Wall Street, let alone that insider trading had nothing to do with the financial crisis. It didn't matter that I'd never sought power or influence for its own sake, or that I'd spent decades working to improve global health, education, and free trade. Bharara's strategy was working: go after the hedge funds and their circle, play up the story in the press, and maybe no one would notice that the big banking executives were continuing to walk free.

Seeing Anita's usually stoic expression giving way to despair, I shook myself out of the spiraling anger, resentment, and gloom that threatened to suck me down. "We can't allow them to destroy our holiday," I said. "No matter what people do to us, we can always choose to respond with grace and spiritual strength." We rejoined our daughters and went to the *puja* room to say prayers. As I watched the flickering flames, my spirit of defiance began to rekindle. I would not be broken by this. *Mind without fear, head held high.* If I were to face a judge and jury, so be it. This time, at least, I would have the opportunity to defend myself.

Part II

Karma Yoga

You have the right to work, but never to the fruit of work.

—Bhagavad Gita, 2:47

6

A Dark Diwali

"Who is there to take up my duties?" asked the setting sun.
"I shall do what I can, my Master," said the earthen lamp.

—Rabindranath Tagore, *Stray Birds,* 153

The day of my arrest was not the first time that the festival of lights turned into a dark day for me. In fact, for most of my life, the joyful Diwali celebrations have been tinged with sadness, because it was on this day in 1964 that I lost my father.

I was fifteen years old. My sisters and I had recently returned to our home in Delhi after a family vacation, while our parents stayed a few extra days in Kolkata with my youngest brother. A sharp knock on the apartment door broke the quiet of the afternoon. The man looked vaguely familiar; he was someone from my father's office. "You must go to Kolkata right away," he told us, his face etched with concern. "Mr. Gupta is very sick."

We were given plane tickets and told to quickly pack some clothes. A car was waiting outside to take us to the airport, and our aunt was already inside. We had never traveled by air before, but what should have been an exciting prospect—my first flight—only served to underscore the seriousness of the situation. My family would never have gone to such expense unless time was critical.

My sisters and I barely spoke a word during the flight, sitting in stunned silence, each afraid to voice our fears lest it make them more real. Baba had been sick on and off for many years, but he had always recovered. This time, however, it felt different. It was dark when the plane began its descent into Kolkata, and the Diwali celebrations were beginning. Sitting in the window seat, I could see fireworks flaring above the streets, looking strangely small from my lofty vantage point. As we skimmed the city, I began to make out dots of light from the millions of little earthen lamps that lined the rooftops for the festival. My younger sister Kumkum clutched my arm as the aircraft wheels struck the tarmac and the heavy plane lurched to a halt. We grabbed our hurriedly packed bag and were carried through the busy airport by the momentum of the crowd until the familiar face of our uncle, Choto Kaka (meaning father's youngest brother), appeared out of the sea of strangers. I didn't want to ask the question, but I had to know. "What's happening with father? Is he alive?"

Uncle's face was somber, but he nodded affirmatively. "You must go directly to the hospital. We'll go to the house later."

As we drove through the city streets, past sidewalks crowded with people in their best clothes, laughing and celebrating, I began to cradle a small flame of hope in my heart. Baba was not dead. Surely this had all been a misunderstanding, an overreaction. After all, when we had left him just a few days earlier, he had seemed fine. We'd just spent several weeks traveling as a family, hitching our little caboose to the trains that criss-crossed the country. It was a happy, carefree trip—falling asleep each night to the rhythm of the train; waking in a new city to the familiar cries of the *chai wallahs* selling sweet, spiced tea in little clay cups. Baba had been with us the whole time—a rarity for a hard-working man who usually only joined our summer vacations for a week at most.

I knew, however, that he was not strong. The many years he suffered in prison during the fight for India's independence had taken their toll, particularly the tuberculosis, which had left him with only one lung. Although he was only fifty-six, his body was failing like that of a much older man.

Earlier that same year, he'd spent several months in hospital in Delhi. I remember that period vividly, because it was the time when I really got to know my father. While we were growing up, he had not been much of a presence in our daily lives. He was often busy writing his editorial for the newspaper when we returned from school, and rarely home for dinner. During his hospitalization, at the All India Institute of Medical Sciences, I visited him every day after school. Sometimes I would sit by his bed and massage his feet or his temples. Other times, when he felt a little stronger, we would walk in the tranquil gardens of the hospital for many hours. It was on these slow afternoon strolls down the tree-lined avenues of the campus that my father came into focus as a person. The vague and slightly distant authority figure of my childhood became more vulnerable, more reflective, and more intent than ever before on imparting his life's lessons to his eldest son.

During those walks, he told me a lot about his life, trying to convey what the struggle for independence had meant to him. He recalled his friends, the sacrifices they made, the years they all spent in and out of jail. He reflected on how he had made a different choice to most of his former comrades—while many had gone on to become leaders of the nation they'd liberated, he had chosen a career in journalism, seeking more stability for his growing family than politics would have offered. He remained closely connected with many of the political leaders of the day, including Prime Minister Nehru, President Radhakrishnan, and Opposition leader Lohia, and would frequently accompany them on official trips.

In the quiet sanctuary of the hospital gardens, he would also ask me about my day, inquiring as to how school was going and encouraging me to think about my future and plan my career. I knew he was proud of my good grades and approved of my choice to follow a science track. In the past couple of years, I'd shed the naughty, headstrong attitude that had characterized my childhood, somehow intuiting that my role was about to change. Now my father's words confirmed my sense of impending adulthood. "Ratan," he would say with great seriousness, using my childhood pet name, meaning "jewel." "It is time for you to become more responsible. When I am gone, you must take care of your mother, your sisters, and your brother."

Those words came back to me as the car sped through the dusty Kolkata streets toward the hospital, the heavy silence inside contrasting sharply with the celebrations all around. In little tents, families were lighting candles for the Kali *puja*. The acrid smell of fireworks hung in the cool night air. I had known the day would come when I would be the man of the family, and Baba had known it too. But surely it had not come so soon?

My mother was waiting in the hospital lobby, at the top of the stairs. Her face was streaked with tears as she gathered us all into her arms. "Baba is gone," she said. My sisters broke down sobbing, but I couldn't take it in. As Ma comforted the girls, I turned to one of the nurses. "Where is he? Which room?" She pointed down the hallway.

When I entered the small room, my father lay before me, looking strangely diminished in the hospital gown. I stood, frozen, for what seemed like an eternity. His face was still and serene. Suddenly, a tiny movement drew my eyes to the tube coming out of his mouth. There were bubbles moving in it. He was breathing! I spun around and ran out of the room, colliding with my mother. "He's not dead!" I exclaimed. "Look, he's breathing!" She gathered me to her, sobbing louder. "No, Ratan, no. He is gone." Finally, I broke down, my flame of hope snuffed out by a wave of grief.

His body was brought home to my uncle's house for viewing. Death is not hidden away in India, but is on display for all the family, including children. Baba was washed and dressed in his clean white *dhoti*. An earthenware lamp was lit at his head, scented water sprinkled over his body, and garlands placed around his neck. As soon as the morning papers published the news, a steady stream of visitors began to appear. Some were friends and family, but many were strangers—people who knew my father by reputation, even some who learned about him just that day, and came to pay their last respects to a hero of the freedom struggle.

As the long day wore on, we prepared for the cremation. Hindu tradition holds that the soul will escape more quickly if the body is burned, and the ceremony must be conducted before a full day has passed. My father's cremation would follow this custom. He was a man of faith, but as a member of the reformist Brahmo Samaj sect, his belief system was non-traditional, incorporating aspects of Christianity and Islam and rejecting the rituals of Hinduism while honoring its Vedantic core. Hence, knowing he would not have wanted it, I chose not to follow some of the traditional Hindu practices, such as shaving my head in mourning. We would have a Brahmo Samaj memorial service later, after ten days of mourning during which we would gather every evening and sing the beautiful music of Rabindranath Tagore that my father had loved so much.

As the eldest son, it was my role to be chief mourner. My mother and sisters did not attend the cremation, since only men were allowed at the burning *ghats*, and my brother was too young. The red sun was sinking toward the hazy skyline as I dressed carefully in a white *dhoti-kurta*, just like the one my father had worn every day, and we began the slow procession to the *ghat*. Here, the body was placed atop one of the wood pyres that dotted a large outdoor area. Some were already engulfed in flames, some were reduced to glowing embers, and some stood freshly built, awaiting their sacred burden. Families gathered around the fires, and the sound of prayers and weeping rose with the smoke into the still night air.

"O Lord, in thy name we consign the mortal to ashes, but the immortal lives in thee." Standing at the head of the pyre, I repeated the prayer that would guide my father's soul to immortality. "Prosper the departed soul in its voyage heavenward and let his blessed memory live amongst us and join our souls to the next world."[1]

The priest handed me a burning taper, and I reached down and lit the pyre. The dry wood quickly burst into flame, and the sweet fragrant incense that was poured into the fire did little to mask the sharp stench of burning flesh. As I stood there silently, watching my father's body turn to smoke and ash, I knew that my childhood was over.

Coming of Age

In the weeks and months following my father's death, there was little surface change in our circumstances. The Sarkar family, who owned the newspaper where my father worked, graciously told us we could stay in the company-rented apartment for as long as we wanted, and they continued to provide a stipend, although my father had had no pension. My mother was frugal by nature, and over the years she had saved money, out of reach of my father's overly generous and always open hands. This, along with her teaching salary and the stipend, was enough for the family to live on. My siblings and I were all offered scholarships so that we could continue attending our private schools. I was in tenth grade at Delhi's Modern School, a very good school where I had many friends and a rich academic and extracurricular life, so I was relieved to be able to stay.

Emotionally, it was a time of tremendous upheaval. I had always been a disciplined and motivated student, but now an unfamiliar sense of lethargy took hold. In the highly competitive academic environment of my high school, this was immediately apparent. My grades plummeted, my enthusiasm for extracurricular activities waned, and I fell into a depression that lasted several months. This was compounded when the names were announced of the six students who would have the coveted leadership role of prefect in the coming year. Everyone assumed I would be on the list, but my name was absent, sending shocked whispers through the assembly. I smarted at the unfairness. I didn't mind being bested in a fair competition, but this felt like an injustice, and there was nothing I could do about it. This wasn't a role one campaigned for; it was a mark of recognition that I clearly deserved. Everyone agreed that I was one of the most qualified students. It only added to my sense that the world was turning against me and no one cared about me any more since my father had died.

At home, I had a similar feeling—as if our family had somehow become irrelevant. When father was alive, the apartment had always been bustling with visitors—senior politicians, civil servants, fellow journalists, and various friends and family members he was helping out. Now, it was just us. As hard as it was for me, in retrospect it must have been harder for my mother. She had been accustomed to a vibrant social life, accompanying father to official dinners, embassy receptions, and other social events. Suddenly, she was a widow, spending most evenings at home, grieving the man she had loved for three decades and trying to remain strong for her children.

In a culture where arranged marriage was the norm, my parents had been a love match, overcoming great obstacles to be together. They met while my mother was a student at Bethune College in the mid-1930s, when my father was hired to tutor her in economics. Their romance blossomed despite the watchful eye of my grandmother, who chaperoned every session. A native of Punjab, Ma broke custom and went against the wishes of her family when she got engaged to a Bengali. That he was a notorious freedom fighter and was in and out of jail every few months only served to reinforce her family's disapproval of their daughter's choice. Keenly aware of his uncertain future, but deeply in love, my father told my mother he could not marry her until India was free. They remained engaged for almost a decade, eventually marrying in early 1947 when independence was in sight. None of her family attended the wedding, although later they would soften and come to love my father as their favorite son-in-law. His loss, at such a young age, was devastating for her, although she tried hard not to show it.

As the spring and summer months passed, my depression slowly lifted. When school began, to my great surprise, the principal announced that a mistake had been made, and I was made a prefect after all. Clearly, there had been protests. Feeling relieved, I trained my sights on the twin tests that would mark the end of my final year: the all-India high school exam and the entrance exam for the prestigious Indian Institutes of Technology.

Like most young people in the Indian education system, by the end of high school my career path had narrowed to a single clear direction. I'd already made the choice, years before, to focus on science rather than humanities. That's what all the boys did, at least those with academic ability, and so naturally I did too. This kind of herd mentality defined educational decision-making in those days. Then, I chose to focus on mathematics rather than biology. Hence, while some of my fellow science students would be applying to medical school, I along with dozens of others would apply to engineering school. And the IITs were the best, so of course we all wanted to go there.

Founded in the 1950s to educate the next generation of India's workforce, this network of engineering schools was seen by many as symbolic of the changing nature of our nation. Nehru, who was instrumental in starting the IITs, called them the "temples of modern India." The IITs were well funded, with state-of-the-art facilities and an unusually meritocratic admissions process that refused to succumb to the corruption and nepotism so prevalent in India at the time. They offered a high-quality engineering program that was supplemented by a very broad-based curriculum, so students were also exposed to history, literature, language, and the arts. Specifically, I wanted to attend IIT Delhi, which was known for its mechanical engineering program, and stay close to my family.

The IIT entrance exam was notoriously tough, and my family could not afford to send me for extra coaching. However, some of my friends were attending a prestigious coaching center near my home, so I invited them to come and visit afterwards and I would help them with their homework. That extra preparation paid off when I sat the entrance exam, along with about a hundred thousand other young would-be engineers; I came first in my school and fifteenth overall. I was also first in the all-India exam for physics, chemistry, and mathematics combined, and was awarded my school's Rudra Prize for best all-round student. I'll never forget the pride on Ma's face when I told her. I just wished Baba could have been there to share it.

IIT Delhi was a residential school, about an hour from home. Moving into the student hostel, along with a dozen or so of my high school classmates, was an adventure, and I quickly became immersed in campus life. Along with student politics, one of my passions was drama, and I acted in several plays a year, in both English and Hindi. At weekends, I would return home, but in contrast to my school life, our home began to feel oppressively quiet.

A strong and independent woman, Ma concealed her grief well, but we would soon realize what a toll it was taking on her. She began to lose a lot of weight and suffer chest pains. Her tall, elegant figure became gaunt and frail. Finally, she went to the doctor and was diagnosed with aortic stenosis—a dangerous narrowing of the arteries. They gave her medication to ease the pain, but surgery was not an option. Later we would learn that she had suffered from rheumatic fever as a child, which had weakened her heart, and the shock of my father's death likely triggered the disease.

During my second year at IIT, I was in rehearsal one afternoon when I received a message that I must return home immediately. Mother was not well. A car and a driver were waiting, but once again I was too late to say goodbye. Only our maid, who cared for her, was with her when she suffered a massive heart attack. Her children came home in the reverse order of their birth, starting with my younger brother, Anjan, who arrived back from school just moments after she passed. Kumkum came next, then me. As soon as I saw people gathered at the house, I knew something bad had happened. Before anyone had a chance to tell me the news, I saw Ma's body in the front room, and my siblings crying.

Didi had received no message, so she arrived home bubbling over with excitement from her graduation ceremony where she'd received her bachelor's degree in chemistry. I was waiting for her on the veranda, not wanting her to find out the way I had. She ran up the steps in her graduation gown, clutching her certificate, but the moment she saw my face her expression changed from joy to trepidation.

At the age of nineteen, I was an orphan.

Orphaned

"We're going to stay together," I insisted, when well-meaning relatives and friends tried to step in and offer homes to one or more of my siblings.

My uncle shook his head vigorously in disapproval. "Anjan needs a father figure and your unmarried sisters cannot live alone at their age—it is not proper." He proposed that I complete my education at IIT while my siblings return with him to Kolkata and move in with various family members.

My sisters and I had already discussed these various options at length and decided that under no circumstances would we allow ourselves to be separated. We would keep the household together until Anjan finished high school. He was only ten, and attending Modern School, as I had done. Both of my sisters were at Delhi University, with Didi just starting her master's program. Four young people living alone was an unconventional choice in the culture of that time, but we were determined. We had also anticipated Uncle's objections and were prepared. For propriety's sake, we decided we would invite an elderly spinster aunt to live with us. Having no children of her own, she was ill-prepared to advise us as we navigated the transition to adulthood, nor was she worldly-wise when it came to handling money. In fact, we ended up caring for her, when her health declined. But her adult presence quelled the opposition to our plan.

My memories of Ma's funeral are less clear than those of my father's, likely because my attention was already consumed with the responsibilities that had fallen on my shoulders. The one thing that stands out above all else was the moment I walked in to the memorial service and saw more than half of my Modern School classmates filling one side of the room. Many of them had traveled across the country to be there. I was overwhelmed by this show of support, and many of those people remain my friends to this day.

Once again, we were blessed by the generosity of my father's former employer, Ashok Sarkar. When I went to see him and told him our plan, he reiterated that we could keep the apartment as long as we needed, rent-free. The bank also showed great kindness, quietly transferring my mother's accounts into my name without requiring that we go through the usual slow succession processes. "It would take a year to go through all the procedures and the lawyers," the banker told me, "so I'm just going to do it." I learned how to manage a strict household budget, something that was new to me. I'd never had to deal with money before. Every weekend, I hurried home across town to take up my role as surrogate father and man of the house.

Anita

One of my great regrets is that two of the most important women in my life never got to meet. I met Anita Mattoo, the woman who would eventually become my wife, in my third year at IIT, several months after Ma's death. Anita and I were cast together in a play. In the early days of our friendship I often called her "Grandma," since she had played the role of my grandmother on stage.

Anita was in her first year when we met, a brilliant electrical engineering student, the only woman in her graduating class of two hundred and fifty students, and one of only a handful on campus. Very few women at that time pursued an engineering career; most went into medicine or other fields. My first impression of her was as a confident and compelling actress, but I soon learned that offstage she was a very shy girl and extremely smart. She too had lost her mother, the same year mine had died, and as the eldest she became like a mother to her youngest brother, who was just a baby, and her sister, who was only four years old at the time. We quickly became good friends.

Indians didn't "date" in the late 1960s, but we became good friends, and our friendship slowly developed into a romance during my fourth year. Every evening, after drama practice, I would walk her back to her dorm, a mile across campus, often lingering in the rose garden on our way.

I learned important lessons in leadership during my third year at IIT. I'd been elected to the position of head of student government, an honor never before held by a third-year student. I quickly found myself at the center of a political standoff. In my view, party politics were best kept out of campus life. We were an educational institution, and I didn't want political agendas derailing the academic focus of the college. However, the campus had a large non-academic staff, perhaps a thousand people or more, who were unionized, organized by one of our professors, Subramanian Swamy, a prominent and ambitious Harvard-educated economist who would later become a national politician. At a certain point, the university staff decided to strike, and there was a strong movement for the students to form a student union and strike in sympathy. Some of my friends strongly backed this idea. "We're not being treated properly!" they declared. "The staff is not being treated properly."

I opposed the idea. "Of course, the staff have a right to strike," I conceded, "but this kind of politics has no place in an educational institution." I'd read so many stories in the papers about strikes on campus bringing everything to a halt, and I felt it set a dangerous precedent to allow those kinds of issues to derail our education.

Things came to a head when three of the pro-union students staged a hunger strike in front of the director's office. I negotiated between the various factions, eventually convincing the student body to forgo the strike. The strike was broken and the three students disciplined. It was a tough situation all round, but it had some positive outcomes. In the course of the negotiations, I was able to use my leverage to tackle some genuine grievances put forth by the student body, in particular a draconian rule that students must attend 85 percent of classes or fail the course. This was simply unrealistic—students miss classes for all kinds of reasons, and I felt that while first-year students might need the discipline of a high attendance requirement, it was unfair to impose it for the entire five years. So I worked with the school to develop a graduated attendance scale, beginning with 75 percent in the first year and reducing each year with no attendance requirement in the final two years. It was quite a revolutionary concept at the time. I was also able to change a rule that said if you failed one subject, you had one chance to retake it over the summer; otherwise you flunked the whole year. A lot of students fell afoul of this rule because English was not their first language, and they had trouble passing the English exam, despite being there to study engineering.

Interestingly, the next year, Subramanian Swamy, the chief proponent of the unions, turned out to be my economics professor. He and I became good friends, with great mutual respect despite our differences of view, and when it came time for me to apply to business school he wrote my recommendation letter.

As my time at IIT came to a close, I faced one of the defining choices of my life: would I apply to graduate school, business school, or seek employment? As I considered my options, I often thought back to those conversations with my father as we walked the hospital gardens.

"Remember this, Ratan," he would say, quoting his favorite poet, Rabindranath Tagore, "'The roots below the earth claim no rewards for making the branches fruitful.' That is the spirit of the *karma yogi*. The karma yogi gives freely of himself without expectation of reward or consequence. There are many paths to God, but this path of selfless service is the path I have walked, and I think it will be your path too. You must strive to do what is right without attachment to the results. Whether you have success or failure, you remain free of outcomes."

My father exemplified this ethos of selfless service—at times, to a fault. He sacrificed his own health and almost his life for the freedom of his country. He lived with an open door and open hands, so unattached to money and worldly goods that my mother had to squirrel away cash to keep the family fed. While I'd taken to heart the spirit of his message, I had also inherited my mother's prudence and pragmatism. As I thought about my future, I tried to marry these two influences. I felt keenly that it was my duty to excel and make a difference to my country. I also felt compelled to be successful—not just for the sake of wealth or achievement, but in order to fulfill my responsibilities and have the greatest impact.

I knew I didn't want to pursue graduate work in engineering or take an engineering job, which left the broader world of business. I had little sense of that world, but it held a certain appeal nonetheless. I intuitively felt that management might be where my impact could be made and my leadership skills refined and tested. In this decision, as with most of my academic choices, I was also strongly influenced by the trends among my classmates. Those going into management were generally taking one or more of three paths: applying to business schools in India, applying to business schools in the US, or seeking employment with one of India's bigger companies that offered management training programs. I decided to do all three.

I sat the entrance exam for the Indian Institutes of Management (IIM) of Ahmedabad and Calcutta and was accepted. I also applied to a long list of American schools, including Harvard Business School. Although I had deep reservations about leaving my family and Anita to study so far away, I thought that this option had perhaps the best long-term prospects. I had long discussions with my siblings about the pros and cons—staying in India might bring more immediate benefit but I'd likely be able to do more for my family over time if I studied abroad. Didi had become engaged to a man she'd met at the Indian Institute of Science, so I knew she would soon be married. But Kumkum and Anjan were still in school, and the elderly spinster aunt also needed care. I hated to leave them, but in the end they were supportive of my decision to apply. Anita steadfastly encouraged me to go, despite the two-year separation it would mean, and the risk of us drifting apart. Later, she would confess that she was convinced I'd never come back, but she still felt it was right for me to go.

The Chance of a Lifetime

Personally, it was my dream to attend Harvard—after all, it was the best business school in the world. But I also knew it was unlikely I'd get in, since they usually chose students with several years of business experience under their belts, and they did not typically offer scholarships. With no money, I would be reliant on financial aid. Nevertheless, I spent several days sitting in a little cafeteria near the women's hostel on campus, crafting the long application essays, with Anita editing. Into each handwritten draft, I poured my hopes, dreams, and ambitions. As I hurried to the post office, right before the deadline, to send it out, I tried hard to take my father's advice to heart and be unattached to the outcome.

While I waited to hear from the business schools, I applied for jobs. Many of India's top employers conducted campus interviews, and for management trainees one of the best options was the India Tobacco Company (ITC), a consumer conglomerate that encompassed hospitality, food, clothing, and other retail lines in addition to its core business selling cigarettes. At the time, everyone smoked, so I didn't give a second thought to working in an industry that I wouldn't even consider today. ITC had a reputation as a great employer, and their management training program was outstanding. They also paid much better than other companies. There were so many applicants in my graduating class that the company decided to conduct group interviews, fifteen people at a time, in a discussion format. From each group, the interviewer, Ramesh Sarin, would select one or two people for the next round. When my group was done, I was not selected.

This surprised me—I knew that objectively I was a much better student than those he had chosen. As the other candidates filed out, mostly disappointed, I sat frozen in my chair. Should I just accept this decision, even though it feels wrong? I asked myself. Part of me was ready to bow my head and slink away, accepting that this was my fate, but another part of me was galvanized by the sense of unfairness. As Sarin was getting ready to leave, I stood up, took a deep breath, and approached him.

"Excuse me, sir, but I think you are making a mistake."

He looked taken aback, but perhaps a little intrigued as well. Since he didn't immediately dismiss me, I pressed on.

"You can't possibly know which are the best applicants from such a short discussion with so many people simultaneously."

No doubt he thought I was arrogant for questioning his interviewing method, but perhaps he knew I had a point. Or maybe he just wanted to get rid of me. "Look," he said, "here's the problem. I have a limited quota and it's already filled. But if space opens up, I'll invite you to the next round."

It turned out he was as good as his word. A week later, I got my invitation, and went to Kolkata for the interviews.

The ITC headquarters impressed me, and I began to feel more confident that I could make a career in management. After all, I'd been in various leadership roles since high school—in student government, in cadets, in the debate team, and in sports. When Sarin asked me to define the term "leader," I tried to sum up the most effective approach I'd learned: "A leader is one who can motivate his colleagues and get things done without making them feel that it was the leader who actually had the idea and got the work done." I forgot about this, until twenty years later I ran into Sarin quite by chance at an airport, and he reminded me what I had told him. By that point, it was a philosophy that I was putting into practice, and one that would serve me well for the rest of my life, in leadership positions I could never have imagined back in that interview. Long before I knew the terminology, I was sensing the power of "leading from behind" and "servant leadership." The ITC executives must have liked my approach, because a few days later I was one of only two people from IIT Delhi they selected for job offers.

Elated, I began to think that maybe this was the right path—staying in India, close to my family and Anita, and building a solid career to support them all. The steady stream of rejection letters from the US business schools seemed to confirm this—thin envelopes that signaled their contents before they were even opened. Most of them told me I didn't have enough business experience, or that they couldn't offer me financial aid. And then one fat envelope arrived: from Harvard. It was a complete surprise—not only did they accept me despite my lack of business experience, but they offered a generous financial aid package. It was a chance I couldn't turn down. Very few of my fellow Indians had taken this path, but opportunity beckoned. As I lay in my dorm bed that night reading and rereading my acceptance letter in disbelief, another favorite quote of my father's came to mind, from the American poet Robert Frost. He would often recite it to me, as we walked in the gardens: "I took the road less traveled by; And that has made all the difference."[2]

With Anita's encouragement and the support of my siblings, I made the decision to go to Harvard. I felt bad about turning down ITC. I wrote to Ajit Haksar, the CEO, and thanked him for the offer but declined.

Haksar was shocked and affronted. "No one has ever turned us down," he wrote in response. "I don't understand this. I want you to come to Kolkata and explain yourself." He enclosed a plane ticket. I knew I wasn't going to change my mind but I also wasn't going to turn down a chance to fly to my hometown and visit my relatives. When I sat down with Haksar and explained the choice before me, his expression softened. It turned out, to my amazement, that he had attended HBS himself, back in the 1940s—one of the first Indians to do so. "Go to Harvard," he said. "It's the chance of a lifetime."

7

Hot Pickle at Harvard

Our life, like a river, strikes its banks not to find itself closed in by them, but to realise anew every moment that it has its unending opening towards the sea.

—Rabindranath Tagore, *Sadhana*

September 1971

"Why are you here? There are no jobs."

Just an hour earlier, I had been marveling at the Manhattan skyline through the window of the plane. I had made it to America, the land of opportunity. My future sparkled ahead of me like the lights on the Brooklyn Bridge. But now I had been brought sharply down to earth, both literally and figuratively, in the grimy streets of Jersey City.

I had left India for the first time two weeks earlier, accompanied by two IIT classmates, Harbinder Gill and Chander Merani. We were all coming to the US to do our graduate work at various colleges. At the airport, we'd been picked up by Chander's cousin, who'd offered us a place to stay for a few days before we each made our way to our respective schools. He pulled up at the terminal in a car that had seen better decades, and as we drove through graffiti-lined, garbage-strewn streets, he regaled us with his tale of woe.

"Me and my friends, we're all engineers too, just like you. We all got good degrees in India and came here with great hopes to go to American grad schools. We studied hard and expected to find good jobs and get rich and live like Americans. Instead, we just have piles of debt. It's been months now, and there are no jobs. Everyone is preoccupied with the war in Vietnam and no one wants to employ foreigners. I don't know why you're here. If you ask me, you should go back to India and get a good job there. Marry a nice girl. You'll do better than this."

Arriving at his home in Jersey City, I couldn't help but think he might be right. My first impressions of America made our modest home in Delhi seem quite luxurious. We dragged our bags up several steep flights of stairs to a cramped, two-bedroom, one-bathroom apartment, where six young Indian men were living, along with an alarming number of cockroaches. I barely slept that night, lying awake on the lumpy couch with Anita's and my siblings' faces in my mind. They had been so strong and supportive, so encouraging. Was it for nothing? I could be working at ITC now, making a nice salary, married to my sweetheart, and supporting my family. I remembered my little brother's tears at the airport. Had I left him behind to live like this?

The next day, Chander asked me to go with him to visit Pratt Institute, the private school in Brooklyn where he would be pursuing his graduate degree in engineering. The streets were intimidating, and the area around his dorm downright scary. We hurried out of there as quickly as we could, and didn't say much as we made our way back to the equally grim streets of Jersey City. I'm sure we were both asking ourselves the same question: Did I just make a huge mistake?

The previous couple of weeks had been an adventure. We'd visited London, Paris, and Amsterdam, getting by on just a few dollars a day, enjoying our freedom to explore these new worlds. I'd known that leaving India would be challenging in some respects, but I had not anticipated the cultural and economic atmosphere I felt on arriving in the US. When we made our way across the river into Manhattan, the iconic landmarks and bustling diversity helped lift our spirits, but I was still keenly aware of the harsh undertones of a country struggling through a recession and embroiled in a divisive war.

After just a few days, I was happy to board a train for Boston. As the grim city streets gave way to rolling hills, brilliant with the first burst of fall, I shook off some of my apprehension. Harvard's beautiful campus seemed like a country club in contrast to the school my friend was attending. I quickly fell in love with the quiet courtyards tucked away in the heart of Cambridge, and the historic buildings overlooking the tranquil Charles River. I breathed a deep sigh of relief as I headed to the administrator's office to register and get my dorm assignment. America may not have been the paradise of my dreams, but neither was it as bad as I had initially feared.

I was greeted on arrival by a familiar face: Harinder Kohli was a second-year HBS student who had been assigned to welcome me. We'd met during the summer in India when he was home visiting family. A brilliant student, he was extremely kind and generous, sharing his meticulously organized class notes with me as well as introducing me around campus, and we've remained friends to this day.

My dorm, Morris Hall, was an elegant, four-story, U-shaped building with a quiet, tree-lined courtyard. Inside, the accommodations were organized in sets of four double rooms that shared a bathroom, known as a "can." My seven "can-mates" and I would call this home for the next year.

We were a diverse group—a Brazilian, a Jewish guy from Texas, a blue-blood American, an Alabama redneck, a Mexican American from Albuquerque, a Boston Brahmin, a New York Jew, and me. Harvard reflected the changing times—to a point. While international students were increasingly common, of our class of more than seven hundred and fifty students, there were only thirty women, and only four Indians. Brown faces were still a rarity in those days—although not as rare as they had been just a decade earlier.

New Rules

On my first day of classes, I made my way into the theater, found a seat, and waited for the lecture to start. I was taken aback when, without a word of introduction, the young professor called on a student a few rows ahead of me to begin the class. The student immediately began to expound upon a business case we'd been assigned to read for the class. I sank back in my seat, hoping I wouldn't be called upon next.

I would soon learn that this was common practice at HBS. Professors would "cold-call" students, and class participation was very much encouraged; it made up a significant part of one's final grade. The teaching method was case-based, which meant that rather than learning rules and theories, we were expected to study real-life business cases and analyze the dilemmas and decisions they contained. I was accustomed to a very different approach that involved listening to lectures, writing papers, and sitting exams. The sheer volume of reading was overwhelming at first: there simply weren't enough hours in the day to read all the cases we were given, and so we lived in fear of being called on to analyze a case we had not thoroughly reviewed or of flunking out before the end of the first semester. Later, I'd realize that this was a deliberate strategy on the school's part, designed to throw students off balance. It was no fun, but in retrospect it was good training for life. After all, we're always having to deal with more than is reasonable. I'm grateful I learned the skill so early.

Despite the heavy workload, I found time for a new fascination: television. I'd hardly ever watched one before. Night after night, as I prepared my cases for the next day, I'd keep one eye on Johnny Carson, trying to figure out American humor. Equally puzzling, at first, was the strange game Americans called football. I'd always been active in sports during my high school and college years, but had never encountered the sport that my can-mates watched with such dedication. As they explained the rules to me, I soon became a fan, captivated by the passion, the pageantry, and the complex strategic layers of the game.

At the end of every evening, when my case work was done, I would sit down and write a letter to Anita. My can-mates were both impressed and perplexed by my dedication to my faraway girlfriend. On Friday nights, when they were all out dating girls, I'd stay back at the dorm, sometimes with a guy called David Manly, who soon became my closest friend. He seemed ambivalent about dating, so I was grateful for his company. Later, he would come out as gay, but back then I'm not sure he was "out" even to himself.

We were less than two months into our first semester when conversations turned to the upcoming Thanksgiving break. The brisk, beautiful fall days had given way to chillier weather and even a few flurries of snow. This was another novelty to me: I'd never seen snow before. Even at its coldest, Delhi rarely gets below freezing. I felt like I could never get warm, shivering in the lecture theaters and running across campus to my classes to escape the harsh wind. My can-mates, especially the East Coast natives, teased me.

"This isn't winter! You have no idea what's coming!"

"Better stock up on that hot pickle you like so much, you're going to need it to keep warm!"

David would paint vivid pictures of winters at his family home near Buffalo in upstate New York.

"You think you've seen snow now, but you've not seen real snow. At home, we get snow so high you can't see out of the downstairs windows. You come outside and your car is completely buried in a snowdrift. It's so cold that even Lake Erie freezes, and it's more than two hundred miles long." During one such conversation, it dawned on him that while he would be with his family for Thanksgiving, I had no place to go.

"Come home with me," he said. "My family would love for you to celebrate the holiday with us." I gladly accepted, and packed every sweater I owned for the trip. This would turn out to be the first of many American holidays I celebrated with the warm, chaotic, delightful Manly family. They quickly made me feel like one of them, assigning me chores so I could pitch in like everyone else, initiating me into family traditions and games. David's stepmother, Anne, cooked enough food for a small army. His father, Doug, who was president of a manufacturing company that made jams and jellies, loved football, and enjoyed teaching me more nuances of the game.

Back at school, I fell into a routine. I'd taken a campus job, known as a "concession," to earn a little extra pocket money. By the time I applied, only one job remained: delivering newspapers around campus each morning. I soon discovered why this job was unpopular—it meant getting up at four thirty every frigid morning to collect the papers, and trudging up and down endless flights of stairs to deliver them to each student's door. It was hard work, and I'd never had a job like that before. In India, it was uncommon for middle-class children to work odd jobs, unlike our American counterparts. But I appreciated the extra money to supplement my limited funds. The executive education students were my favorite customers, because they always ordered all three papers—the *New York Times, Boston Globe*, and *Wall Street Journal*—and they had mailboxes on the first floor. Plus, they tipped well when they graduated.

I soon made friends with the other three Indian students on campus, particularly a guy named Prafulla Gupta (who has remained a friend to this day). Bonding over our disdain for the blandness of American food, we would share an occasional spicy Indian meal that he would cook in the dorm room before walking over to the neighboring MIT campus to watch Hindi movies. Another guy, Mithilesh, was married, and would sometimes invite me over for his wife Pratima's home-cooked meals. The fiery flavors temporarily eased my homesickness, but I missed Anita and my siblings intensely. We rarely spoke on the phone, since international calls were expensive and difficult to schedule, I kept up my daily letter-writing throughout my two years at HBS. Later, she told me that she had been prepared for me to drift away, to get caught up in American life and forget her. But not a day went by when she wasn't on my mind. I couldn't wait for the two years to be done so we could marry and start our life together.

Deal-making

My time at Harvard was deeply formative, both personally and professionally. Once I became accustomed to the learning style, I realized that it was in fact much less demanding than IIT. The cases we were dealing with didn't involve complex engineering and math—from a certain perspective, they were just applied common sense. I'd known relatively little about business before I arrived—I didn't even know what a stock market was—but I found that I had a natural aptitude for the topic. I was able to effectively analyze the dilemmas described in the cases and often see more effective solutions than the ones presented.

However, I continued to struggle with the requirement for classroom participation. Back home, I'd been quite comfortable speaking in public on stage when I'd had a script to follow. But my confidence deserted me in the midst of this unstructured free-for-all. My American classmates were so competitive—vying to get the professors' attention and be heard. They would ramble on and on, taking up airtime with superfluous comments. What am I supposed to learn from this, I wondered? Indian students didn't speak unless called upon. My father and my teachers in school had always taught me that it befitted a man to be humble and self-effacing, not brash and assertive. If you worked hard and lived with integrity, you would be rewarded and recognized without having to push yourself in people's faces. This opinionated game of classroom one-upmanship seemed crass and awkward to me. Plus, it puzzled me that Americans were always so confident even when what they were saying sometimes made little sense.

Midway through my first semester, Earl Sasser, professor of

manufacturing management, pulled me aside after class and told me I needed to speak up more or my grade would suffer. "You're smart and hard-working," he told me, "but you need to participate in the classroom." So I swallowed my discomfort and made an effort to do so, speaking up in every class. After a few weeks, however, I noticed something strange: the professors in several of my classes had stopped calling on me, even when mine was the only hand raised.

Puzzled, I finally asked Sasser what was going on: "You wanted me to speak up, but now you don't ever give me a chance."

"You confuse the class," was his reply. Seeing my crestfallen look, he quickly explained, "It's not that your ideas are wrong. They're just more complex and nuanced than the basic concepts I'm trying to get across."

I thought about this for a moment. Surely it wasn't fair that I was disadvantaged for having a more advanced understanding of the subject matter. So I made a proposal to the professor: "Grade me only on my final exams and I'll stay quiet in class." To his credit, he agreed to my unconventional deal, and I ended up making the same agreement with a couple of other professors as well. This gave me a great advantage, because I could quickly skim the cases for those classes, knowing I didn't have to worry about being called on, and concentrate on other topics. My can-mates could never figure out why I had so much time on my hands to watch television, when they were working through piles of cases. When the exams came around at the end of my first semester, I was one of only two people who got all "excellent" grades (at HBS, "E" comes above A, B, C, etc.). After that, both my professors and my classmates respected me and would carefully listen whenever I spoke. It was my first lesson in how to assert myself in a culturally unfamiliar environment—rather than trying to be like everyone else, I could focus on my strengths and use my difference to my advantage.

Harvard's teaching style, while less mentally challenging than IIT, was critical in broadening my worldview. Often, the problems we considered had no "right" answer and could be approached from several equally valid perspectives. In analyzing business cases, I learned the importance of gathering and presenting all the evidence possible before making a recommendation or decision—a practice that would serve me throughout my career (and make it all the more frustrating when, forty years later, a jury would pass judgment upon me without being allowed to review all the evidence). Although always reticent in the classroom, I enjoyed discussing and debating the cases with my can-mates, and quickly learned that in helping them with the course work I also deepened my own understanding. Our heated debates continued every evening as we walked the quarter-mile across campus through Harvard's famous underground tunnels, and over dinner in the cafeteria.

A Consultant in the Making

As my first year drew to a close, I started looking for a summer job. Unfortunately, without US citizenship or a green card, most companies wouldn't even consider me. I badly needed the work experience and the money, but it seemed hopeless. Frustrated, I considered returning to India for the summer, when David came to me with a proposition: "My father will give you a job at the factory. He needs someone to help him figure out how to make the production line more efficient." Even better, his family would give me a place to stay. I happily accepted, and we agreed I would start in July, after a short visit to India to attend Didi's wedding.

I was a mechanical/industrial engineer by training, so the job at Red Wing, the jam and jelly manufacturer, turned out to be right up my alley. Their production line was not running efficiently, because they had to keep switching flavors of jam each time they got a new order from one of the many labels they supplied, and every time they switched, they had to wash the whole line, which took several hours. As a result, they were falling short on inventory and couldn't fill orders promptly. For the first time, I was able to put my problem-solving ability to the test in a real business environment. Scheduling and inventory management dilemmas were simply a matter of linear programming, and I'd solved dozens of such problems in the abstract.

During my eight weeks with the company, I designed a new system and tested it. Rather than making the jams in response to orders, they would produce each flavor for a certain time based on aggregate demand. They could store some of the jars unlabeled and then create a separate labeling line to label them for a specific brand when an order came in. And by progressing from lighter flavors to stronger flavors, we eliminated the need to wash the line every time the fruit changed—the first few jars would just "flush" the line and be discarded. The new system worked. Everyone was delighted, and Doug Manly asked me to come back every few weeks to check on the system, a welcome source of extra income during my final year. I was glad I'd done a good job for a man who'd been so welcoming to me. A decade later, I visited the factory and was amazed and gratified to see my faded, handwritten scheduling system still on the wall and still running the production line. "We call it the Rajat System," Doug told me proudly.

My summer job success gave my confidence a much-needed boost as I began my second year at HBS, and I continued to do well. As graduation approached, everyone was talking about their employment prospects, and recruiters were visiting campus every week. I wanted to stay in the US—Anita was talking about coming to an American college for her master's and I was eager for us to make a life together here. However, few companies wanted to deal with the complexity of hiring an immigrant and sponsoring a green card application. Doug Manly offered me a permanent job at the factory, but while I'd enjoyed my summer there, I'd set my sights on something more.

It seemed there was only one option for non-American MBAs: the consulting companies. These were a relatively recent emergence in the corporate world: a fast-growing new class of professional business experts who made their living providing advice. There were three major players in consulting at that time: McKinsey, Booz-Allen, and

Boston Consulting Group (BCG). Of these, McKinsey was the oldest and most respected, and its values appealed to me. I didn't know if I'd have much of a chance there: the firm had a reputation for being elitist, with a preference for pedigreed white male Ivy League graduates. But when I read up on Marvin Bower, who had taken over from the firm's founder, James O. McKinsey, and led from 1950 to 1967, I was immediately inspired. Bower, whose vision shaped the firm, articulated what it truly meant to be a professional—he talked about *serving* clients, putting their interests above those of the firm, letting financial reward be a byproduct of providing an excellent service. I felt an immediate calling to what felt like a dignified, even noble, profession, and I set my sights on becoming a McKinsey consultant.

All these companies conducted campus interviews, and those candidates who made a favorable impression would get an "ask back"—an invitation to attend a day of follow-up interviews at the firm's offices. I thought I'd done well in my McKinsey interview, but at the end of our conversation, the recruiter told me I should go away for a few years, get another job and some experience under my belt, and then apply again. But how could I get experience when no American company would hire me? Feeling depressed, I made my way to class, wondering what this had all been for. Was I going to end up like those guys in Jersey City? Or would I be forced to return to India and take up the kind of job I'd walked away from?

My teacher that day happened to be the marketing and retail guru Walter J. Salmon. I didn't know him well, but I'd enjoyed his classes and had a great deal of respect for the brilliant, rather scruffy-looking red-haired professor. That day, however, the class was a blur. It seemed pointless to pay much attention or make the effort to join the discussion. As I was packing up my books and notes at the end of class, he approached my desk and sat down beside me.

"Rajat, what's going on?" he asked. I was taken aback—I didn't think he'd been paying that much attention to me. We'd never had a one-on-one conversation before, or interacted outside of class. "I couldn't help but notice that you're looking dejected," he explained.

"I didn't get any ask-backs," I told him, recounting what the McKinsey recruiter had told me. "What am I supposed to do? He wants me to go away and get some experience, but no one will hire me because I don't have a green card."

Salmon shook his head. "Come with me," he said, striding down the hall toward his office. He dictated a three-sentence note to McKinsey's New York office manager, Ron Daniel, who happened to be a classmate and friend of his: "You're making a mistake. Rajat is one of my best students. I would strongly encourage you to invite him for another interview."

Because of his kind gesture, I was indeed invited to McKinsey for a full day of interviews, and was subsequently offered a job. Now, I could return to India with my head held high and marry Anita.

Monsoon Wedding

Long before there was a movie by that name, Anita and I had our own "monsoon wedding." Her father had chosen a date he considered auspicious, which happened to be August 5, at the height of the rainy season. We didn't try to oppose him; we were just glad he seemed to have accepted our intention to marry. In a culture where engagements were still usually arrangements made between parents, Anita and I were unconventional. She came from a very traditional and well-known Kashmiri family, and I'm sure that her father would have preferred her to marry one of her own people.

He and I had only just met for the first time, but she had told him about me and he had done his background research. Unfortunately, he couldn't go and talk to my parents about it, since they were both dead. However, it turned out that Anita's uncle, A.N. Dar, was a journalist who had known and respected my father, so that helped. Plus, I had a well-paying job and could clearly take care of his daughter.

I didn't see much of Anita in the month leading up to the wedding;

she was busy with arrangements, shopping, dress fittings, and an extended trip to Kashmir where she had to invite all her family personally. Plus, we suddenly had to be chaperoned, something we'd never dealt with at IIT. The guest list kept expanding, until we had almost a thousand guests expected to join the week-long celebration. There were a series of traditional Kashmiri celebrations, and then we decided to do all the Bengali ones too.

A vast tent had been set up on the lawn outside Anita's father's house, but on the big day it rained so hard the tent collapsed and had to be rebuilt. The only consolation, we reminded ourselves, is that rain is considered a blessing on such important occasions. Having waited for the auspicious day, we also had to marry at an auspicious hour, which for some reason turned out to be almost midnight. So we planned a dinner and reception ahead of the wedding, which went off smoothly. The downpour began again later that night, however, and the wedding itself had to be moved into the house, lasting four hours. But nothing could dampen our spirits. Our new life was about to begin.

8

The Firm

The roots below the earth claim no rewards
for making the branches fruitful.

—Rabindranath Tagore, *Stray Birds,* 134

Fall, 1973

Maybe McKinsey hadn't made a mistake after all when they initially turned me down. This was the thought that ran through my mind when I arrived at the New York office on my first day and was introduced to my office mate and fellow new recruit, Karl Wyss. At least ten years my senior, Karl was a tall, imposing, confident veteran of IBM, where he'd worked for a decade before joining the firm. At one point, he'd had more than a thousand people reporting to him. I, on the other hand, had never worked anywhere but the jelly factory, for a total of six weeks. I was just twenty-four years old. It seemed ludicrous to me that now we shared not only an office but the same title of Associate.

I was the only HBS graduate to join McKinsey's New York office straight out of school that year. The firm was going through a tough period in its history, as upstart rivals encroached on its market share. The growth it had enjoyed throughout the previous decades had slowed perilously and even slipped into decline. As a result, it was hiring fewer consultants overall, and focusing on experienced hires rather than business school graduates. All the other new recruits, like Karl, had several years of real-world experience under their belts. They were also almost all pedigreed white American men.

I felt out of my depth immediately, my natural confidence deserting me. There was only one other Indian in the office, Tino Puri, who was several years my senior and took me under his wing. I was keenly aware of my youth, my inexperience, and the color of my skin. Even my brand-new suits, which I'd had specially made in India, weren't cut quite right, and they were conspicuously lighter in color than the conservative dark gray or pinstripe suits that most partners wore. While McKinsey had abandoned its official "uniform," including mandatory fedoras, in the early 1960s, the partners all looked like they had stepped out of a Brooks Brothers catalog. Meanwhile, my shirts cost $2 each at Filene's Basement, but it's likely no one noticed those since they were eclipsed by my loud batik-printed ties.

Despite my insecurities, my new colleagues were welcoming and for the most part generous in their mentorship. I got into the habit of taking breaks and walking the hallway that ran the circumference of the firm's Park Avenue offices, dropping in on various colleagues. Most partners left their doors open, emblematic of the friendly and collegial atmosphere that the firm encouraged. Visiting the various partners' offices, you could learn a lot about the people from the décor. Upon election, every partner was given a budget to decorate his office. Some were ultra modern, others more traditional. Some had comfortable couches, while others didn't even have a desk.

Consulting is a profession that is learned on the job; while I'd gained general problem-solving skills and studied business cases at Harvard, I had little sense of what it took to be a successful "client guy." After completing my two-week introductory training program, I was expected to choose from among the available projects and jump in. At McKinsey, client projects (or "engagements" as they were known) would be assigned to a team made up of a vertical slice of the firm: a senior partner, who oversees client relations; a junior partner, serving as engagement director; an engagement manager, who was essentially project manager; and one or more associates, entry-level consultants like me who would do the research and analysis and learn the ropes. I wasn't expected to manage client relationships right away, but I noticed how much more comfortable my peers were interacting with executives. Many of them had years of business experience by the time they came to McKinsey, while I was fresh out of school.

My first assignment was a cost-reduction project for a company called Food Machinery Corporation (FMC). It was not a particularly exciting task—most of it pedantic analytical work, such as examining the purchase activity of the various plants and assessing how they could combine to get better rates. However, it did help to boost my confidence. I began to think that perhaps I could succeed as a consultant after all. I found the work extremely easy, often finishing my assigned tasks soon after lunch. "What should I do now?" I asked my engagement manager.

"Go home!" he replied. "So long as you do your work, no one cares when you come and go." So I happily left the office early to meet Anita and explore the city.

Besides adjusting to my new job, I was also adjusting to married life and to my new home. Anita had turned down an offer from MIT and instead accepted a place in the engineering program at Columbia, since my job was in New York City—one of the many professional sacrifices she would make over the years in support of my career. We had arrived with two suitcases and no plan as to where we would live. I'd figured we'd just get there and find a place. Luckily, a friend of a family friend had offered us a place to stay while we searched for an apartment up near Columbia, which, it turned out, was a pretty bad neighborhood in those days. After a dispiriting couple of weeks looking at decent apartments that we couldn't afford, or miserable apartments we could afford but couldn't bear to live in, Anita managed to get us a little furnished studio close to the campus through Columbia's student housing program. I think the woman in the housing office must have taken pity on this poor girl in a sari and found a way to give us a decent place.

We lived simply, often sharing our tiny one-room apartment with visiting friends and family from India. At first, Anita had no financial aid, since she'd only chosen Columbia at the last minute, but in her second semester she was offered a scholarship, which helped. Still, I was paying off my own student loans and sending money home to India, where my siblings and I were building a house on the land our father had left us, so we took care to keep our costs minimal. Luckily, we soon discovered that American portions were huge, so when we ate out we'd share a sandwich. There was a Baskin-Robbins ice-cream shop below our apartment, and we'd order one cone between the two of us. Seeing no point in spending money on lunch every day, I'd often show up at work with a brown bag, to the bemusement of my McKinsey colleagues. No one else in the office would even think of such a thing—lunch was a time for developing relationships and wining and dining clients.

Every night, Anita would study, and I'd watch television with the volume down low. I was responsible for doing the laundry, which I accomplished to the point that it was clean, but it took some time before I learned to fold. The piles on the kitchen table grew and I thought wistfully of my father's three simple dhotis: one to wear, one to wash, one spare. Maybe I should try his minimalist approach.

As the FMC project came to an end, I started thinking about what to do next. Like most young associates, I was eager to cut my teeth on the most interesting assignments with high-profile companies. I met with Bud Miles, the staffing coordinator, who offered me several potential engagements. I spent a few days talking to colleagues about these options, trying to figure out which would be most advantageous to me. Hearing about my inquiries, Mike Murray, a senior partner I had already come to like and respect, called me into his office one day and gave me an invaluable piece of advice. "Don't worry about choosing the best projects," he told me. "You can't know in advance which assignments will turn out to be useful, or which clients you'll get along with. Sometimes the engagements that sound interesting turn out to be dull and routine, while those that sound boring end up offering invaluable challenges and opportunities for development. And more importantly, if you go in with an open mind, you can learn from any assignment you get. So just take what you're offered." This proved to be wise counsel and would become a pillar of my approach to business: always have a learning mindset and don't try to predict what will be best for you, career-wise.

Another early assignment was with AT&T Corporation, on a team led by senior partner Fred Gluck, who would later be elected managing director of the firm. They came to us with a specific problem: three million lost phones. In those days, their customers rented handsets from AT&T along with paying for the service. But when people moved house, they often took the phones with them, and the company was losing a lot of money on those that went astray. I decided that in order to help, I needed to observe the problem directly, so I accompanied a team from AT&T on house calls, as they attempted to retrieve some of the missing phones. What quickly struck me was how much time was being spent in this often fruitless pursuit. Surely this time was more valuable than the lost handsets?

I returned to my fellow consultants with this analysis: AT&T needed to create a system to strategically assess when it made sense to try to collect a phone and when it made sense to just let it go. This project taught me one of the fundamental lessons of consulting: the problem the client presents may not be the actual problem. To do my job, I needed to be able to see beyond the apparent problem to the actual problem, and help the client put aside their own assumptions in order to see the deeper issues to which they were often blind. Problem definition became central to how I approached every subsequent assignment.

This lesson served me well on another early engagement involving a company that made processed meats—ham, salami, bacon, and so on. The problem they presented to us was that they were running out of capacity and wanted to build another plant. Our assignment was to advise them on where they should build it, how big it should be, and other specifics, in order to ensure that they made a good investment. When we took a closer look at the company, however, what became clear was that their existing plants were far from functioning optimally. We analyzed their use of critical resources, like the smokehouse and the cooler, their production schedules, and even the way they positioned the products within the cooler. Just as I had at the jelly factory, I sketched out a more efficient production schedule. With all of this in hand, we proposed changes that we felt would result in such a dramatic increase in output that not only was the new plant unnecessary, they should actually consider closing one of their existing plants.

When I presented these findings to my engagement director, Paul Krauss, he was excited.

"That's brilliant," he exclaimed. "Rajat, I want you to present this to the CEO right now."

I wasn't expecting that. Associates like me didn't usually present to client CEOs. Plus, what I'd shown Paul was just a preliminary desk analysis—I hadn't talked to anyone on the ground to verify my ideas. But he didn't seem worried about that.

I followed him to the meeting, terrified. Paul introduced me to the client, and announced: "He's going to tell you why you actually need to close a plant, not open a new one."

The client looked taken aback. "I don't believe you," he said bluntly.

I walked him through my analysis, but he still looked skeptical. He'd been a plant manager himself and knew his business inside out. I could almost see him thinking, why is this kid with the strange tie and the funny accent, who's never even seen the inside of a smokehouse, telling me how my plants should run?

"You're wrong," he said. "There's no way those plants can produce the volumes you're describing. I know that for a fact from my plant manager days in Phoenix. Go talk to my guys on the ground and you'll see."

As we left the meeting, I glanced at Paul. Clearly that hadn't gone the way he'd planned, and he was probably realizing we should have handled this client more carefully. But when we were outside, he just said to me with a laugh, "Well, Rajat, you've got a one-way ticket to those six plants and if you can't prove you're right, don't come back!" Paul had a great sense of humor but I was left wondering whether he was really joking.

So I flew to each of the plants, talking to the managers and the guys on the production lines. At five of the six, I found that I'd been right; in fact, my estimates of how much more they could produce had been conservative. But at the sixth plant, in Phoenix, there were some constraints I hadn't considered, and I was forced to modify my analysis. The CEO had been correct about that particular plant. I was still confident in my conclusions, but when I returned to meet with him and present my findings, I began by saying, "You were right."

As I explained what I'd learned at his plant, I could see the satisfaction in his face—he was proud of his own hands-on knowledge, and our cavalier approach had offended him. This was an important lesson in client relations—never forget, the client knows their business better than you, so tread lightly and do your homework before proposing radical changes. My engineering background had prepared me to do linear programming and analysis, but I had a lot to learn about the human side of my new career. After I'd acknowledged the CEO's expertise, he was much more open when I went on to say that my analysis had proven correct for the other plants, and my proposal still stood. They ended up taking my advice and closing a plant.

Up or Out

In those early days at McKinsey, my problem-solving skills served me well, but my career trajectory moved more slowly than that of most of my colleagues. Consulting, I soon discovered, was a competitive, status-driven business. You were expected to progress to certain milestones within a particular time frame, or else you weren't likely to succeed—an attitude captured in the phrase often used to describe McKinsey's culture: *up or out.* It was a well-earned reputation: five out of six associates never made it to partner. Throughout my early years at McKinsey, I was convinced that I was destined to add to that statistic. I was often worried that I wasn't advancing fast enough to keep my job. I got great evaluations on problem-solving and was learning the ropes of project management, but the reticence that had hampered me at Harvard was also an issue in my new role, with my colleagues regularly telling me that I was too quiet in team meetings. More concerning was my natural reserve, which made it hard for me to embrace the important task of introducing and developing clients. My lack of business experience made it more difficult—I simply didn't have a big network to tap. It took me four years to be given the role of engagement manager—an important step on the McKinsey ladder, and a role that my office-mate Karl Wyss had attained before his first year was out. However, I was good at my work and well liked among my colleagues, and I always felt the evaluation system was fair and unbiased. As the years passed, I grew more confident that I had a future with the firm.

The milestone that mattered most was being elected partner, and the typical time frame within which associates were expected to achieve it was five to seven years. As I approached the five-year mark, I began to hope that my name would come up at one of the twice-yearly elections, but several cycles passed without any change in my status. I watched people who'd come on board the same year as me make partner before I did. As someone who was accustomed to being, as we say in India, a "topper"—leading my class in exam results—this was challenging for me, but I developed a philosophical attitude. It became an essential defense mechanism—with such a small chance of success, one didn't dare get too emotionally invested in a future with the firm. All I could do was give myself fully to the tasks in front of me, and then let go of the results. If it was my karma to succeed at McKinsey, it would happen, and if not, then I would do something else.

I was blessed with several mentors during my early years at the firm, including Mike Murray, Mike Bulkin, Carter Bales, Fred Gluck, and Jon Katzenbach, to name just a few. Each engagement, in addition to experience and learning, offered an invaluable opportunity to build a relationship with my seniors. In retrospect, however, this multiplicity of mentors may have worked against me, since there was no one person advocating for my advancement, and each may have assumed the other was doing the necessary pushing on my behalf.

One of my mentors, Mike Murray, was the senior partner who managed the firm's extensive engagements with GE International. I had accompanied Mike on several trips to work with the client, and so when they offered us a new assignment in the late 1970s, I was one of his natural first choices. There was just one issue: the assignment was in South Africa. The firm had a policy of not working with South African companies during the apartheid era, but Mike felt that maybe this was different. After all, GE was an existing client and not a South African company. Besides, they were the firm's biggest client, and he was hesitant to say no.

He called me into his office to tell me about the assignment. The scope wasn't clear yet, but the first step was for us to fly out there and figure out what made sense with the client. What Mike clearly didn't realize was that I couldn't fly to South Africa on my Indian passport. And even if I could, I'd be subject to institutionalized discrimination every step of the way. Resisting apartheid wasn't just a matter of principle for me—it was personal.

"Mike, do you realize that if we take this assignment, you and I might be forced to stay in different hotels and travel on different transportation?" I asked him. He looked shocked—I don't think that had occurred to him when he selected me for the project. A couple of days later, he called me into his office again and told me that the firm had turned down the assignment. He could have just taken a different team, but to his credit, he decided against going at all. That was McKinsey at its best, and I felt very proud to work for a firm that stood up for principle at moments like that.

Finally, after I had been with the firm almost seven years, I was elected junior partner, in January 1980. It was a relief to have reached that critical rung of the McKinsey ladder, albeit a little late. Many of those elected with me had joined after me, including some from the class behind me at HBS. Funnily enough, when the election day came around I had forgotten the precise date. It was a Saturday, and I was recovering from some dental work that morning. When Jon Katzenbach, the head of the office, called to congratulate me, I was speechless—literally, as my mouth was still numb from the Novocaine. I attempted to mumble a response before handing the phone to Anita, who explained my predicament.

Geetanjali

While waiting to be elected partner, I'd reached another milestone of a more personal nature. In early 1978, Anita and I had learned we were expecting our first child. We had recently moved out of the city and bought our first house, in Middletown, New Jersey. Anita had taken a job at nearby Bell Labs, working on designing satellite communication systems, and was also working toward her PhD. It was a long commute for me—almost two hours each way—but her office was just five minutes from home, which would be perfect after the baby came.

Our daughter was born that fall. She took her time coming—Anita and I spent a long day playing cards and waiting for the labor to begin in earnest. I was at the hospital for the birth, but after just a few days I was forced to leave for a business trip. When I returned, I requested assignments that were less travel-intensive, which the firm generously agreed to, and was able to spend more time at home.

I was mesmerized by the small, exquisite human who had joined our family, and spent many hours lying on our couch with her asleep on my chest. Watching her expression change, I thought of Tagore's musings on the origins of the smile that flickers on a sleeping baby's lips. "There is a rumour," he wrote, "that a young pale beam of a crescent moon touched the edge of a vanishing autumn cloud, and there the smile was first born in the dream of a dew-washed morning."[1] We named her Geetanjali, after Tagore's poem, but with a twist in the spelling. Like most Indian children she quickly became known by a pet name, Sonu, which began as the Bengali endearment Sona, meaning *golden*.

Both Anita and I keenly felt the absence of the extended families that naturally help with the work of child-rearing in India. I tried to help out more around the house, but the reality was that my work was demanding and my days were long. Our new home was a modest house by American standards, and it had some issues. Anita hated the linoleum floor in the tiny kitchen, and after listening to her complaints for several weeks I decided to take it on myself to replace the flooring. The guy at the hardware store assured me it was a simple job, and sold me various tools I would never have expected to need. I would soon learn that home improvement projects are never as simple as they seem. A series of setbacks and several more trips to the hardware store culminated in a collapsed basement ceiling, which left us without a workable kitchen for several weeks. Anita shook her head and told me that in future we would hire a contractor. But when I finally installed our new shiny tile floor I was extremely proud of the result.

Unlike many of my colleagues, I made a conscious choice to keep my work and personal lives quite separate. Early on, I made an important decision that I stuck to throughout my career: I would not take up golf. Whatever advantages my colleagues may have gained on the golf course, I preferred to spend my weekends with my family. I also rarely met my clients socially, although it was common practice for my colleagues to use the firm's generous expense accounts to develop clients over dinners. As my career progressed, I never found my difference to be a disadvantage—clients seemed to appreciate the fact that I was not like my fellow consultants, and they found it fascinating. A story about what it's really like at an Indian wedding was much more interesting than yet another discussion of a golf shot. This became another key lesson: use difference to your advantage.

An Unforgettable Engagement

In early 1980, shortly after my election as partner, I took on an assignment that remains among the most unforgettable of my entire career. The company was Arrow Electronics, based in Long Island, New York, a distributor of electronic components, semiconductors, computer products, equipment, and so on. They were relatively small by McKinsey's standards, but one of the senior partners, Carter Bales, had gone to school with the three guys who owned the company, so he took on the assignment as a favor. Our task was to help them with their strategy and forward planning.

On December 4, 1980, we were due to make a presentation at the company's annual management meeting at Stouffer's Inn, a quiet, upscale country hotel in Harrison, New York. I had a scheduling conflict: my other client, GE, needed me to give a speech at a conference in Bermuda the day before, so it was decided that my colleagues would handle the Arrow presentation while I served GE. On my return, I got in my car and turned on the radio to hear a news announcer reporting on a tragic fire that had occurred—at Stouffer's Inn. "Multiple casualties . . . electrical fire . . . conference center . . ." I listened in shock. These were the days before cell phones, so I had no way of finding out if my team or our clients had been hurt. I changed course and drove directly to the inn.

As I pulled up at the hotel, the smell of smoke hung thick in the air, and fire trucks blocked the driveway. Jumping out of my car, I was relieved to see my team standing outside, but my relief turned to horror when they told me what had happened: they had been on their way to the meeting when they saw flames in the hallway leading to the main conference room. They ran to alert the hotel staff and get help, but it was too late. The fire had consumed the windowless conference room and twenty-six people had died, including thirteen of Arrow's senior executives. I knew all of these people, and had worked closely with some of them for the past year.

Only one of Arrow's owners escaped the tragedy—John C. Waddell, executive vice president, who had returned to their offices the night before to deal with media questions regarding a stock split that had been announced earlier that day. Waddell had joined Arrow in 1968 with his venture capital partners Duke Glenn and Roger Green, who had served as chairman/president and executive vice president, respectively. Although all three were in their early forties when I met them, Waddell struck me as a somewhat old-fashioned character, more comfortable out of the limelight. He had been the least involved in the day-to-day running of the company. Now, he found himself alone at the helm.

The next day, we showed up at their headquarters to see how we could help. Waddell had gathered all the employees and Duke Glenn's widow, Lynn, had come to speak to them—an extraordinarily courageous thing to do on the day after she lost her husband. She urged unity and resilience, asking the assembled workforce to "keep the faith" and not get spooked, even if competitors came calling and the future of the company looked uncertain. After her moving speech, we met with Waddell and he asked us to help. Essentially, my team and I stepped in and helped run the company for the next six months.

The business of consulting suddenly became very personal, and I grew up fast during that assignment. Nothing in my Harvard education had prepared me for dealing with a company that had been, as the *New York Times* bluntly put it, "beheaded."[2] How were they to rebuild? What could they do to support the widows and families of their lost colleagues? How could they pull together and motivate a shell-shocked and grieving workforce? How could they give investors confidence as their stock price tumbled? And how were they to fill the gaping holes on their board and in their executive offices? We helped them to navigate all of these issues, eventually recruiting an ex-McKinsey guy, Steve Kauffman, to take over as CEO. Arrow survived that traumatic episode and today is a Fortune 500 company with more than $23 billion in annual revenue.

An Unexpected Invitation

"How would you feel about transferring to the Scandinavia office?"

Scandinavia? The question took me aback. When Jon Katzenbach, one of my early mentors who had recently become head of the New York office, asked to meet with me in the spring of 1981, I had hoped for a new challenge, but I'd never expected something like this. Why me? I asked him. Surely an Indian would not be the most natural fit for the Scandinavian culture. He explained that a partner named John Forbis, with whom I'd worked in New York, had recently transferred there, and had asked for me. I was flattered but very hesitant. Was I ready to once again move to a new country and adjust to an entirely different culture? Would my career languish, so far away from the power center of the firm? And more importantly, how could I ask my wife to uproot herself and the baby, when we'd only just bought the house and settled down? Anita had recently returned to her job at Bell Labs, after six months of maternity leave. She couldn't have asked for a better situation—her commute was short, she was working for a great company, and she was finishing her PhD. I thanked Jon for the opportunity, but told him I would have to ask my wife—fully expecting that her answer would be a firm "no" and I could elegantly excuse myself.

Anita's response, however, surprised me even more than Katzenbach's original offer. "Well, why not? Let's go." I was out of excuses, so I accepted the position, though not without some trepidation about whether I'd be able to fit in and succeed there.

Later, I would find out the real reason for Anita's unexpected willingness to make the move. Initially, when she'd gone back to work, we'd hired a wonderful Italian grandmother to care for Sonu, and Anita felt at ease leaving the baby in her very capable hands. But then this woman's son persuaded her to come work at the family restaurant (she was a fabulous cook), and we lost our babysitter. Since then, we'd been through several unsatisfactory replacements, and Anita was feeling increasingly like she should be home herself. The proposed move gave her the excuse she was privately seeking to quit her job and be a full-time mom.

In 1981, we packed up and moved to Copenhagen, Denmark, where the firm's Scandinavia operations were based. The initial plan was for us to stay two years. If the US had been a culture shock, Scandinavia was another planet. As I'd expected, it was a very homogenous population. I suspected that many of the local people we interacted with outside of the business community had never seen a brown face and I often noted the looks of surprise when I met clients for the first time.

When I first joined the office, it was a small team of about twenty professionals, operating out of one room. As it turned out, by the time I got there, the senior partner who had asked for my transfer, Forbis, had left, along with several other principals, so although I had less than three years' tenure, there was only one partner above me, the head of the office. A tall, charismatic Norwegian who had opened McKinsey's Copenhagen office, he would quickly become a mentor to me, particularly when it came to his greatest talent, introducing and developing clients. This had never been my strength, and I was grateful that he invited me to work directly with him and learn from one of the best. He also introduced me to another great client guy, Christian Caspar, a Swede based in the Stockholm office. Christian had been elected six months after me, but when it came to developing clients, he was already a master and a rising star in the firm.

I set up a meeting with him, but was put out when he canceled at the last minute. We rescheduled, and I traveled to Stockholm, only to find that he wasn't at his office. How is he some great client guy when he can't even keep an appointment? I wondered, infuriated. When he finally arrived, he didn't seem too concerned that I'd been waiting for several hours. I'm not usually a confrontational person, but I told him flat out: "If you ever do this to me again I'll never work with you again."

Christian's charm soon softened my irritation, and he took me to his office, where he showed me a complex graphic from the Swedish financial newspaper that analyzed the network of companies owned by the Wallenberg group, Sweden's wealthiest business dynasty. He began to talk me through it, explaining who he knew at each company and how they were all connected. Get to know the right people, he said, and your influence and reputation would ripple through dozens of companies. It was a powerful lesson in networking, and I would later witness its truth. I took on an assignment with a tech company within the Wallenberg empire and became connected to two of the team members assigned to our study—Leif Johannson and Lars Ramqvist. Several years later, Johannson would become CEO of Electrolux, Ramqvist would become CEO of Ericsson, and through them, I would go on to serve two of Sweden's most prominent companies.

Besides Christian, there was one other partner on the team during my early days in Scandinavia, Jan Aarso Nielsen, who had a year less tenure. I became good friends with both of them, and together we were the young Turks of the office.

Although the office manager was brilliant and charismatic, he was also erratic. He'd run hot and cold, sometimes blowing up without warning. We'd arrive at the airport to take a flight and he'd be missing. He'd show up late—or not at all—for client meetings. I soon began to notice that he had a tendency to drink a lot. At first, this hadn't seemed that unusual—everyone in Scandinavia seemed to drink more than Americans did. But soon, he started to become an embarrassment to the firm. At office dinners, he would drink far more than anyone else at the table, becoming incoherent and sometimes highly inappropriate.

We never discussed his behavior—it seemed taboo to do so—but we did our best to cover for him.

Things came to a head at our annual office offsite meeting, which was held that year at the ski resort of Courcheval in France. The office manager began drinking on the bus journey. That night, he was supposed to introduce a speaker, and he made a fool of himself—his remarks were rambling, incoherent, and peppered with insults. After we got him back to his room, Christian, Jan Aarso, and I looked at each other and knew we couldn't keep quiet any more, however much we respected our partner professionally and liked him personally. We were the most senior people in the office besides him, so the intervention fell to us. Looking out over the moonlit ski slopes late that night, we debated the best course of action.

I felt that we had an obligation to at least inform the firm's managing director, Ron Daniel, who had been office manager during my time in New York. I was prepared to call Daniel myself; however, I was worried that if I acted alone, it would be seen as a personal betrayal. Plus, if the firm decided to do nothing, I didn't want to be singled out for retaliation. We agreed that we would make the call together, the next morning, presenting a united front.

Daniel happened to be in Paris when we called him. "Ron," I began, "this is a delicate matter, but there's an issue with—"

"I know," he replied. We didn't need to say more—he was already aware of the problem and had guessed the reason for our call. He invited me and my colleagues to meet him in Paris the next day. "Don't say anything to him, just come." This was a little awkward, since it meant disappearing in the middle of our retreat, but things were going to get a lot more awkward if we didn't intervene. We booked the first flights to Paris the next morning. When we met with Daniel, he informed us that he'd already discussed the issue with the firm's executive committee. The office manager would be relieved of his duties immediately and would be checking into the Betty Ford Clinic. (He would go on to make a full recovery and have a very successful business career. Two years after the intervention he returned to Copenhagen and invited me and my colleagues to dinner, thanking us for saving his life.)

"We've also decided it's not in the firm's best interests to send a senior person to Scandinavia to replace him." Ron turned to me. "Rajat, we'd like you to take over as office manager."

I was taken aback, to say the least. Yes, I was the most senior person left in the office, but I'd only been a partner for three years, and I was just thirty-three years old. No other McKinsey office was managed by a junior partner.

Ron Daniel had always had confidence in me—at times more than I felt I deserved. He had been the one my professor at Harvard approached to ask for a second chance on my behalf. He'd consistently encouraged me through the uncertainty of my early years with the firm. Once, a fellow young associate and I had time on our hands and took it upon ourselves, uninvited, to do a strategic review of the growth potential of the firm in the US. We concluded that the market was saturated, new competitors had entered, and McKinsey would have a tough time growing. Ron graciously heard us out, even though our analysis turned out to be way off the mark. I think he appreciated our initiative. If Ron thought I was up to the task of managing the Scandinavia office, I told myself, I should at least try my best.

Arriving back at the office Monday morning, we felt daunted by the task ahead of us. We were bright and full of zeal, but we were inexperienced. And the office, at that point, was just limping along. Did we have what it took to develop new clients, make the office truly successful, and keep our team busy? We resolved to give it our best shot and prove to the firm that we could manage without a senior partner, and not only sustain but grow the office.

Learning to Lead

I had never been in a managerial role before, and with no one to tell me how to do it I had the opportunity to develop my own particular leadership style and practices. I had always been a team player, oriented toward collaborating and uplifting others, and I decided that this was the culture I wanted to foster in the office. Christian and Jan Aarso enthusiastically signed on to this team approach.

An early opportunity came when the annual partner elections arrived. There were three associates on our team who were candidates—two Americans, Bill Hoover and Tom Wylonis, and a Swede, Micky Obermayer. If all of them were elected it would have effectively doubled the size of our partnership, and many would have argued it made sense to delay some of their elections so we could grow more slowly. But I respected all three and wanted to show my faith in them and the office, so I recommended that they all be made partner. I felt confident that they would be approved, because they deserved it, and I thought the firm should support our fledgling office.

I went ahead and scheduled a party to celebrate, on the Saturday night that marked the end of the board meeting. News of the elections usually came on Friday night, so it would be official by then, I reasoned. But Friday came and went, with no call. On Saturday, with the office decorated and refreshments waiting, I began to worry. At six o'clock, I told Anita to go ahead, and was left alone, pacing the halls of my house. Finally I called the New York office, only to be told the board meeting was still in session. I went back to pacing, even more anxious now. Was I going to have to cancel the party, and embarrass myself and publicly humiliate some of my colleagues? Had I acted with too much confidence? I called New York again, and this time insisted that they get Ron Daniel out of the meeting to speak with me. He was not too happy about it, but he understood, and, thankfully, the news was good. We had reason to celebrate after all.

McKinsey guys tended to be generous in their mentorship when working on the same teams, but many of them guarded their own client relationships and kept their cards close to the vest. We instituted a different approach. Each week, we would hold a meeting involving the entire professional staff, and we would go around and discuss every client and every prospective client, all weighing in and helping each other out. It was my strong belief that if we supported each other, we would all succeed beyond our wildest expectations.

While I fostered a collaborative spirit within the office, I encouraged a highly competitive attitude outside. At that time, McKinsey was the only consulting firm with a local office in Scandinavia. Our main rivals were firms with offices in London or Germany, who would send out teams to Scandinavia. To shore up our position as the dominant firm in the region, we decided to corner the market on Scandinavian talent. This was a preemptive strategy designed to prevent our competitors from establishing themselves in the region. We'd go to the top US and London business schools and hire every decent Scandinavian graduate. We also approached every competitive negotiation with a win-at-all-costs mentality, aggressively underbidding our competitors if that was what it took to prevent them from getting a foothold. We almost never lost a client.

I remember one particular weekend when we were working on a proposal for a client we were determined to win. We spent two days poring over it, and because we were all smokers at the time, the room in which we were working, which had no air conditioning, became thick with smoke. It was only when we finally stepped out into the sunlight at the end of this marathon work session that we realized how bad it had been in there. We looked at each other, and right then and there, we agreed that if we won the client, we'd all quit smoking. That was indeed my last weekend as a smoker. We won that client, and many more—in fact, our strategy worked so well that no other firm even opened an office in the region for at least ten years.

As a result of this strategy, the office grew rapidly in my first few years as its leader. We increased our staff from twenty to 160 people in three years, at the same time importing dozens from other offices on temporary assignments. Our client base was growing rapidly as well. Christian and I got to know the influential Wallenberg family, who dominated the Scandinavian industrial scene. Christian worked closely with the grandfather, Marcus Wallenberg, Sr., and I served his son Peter Wallenberg, Sr. quite extensively. Soon, we had become the fastest growing and most profitable office in the firm, and, most importantly, we had a truly enviable, high-quality client base.

In the early days of my leadership in Scandinavia, we had a disproportionate number of Norwegian clients and associates. The first leadership challenge I faced was when the talented Norwegian associates got together and told me that the establishment of an Oslo office was critical if they were to stay in the firm. I did not like the ultimatum, but I knew they were right in asking for the office, so I relented. In addition to Oslo, we went on to expand our office in Stockholm and open one in Helsinki as well. The original Copenhagen office became quite secondary.

It was in Scandinavia that I honed the entrepreneurial skills that would serve me through the next several decades. I became accomplished at understanding and leveraging business networks, and gained confidence in introducing clients. Had I stayed in New York, I think it would have taken much longer to gain those skills, because there were so many senior partners doing the work of bringing in the big clients. In Scandinavia, there were so few of us that I was forced to put my natural reticence behind me once and for all and get comfortable meeting new people and convincing them to work with us.

I was fortunate to work with some very talented colleagues and interesting clients. Christian Ringnes and I served Norgas, one of the industrial conglomerates in Norway. They owned a tiny company called Nycomed and hired us to do a small study to determine its potential. Together with another colleague, Gert Munthe, Christian and I did the study and in the process realized that this little company, with only around $25 million in revenue, had a unique product with huge global potential. Under Gert's guidance, they expanded to eventually become the most valuable company in Norway, besides the oil companies.

During my time in Scandinavia, my career development gained some momentum as well. Only four and a half years after I'd become partner, I was elected director, and for once I was ahead of my peers. Our planned two-year stay quickly turned into six, with our family welcoming two more daughters during that time. Megha was born in 1982, and Aditi followed in 1985. We also became surrogate parents to Anita's younger siblings, after her father died unexpectedly from a brain hemorrhage in 1984. Her brother Arvind was just sixteen at the time and her sister Aninda was twenty. Anita had always been like a mother to them. Now they were orphans, and we felt responsible for raising them as we would our own girls. Over time, Arvind stopped calling me Bhaiya, which means elder brother, and began to use Baba instead. Aninda also visited us regularly in Denmark, where she would first meet Ajay Kaul, the man she later began to date and eventually married.

By the late 1980s, everyone in the firm expected me to stay in Scandinavia, since I'd established myself there and made a name for myself. I loved the work and was proud of my team and our accomplishments, but I knew that Anita and the girls were not nearly as settled as I was. While everyone in the business community spoke English, the same was not true of the locals, and simple tasks like grocery shopping were a challenge. In those days, English-language newspapers were hard to come by, and there were no English television channels. There were five Indian families in the entire city, and during our time there we connected with all of them and became good friends, which we remain to this day. Every weekend we would gather to cook Indian food and play bridge. Although we had a network of friends among the families of my fellow partners, and our family from India visited when they could, it was clear that Anita often felt isolated. If we were to stay much longer, we should probably consider this our home for life, and that was not what she wanted. After much discussion, I decided that it was time to return to the US and let the Scandinavians run their own office.

Most of my colleagues and mentors advised against the decision. "Why would you walk away from what you've built?" they asked. "Why would you leave such a nice situation and such prestigious clients? Everybody loves you there." But my instinct told me: don't settle—get out of your comfort zone. I decided to trust my gut, and respect my wife's preference, and so we chose Chicago as our next home.

Just before I left Scandinavia, I had two surprises. The first was a call from Ron Daniel informing me that I had been elected to McKinsey's board, something almost unheard of for a thirty-seven-year-old. I almost fell off my chair. The fourteen-person board was mostly comprised of senior partners with a decade or more tenure and life experience than I had. I knew my success with the office had made an impression on the firm's leadership, but this was unexpected, to say the least.

The second surprise occurred during my farewell party, organized by my good friend Christian Caspar, who would succeed me as office manager. It happened to be Christmas, and so the party had a festive theme, complete with carols and a Santa Claus. In the middle of the party, Christian told me it was up to me to guess the identity of Santa. He hadn't said a word, and I could not see much of a face behind the flowing white beard and fur-trimmed hat. After a few tries, I admitted defeat, and Santa reached out and shook my hand. The moment he spoke, I knew who it was, although I could scarcely believe he had flown halfway around the world to attend my party. Marvin Bower, McKinsey's early leader and the widely acknowledged father of modern management consulting, thanked me for my service in the region and raised a toast to my future. It was the most moving moment in my McKinsey career.

9

Chicago

[W]hen old words die out on the tongue,
new melodies break forth from the heart;
and where the old tracks are lost,
new country is revealed with its wonders.

—Rabindranath Tagore, *Gitanjali*, 37

Christmas 1986, Chicago

No clients. For a McKinsey consultant, that's the worst possible situation. Yet that was the predicament that confronted me when I arrived in my new home. When I showed up for work on my first Monday morning in the Chicago office, I had nothing to do. There simply weren't enough clients to go around. And I soon realized that no one was going to help me—they were all trying to keep the clients they had. Even my friend and mentor Mike Murray, who was head of the office and had convinced me to come to Chicago, wasn't busy enough to share.

From a business standpoint, McKinsey's Chicago office was the polar opposite of Scandinavia. The birthplace of the firm, it was a very mature office with about sixty professionals and a heavy preponderance of long-time partners and directors—too many, in fact, to serve the firm's limited client base in the city. Why had Mike encouraged me to come here? The office clearly didn't need yet another partner.

Luckily, I had anticipated that it would take me a little time to get established in my new city, so I had not given up my key Scandinavian clients. For my first year in Chicago, I basically commuted to Scandinavia, continuing to serve Ericsson and others. I even started taking some of my colleagues from Chicago with me to help, since they had time on their hands. In between trips, remembering everything I'd learned from my colleagues in Scandinavia, I set out to build a new client base in my new home.

As a first step, I got out the HBS alumni directory and looked for people I knew in the city. Soon enough, I discovered that one of my classmates, Steve McMillan, was head of strategy at Sara Lee Foods, one of the biggest consumer product companies in Chicago at the time. He'd joined McKinsey the same year as me, but had left to work at Sara Lee. I knew he'd understand my predicament, so I called him up.

"I just landed here, I don't have any clients yet, so if you need anything, please let me know."

Steve was happy to hear from me, but he said he didn't really need a consultant right now. "Besides," he added, "our CEO, John Bryan, doesn't like McKinsey."

When I inquired as to the reason for this antipathy, Steve explained that John had hired a McKinsey guy to be his number two and the guy had tried to overthrow him. "I doubt I could convince him to work with anyone from the firm again." A week later, however, he called me back with the offer of a small six-week project—an acquisition evaluation. "This is an opportunity for you to impress John. He doesn't have to sign off on it beforehand, but I'll make sure you have an opportunity to present to him so you can meet in person and perhaps dispel some of his negative feelings toward McKinsey."

The project was successful, and when I met with John I laid my cards on the table. "I understand you've had a difficult history with the firm, but I'd like to have the chance to serve you."

John, then in his forties, was a shrewd, soft-spoken Southern guy. He'd joined Sara Lee as a young man when the company had acquired his father's meat processing business, and become a favorite of the CEO, eventually being tapped to succeed him at the unusually young age of thirty-nine. He told me about his unhappy history with McKinsey, but agreed to give me a chance. I thanked him and also asked for his help: "I'm new in this town. I have no work and my partners are not in a position to help. Can you make some introductions for me in the business community?"

John seemed surprised by my request. McKinsey consultants have a reputation for arrogance, and never want to show weakness. I guess my asking for help was unexpected, but it's always been my experience that when you're honest and vulnerable about your needs, people want to help. And John was no exception. "Okay," he said. "I'll help you." We became good friends, and McKinsey would go on to do a lot of work with Sara Lee. He was also as good as his word, introducing me to many CEOs in his circle. Within a year, I'd become a big client producer.

A Premature Nomination?

In 1987, Ron Daniel's final term as managing director was coming to an end. The firm had an age limit of sixty for the role, and Ron was fifty-nine. An election was scheduled for the end of the year to choose his replacement. McKinsey's managing director election is often compared in the press to the papal conclave, but it's actually a fairly simple process. There are no smoke signals or sealed doors. However, like prospective popes, McKinsey partners know that it's considered poor form to publicly campaign for the role. That's not to say there wasn't subtle jockeying for position, of course. The process began with a nomination round, in which anyone's name could be put forward.

The seven most popular would become the nominees, and then several rounds of voting would follow, with the person with least support dropping out each time until a managing director was elected. I was sad to say goodbye to Ron, who had been such a champion of mine, but curious to see whose names would come up. When the nomination ballot was revealed, the one name I absolutely had not expected to see was my own. But there it was, on the ballot, alongside some of the giants of the firm, many of whom were a decade or more my senior.

My board election had been a surprise; this seemed absurd. It seemed I'd gone from being late to reach every milestone to being early. I was not yet forty. Although I had an impressive track record with the firm, I did not think myself ready to lead it.

Mike Murray seemed to agree. He was unable to hide his genuine surprise and told me bluntly: "You're not ready." I shrugged—this was probably true. Mike was a supporter and a good friend, so I didn't take it personally. Perhaps it was just a fluke that I'd gotten a few votes and somehow ended up making the cut—if so, I'd be out in the next round. However, clearly some among the partners didn't agree with Mike's assessment of my readiness, as my name stayed on the ballot for two rounds before I was voted off in the final four.

In retrospect, I think my nomination said less about my personal readiness and more about a growing readiness in the firm to pass the baton to a new generation of leaders. Until that point, McKinsey's managing directors, like the others on that 1987 ballot, had come from the generation who had worked directly with Bower and they'd been shaped by his influence. But times were changing, the firm was changing, and some people felt it was time for younger leadership. While perhaps premature, my nomination would prove prescient. McKinsey was not quite ready for a young, non-American, non-white leader, but it would be before long. In the end, the election came down to Fred Gluck and Jon Katzenbach, and Fred prevailed.

The new managing director had been an early mentor to me, and we had a good relationship, but we didn't always see eye to eye. In particular, I remember an incident not long after his election involving my Danish colleague Jan Aarso Nielsen. It turned out that Jan had been serving two clients who were competitors, albeit in different countries—a practice that was frowned upon, although not a direct infraction of McKinsey's rules. To be honest, I'd seen many partners work in similarly gray areas, and while Jan clearly should have been more careful, it didn't strike me as cause for overly severe punishment.

Others felt quite differently, however. An evaluator was sent to the Scandinavia office, and he recommended that Jan should be fired "with cause." The directors committee agreed, and their recommendation came to the board, at which point I raised an objection. "This seems excessive. Surely the punishment is not proportional to the infraction. And besides, if we're firing Jan for this, we need to question a lot of other partners as well, including ourselves." I felt Jan should be reprimanded, the incident should be reflected in his evaluation, and, more importantly, the gray areas should be clarified.

Privately, I suspected that the firm's leaders were looking for an excuse to show Jan the door. I considered him a good friend and had great respect for his professional aptitude, but I knew that many of the partners were not so fond of him. He was not the typical suave, self-effacing consultant type; his personality was rather abrasive and domineering. But he was extremely good at his job and his clients liked him. I considered it one of the firm's weaknesses that it tended to select a particular personality type. It was my personal policy to never judge others by surface characteristics alone or be too quick to dismiss someone because he had rough edges.

In Jan's case, the board overruled my objection, and it was decided that he should be fired. I was disappointed, but there was not much I could do other than make my feelings clear. After the meeting, Fred pulled me aside.

"You know, Rajat, if you're thinking about your future as a leader in the firm, you might want to reconsider your position. You don't want to be supporting that guy."

"Is this a threat or is this a piece of advice?" I asked him, only half joking.

Fred just repeated his warning.

"Okay," I conceded, "but he's a very competent consultant and he built that office with Christian and me. But it's not up to me, so you do what you think is right. I've said my piece."

At the next board meeting, Jan was on the agenda again. He had been fired, and not surprisingly, from my perspective, he had sued the firm for wrongful dismissal. He had a very strong case. His performance had been outstanding, he'd been given no warning, and the worker-friendly Scandinavian labor laws were clearly in his favor. The firm was going to lose, and it would be costly. I refrained from saying "I told you so," since it would not have served any purpose, but I hoped Fred was at least a little aware of the irony when he turned to me and said, "Rajat, I need you to get us out of this. You're the only one he trusts and the only one he'll talk to." I invited Jan and his lawyers to immediately fly to New York, and even while the three-day board meeting was in process, I was able to negotiate an acceptable settlement for both parties.

"I Won't Step Aside"

McKinsey's managing director does not have much power to make unilateral decisions; most important matters in the running of the firm are handled by various committees. However, there is one area in which the managing director can call the shots: appointments. It was Fred's prerogative, as the newly elected leader, to appoint people to all leadership roles in the firm. He decided that it was time the Chicago office had a new manager. Mike Murray was initially resistant to the change, but eventually acquiesced, telling Fred that he should make me office manager, based on my success in Scandinavia and client record in Chicago.

Fred, however, had someone else in mind. He could have just gone ahead and made the appointment, but clearly he was uncomfortable about it and felt he owed me an explanation. Perhaps he was also hoping I'd make it easy for him by telling him I wasn't that interested in the role anyway. "You've already managed an office," he told me, "so you really don't need any more management experience. I'd like to give someone else this opportunity."

I was disappointed. I'd enjoyed running the Scandinavia office and would have relished the challenge of taking on Chicago. I felt I'd earned it and had trusted that McKinsey's meritocratic system would recognize and reward my hard work. But I tried not to let Fred see how I felt. "Okay, do whatever you want; it's up to you," I told him.

Over the next couple of days, however, my response didn't sit well with me. I felt I was not being honest—I wanted the job and I felt I was the best candidate. Some instinct told me that if I didn't fight for this, my career would stall. Plus, my sense of fairness had been offended. It wasn't right that I simply step aside. Perhaps it was too late and Fred's mind was already made up, but if I'd learned anything from my early experiences with ITC and McKinsey, it was that asking for a second chance can pay off.

I called Fred back. "To be honest, I would like to be head of the office. Ultimately, it's your choice, but I want you to know that I will not step aside and take myself out of contention."

This put Fred in a tough position. Although the appointment was his prerogative, it was important to him to be seen to be making the right choice with the support of the partners. He sent one of his colleagues to Chicago to talk to the rest of the partners and find out their preferences. This process went on for several days.

In the end, the majority of partners expressed a clear preference for me. To his credit, against his own wishes, Fred gave me the job. I was glad I'd told him what I wanted—I think I would always have regretted it had I not stood up for myself at that crucial juncture.

Managing Chicago

The Chicago office was a challenge. It hadn't really grown in ten years. I decided to try some of the strategies that had worked so well in Scandinavia, starting with changing the culture to encourage more collaboration. My own experience upon arrival had revealed just how territorial most partners were. They protected their existing clients, and staked out "their" prospective clients, even when they were being quite ineffective about developing them. Many would insist they were "in talks" with a particular CEO, but nothing ever seemed to come of it, so that no one else could step in. So I instituted weekly partner meetings, held on Saturdays so everyone would be able to attend, at which we would discuss every client and potential client.

At the first of these meetings, we gathered in Mike Murray's living room. "Openness and honesty are critical," I told everyone. "This will only work if we're straight with each other about what's actually going on in these client relationships—the good, the bad, and the ugly—and what we can each realistically commit to achieving."

The partners were initially very reluctant, but as the process began, they soon found it cathartic. It was like a form of group therapy, as people began to admit that they were stuck in developing particular clients, or were trying but failing to close a deal with new ones. It was a relief to many to be able to say they weren't sure how to achieve the desired results, and to ask others for help and suggestions. A spirit of camaraderie began to emerge in the office.

We were still struggling to be a well-performing office, however. Well, we were the master consultants, I thought, so we should be able to figure out what the issue was. I decided to ask the firm to do an analysis of the office and see if it could pinpoint the problem. It came back with a clear conclusion: our underlying problem was that we had too many partners—three too many directors, to be exact.

I presented the report at our partner meeting. There was a silence as I finished, and as I looked around the room, I could tell that most people were immediately worrying about whether they were among the "too many" and wondering who would be asked to leave. Those were not the questions I was asking, however.

"I don't believe a word of this report," I told the surprised partners, recalling how Ron Daniel had once said the same words to me in response to my youthful, inaccurate assessment of McKinsey's future. "It makes no sense. There's a huge client potential here. Why would we ask three directors to leave, rather than increasing our client base and growing into the number of directors we have—or more?"

Over the coming years, that was the strategy we adopted, and it worked. In fact, three years later we'd gone from sixty professionals to 160 and become one of the best-performing offices in the US. I brought in some new blood from other McKinsey offices and developed a lot of the younger associates and partners. The team-oriented culture continued to thrive, and we developed many new clients. We also forged friendly relationships with the neighboring offices in Toronto and Cleveland, forming a kind of Great Lakes collaboration.

As office manager, I could have cut back on my own client work—many office managers did. But I decided to do the opposite. Serving clients was the heart and soul of what we did, so why should the leader be exempt from that work? Besides, I loved the client work. I began to work the Chicago business networks as I had in Scandinavia, to similar effect. One memorable engagement was with Nutrasweet, then a tiny division of the giant Monsanto. Nutrasweet's CEO was a razor-sharp lawyer and I worked hard to help him develop strategies to combat competition as his patent came to expiration. A few years later, he would be handpicked as the next CEO of Monsanto, and the firm landed a very big client.

As a family, we enjoyed our time in Chicago. Anita was happy to be back in a country where she could simply pick up the phone and call a plumber, and didn't have to go to the train station every day to get a single English-language newspaper. Despite an invitation to join a prestigious country club, of which I would have been the first non-white member, I remained firm in my decision not to play golf but to dedicate my weekends to my family. No doubt the fairway would have been a great place to meet clients, but I was doing quite well in other settings, and I cherished my time with my wife and girls. Our youngest daughter, Deepali, was born in 1990, completing our family. Her chubby body and exuberant hair reminded us of a "koosh ball" toy, and she soon gained the pet name "Kushy," which has stuck to this day. Anita stayed a full-time mom to the four girls, and a full-time job it certainly was, especially as my job increasingly demanded me to travel.

When I was home, I tried to spend as much quality time with them as I could, including helping my daughters with their schoolwork. Sonu had always had an unusual gift for pattern recognition, solving puzzles since she was a year old. She was extremely good at math, and I always proudly thought she took after me, since I had scored the highest in an all-India math exam. In middle school, she was given the opportunity to attend an advanced math class at the local high school, and I loved helping her with the problems she brought home, until one day I had the uncomfortable experience of staring perplexed at her homework, unable to solve the problems. "Baba," she said, catching my look of dismay, "what's wrong?" As she figured out the answer on her own, I had to admit that my teenage daughter had surpassed me. I could no longer help her with her homework, but I was even more proud of her prowess.

McKinsey Looks East

In the early 1990s, the firm served its first Indian client: a software company called HCL that wanted to expand into the American market. I was overseeing the team, and soon became friends with the CEO, Shiv Nadar. It was on this engagement that I made the acquaintance of a young engagement manager from our San Francisco office named Anil Kumar.

Around the same time, the firm's leadership was talking seriously about starting an office in India. My New York mentor and colleague Tino Puri decided to make the move and head up the office, along with a few other Indian partners who were happy to go home. When Anil reached out to me saying that he was considering asking for a transfer to the new office, I encouraged him, and put in a good word with the relevant people. For myself, the India office never beckoned. I was too busy in Chicago, and saw my opportunities as firmly rooted in US soil.

The establishment of the India office was just one example of McKinsey's increasingly global outlook. The firm was becoming truly international. Of the thirty-three new offices that had been opened in the 1980s and early 1990s, only six were in the US. Seventy-eight of our 148 senior partners lived outside the US. As Fred Gluck's second and last term as managing director approached its close, there was a lot of speculation about who would replace him, and whether the firm might finally look beyond the US for its next leader. In late 1993, I came to work one day to find the office abuzz with gossip about an article in *BusinessWeek* entitled "The McKinsey Mystique."

"Many insiders believe McKinsey may well elect the first non-American to lead the firm," the article declared, and went on to identify four potential candidates: my old friend Christian Caspar in Scandinavia; Lukas Muhlemann, who had made quite a name for himself in Switzerland; Norman Sanson in the London office; and the formidable Herb Henzler from Germany.[1] Despite my previous appearance on the ballot six years earlier, I did not seem to be on their radar, but this time I privately thought that I had a good shot. My success in both Scandinavia and Chicago—two very different offices—had made an impression, and I knew that many people supported me. I now felt ready, but I didn't know if the firm was ready for a leader so far outside the McKinsey mold. When the ballots came back, however, the choice was between me and Don Waite, head of the New York office. No one else, including all of *BusinessWeek*'s projected favorites, even made it to the nomination.

Don Waite was a blue-blooded American in the classic McKinsey mold and part of the older generation. His election would have represented a continuation of the firm's history, rather than a changing of the guard. I, on the other hand, was only forty-five and considered by many to be the new face of the firm, an appropriate choice to lead McKinsey in the globalizing world. In March 1994, the second round of voting took place while I was vacationing with my family at our ranch in a remote part of Colorado.

The day the votes were counted, I was alone in the house, having injured my back the previous day while teaching four-year-old Kushy to ski. The rest of the family had gone to the slopes without me, so there was no one around when the phone call came from my long-time mentor Ron Daniel, who was head of the election committee.

"Congratulations, Rajat," he said. "I'm calling to tell you that the partnership has chosen you to lead the firm. I'm very happy for you and for the firm. I assume you will accept the role?" I told him I would be honored. Who would have imagined, back when Ron had given me a second chance to interview at McKinsey, that twenty-one years later he would be making this call?

Not wanting to call anyone before I'd told my family, I had several solitary hours to reflect upon this remarkable turn of events. I was the first non-American-born managing director of the firm, and the first Indian to ever lead a global company of McKinsey's stature. I was also the youngest leader the firm had elected in the modern era.

As I sat on the deck, looking out over the grandeur of the mountains, I thought of my parents and how proud they would have been. My path had led me in such a different direction to the one my father had taken, but I hoped he would have appreciated that in my own way I was attempting to serve my family and my country, just as he had done. My mother, too, would have been gratified to see that the resourcefulness and dedication she taught me had brought me so far.

I felt a deep gratitude for the genuine meritocracy that the firm had proven itself to be. My peers had done me this honor on the strength of my leadership record, my problem-solving abilities, the relationships I'd built, the clients I'd introduced and served, and, most importantly, the trust I'd earned. The color of my skin and the country of my birth had not mattered, in the end. I could hardly believe this had happened. Even after I told my family later that afternoon, it still felt surreal. The reality only began to sink in when several journalists and photographers showed up on our doorstep the next day, having heard the news and tracked me down at our remote little mountain retreat.

As soon as we left Colorado, I booked a ticket to Boca Raton, Florida. I felt strangely nervous as I sat on that flight, less like the soon-to-be-leader of an international firm and more like a humble student making a pilgrimage to meet a great teacher. When I stepped out into the Florida sunshine, I was taken aback to see that the teacher had come to greet me. McKinsey's patron saint, Marvin Bower, then in his nineties, was standing on the sun-baked sidewalk waiting for me.

When he saw me, he came forward and clasped my hand, congratulating me on my election. We spent several hours together that day, discussing the future of the firm. He told me he was concerned that the firm could be growing too fast, and that partners might get too focused on increasing revenues at a cost to the quality of client service. I shared with him the plans I was formulating, and we talked about the importance of keeping the McKinsey partnership intact and its values solid, even as it became more diversified and global. By the time I left that evening, with Marvin's blessing, I felt the mantle of leadership beginning to settle a little more comfortably on my shoulders.

10

Unity in Diversity

Let us unite, not in spite of our differences, but through them. For differences can never be wiped away, and life would be so much the poorer without them.

—Rabindranath Tagore, *Talks in China*

I was late for my first day as McKinsey's new leader—two weeks late, to be precise. I'd gotten sick earlier that month, a gall bladder infection that I didn't seek treatment for quickly enough. Right as I was getting ready to take up my new role, my gall bladder burst and I contracted a staph infection that almost killed me. On the day I should have officially taken on the role of managing director, I was in a hospital bed. Thankfully, I made a full recovery and was eventually able to return to work.

During the previous few months, I'd taken a fascinating and important journey, visiting every one of the firm's sixty-two offices in thirty-one countries and talking with almost all my partners. I was in the unusual position of knowing almost every senior partner in the firm directly, having worked in Scandinavia, Europe, Asia, and the US, as well as served on several committees related to personnel and compensation issues. I made sure to spend time with the young directors, principals, and associates as well. This was a practice I'd adopted as a consultant—you can learn a lot more about a company by speaking to those on the lower rungs of the ladder than by speaking only to the leadership. This journey confirmed my sense that the firm was truly evolving into something far removed from its traditional, pedigreed American reputation. I was becoming leader of a truly global partnership; in fact, more of our senior partners lived and worked outside America than inside, and 60 percent of our revenues came from overseas. My election reflected this reality. I felt like a global citizen more than I felt Indian or American. When I told the press that I took all the congratulations as a great compliment to the firm, I wasn't just affecting modesty. I was genuinely proud of the firm for having proven itself to be the meritocracy I'd always believed it to be, rather than affirming its reputation as an old boys' club.

At the end of my travels, I felt I'd taken the pulse of the firm and was ready to meet with the directors and formulate my priorities as the firm's new leader. I summed these up in a memo to the partnership that I sent out in July 1994. I intended to enhance collaboration, beginning with building genuinely global client service teams, institutionalizing client impact reviews so we could measure the actual effects of our work; improving our functional knowledge development efforts to become a firm of innovative ideas; reaffirming our commitment to geographic entrepreneurship and being present in every major economy in the world; rendering governance flatter and more transparent and building on our partnership values; and reducing unnecessary costs, since we were the custodians of our clients' money.

During my travels, I'd also made an important personal decision that surprised a lot of people: as managing director, I would not relocate to the New York office. At first, I'd assumed I'd have to move. Leaders of the firm had been elected from the New York office and had run the firm from there since 1939, when Bower relocated from Chicago after the founder's death. I wasn't too happy about the idea of uprooting my family again, however. The girls were all settled in school, and we loved our home and community of friends. I was explaining as much over dinner to my Scandinavian friend Micky Obermayer, when he asked, "Why do you have to move? There's no rule that says you need to be in New York." Micky is a true out-of-the-box thinker, and to this day he comes up with unexpected perspectives on many aspects of life. The more I thought about his question, the more it made sense—and not just personally but philosophically as well. If the firm was truly a global partnership, then it need not have a geographical headquarters.

So I decided to stay in Chicago, while the rest of the administrative staff remained in New York. My first appointment as managing director would be to make Dick Ashley the Chicago office manager, giving him an opportunity he richly deserved.

They say "keep your friends close and your enemies closer," but to be honest I never thought of any of the partners as my enemies, even those against whom I competed in elections. Those names that had appeared beside mine on the ballot, I reasoned, were there because they were the others most qualified for the job I was now doing; therefore, they would likely be my best sources of counsel. With this in mind, I decided to establish a "kitchen cabinet" to advise me in my new role, and the first person I invited to join was the man I had beaten out for the job—Don Waite. It was time for him to leave the New York office and let someone else take the lead, but I felt it was important to offer him a new position to move into. As a leader, I felt it was as much my responsibility to find roles for those displaced by my appointments as it was to make the appointments. Plus, I'd heard Don had been very disappointed after he lost the election; he couldn't understand how he'd lost to someone so much younger and less experienced. I also asked my old friend Herb Henzler from Germany. Later, as part of our governance initiative, we expanded this group and established a more formal Office of the Managing Director (OMD).

The Eight Laws of Rajat Gupta

In my office there hangs a framed document that was presented to me at a party to mark the end of my tenure as Chicago office manager. My good friend Atul Kanagat and his wife, Bina, were responsible for its creation. Entitled "The Eight Laws of Rajat Gupta," and inscribed in elegant calligraphy, it reads:

1. If someone else wants to do it, let him
2. If you have ten problems, ignore them – nine will go away
3. Being there is 90% of the game
4. You can't push a noodle; find the right angle and pull
5. The softer you blow your own trumpet, the louder it will sound
6. There is no such thing as too much work or too little time
7. Listening takes a lot less energy
8. When in doubt, invite them home.

This made me chuckle; my friends knew me well. It also made me reflect on my leadership style, which they had succinctly captured, and how it might serve me in my new role. The "noodle" rule, in particular, was going to be critical. Leading McKinsey would require skillful pulling from many angles. The firm was a partnership, so while I was nominally its leader, in reality it had at least as many leaders as it had senior partners. You couldn't just sit in a New York office—or a Chicago one—and direct the partners. Pushing had no effect. Even making appointments and selecting committees, the one power vested in the managing director, usually required consulting with a lot of people and gaining their support. It was rarely a unilateral decision. And once you appointed someone to a position, there was no expectation that they would vote with you or serve your agenda. Every partner was fiercely independent and entrepreneurial-minded.

I always thought of the managing director as "first among equals" and knew that my effectiveness in the role would be directly proportional to the strength of my relationships with my partners and my understanding of their viewpoints and the issues they were dealing with. Listening does indeed take a lot less energy than talking, and it also allows you to understand the aspirations of your partners and to effectively lead from behind.

However, I also knew that there was plenty of speculation, both in the papers and behind closed office doors, about whether I was tough and assertive enough for the job or too much of a "nice guy." I did tend to blow my trumpet quietly. The *Chicago Tribune*, with reference to my admiration for Swami Vivekananda and Mother Teresa, mused that "running McKinsey & Co. with its gung-ho battalions of princely consultants with lofty degrees . . . would seem to require someone whose idols are Napoleon and Lucretia Borgia, not a swami and a nun."[1] Perhaps. But the folks at the *Tribune* didn't seem to realize what determined characters both Swami Vivekananda and Mother Teresa were.

As I contemplated the challenges of my new job, I often thought of a phrase from Tagore that my father liked to quote: "unity in diversity." Tagore spoke out fiercely against what he saw as the scourge of nationalism, affirming a greater human unity that embraced and celebrated our differences. It was an idea well-suited to McKinsey in that era—we were growing more diverse by the day and yet our success, as Marvin Bower had counseled me, would depend on finding ways to remain unified.

Clients First

One of my concerns, when I took office, was how bureaucratic the firm had become and how much time partners were spending on administrative tasks, rather than serving clients. I was a firm believer that everyone should be client-focused, including the managing director. We were a client service firm, first and foremost, and so if someone wasn't really serving clients it was inevitable that they would slowly but surely lose the respect of the partners. I was aware that there were several older office managers who hadn't served a client in a decade. Why should the young partners take direction from these guys if they were so out of touch with the actual work?

Previous managing directors had all stepped back from client work after election. I'd been the busiest client guy in Chicago even while running the office and I intended to continue to set that example. I made it clear that this was expected from every partner. The only person I allowed to be exempt from this requirement was my chief of staff, Jerome Vascellaro.

In line with this principle, I felt we needed to shake up the firm's relationship to appointed positions. It was basically a collection of fiefdoms, and once someone was in an office manager role, for example, there was no simple way to move them on unless they weren't doing a good job. I felt that every role should rotate regularly. After all, everyone had their own biases and particular strengths and weaknesses, so it was good for there to be regular change.

Managing directors tended to change regularly simply because of the age limit, but when I was elected, at forty-five, I realized I could end up serving five terms. It was a good test of my belief in the idea of rotation. Was I ready to impose term limits on myself? I decided I was. Eventually, as part of a governance initiative during my second term, we created a policy stating that the maximum time any individual could serve as managing director was three terms. This principle of rotation applied to all appointed and elected positions, with varying terms, including the board, which upset some long-standing board members.

True to my word, I continued to serve clients and to introduce new clients throughout my time as managing director. I loved the work and took great satisfaction in the networking that had once seemed so foreign to me. I would never approach it in the same way as my American counterparts, but I'd always find ways to use my difference to my advantage. Indeed, the last of the "eight laws" referred to my signature way to close a deal with a hesitant client: rather than taking them golfing or wining and dining them at trendy restaurants, I'd invite them to my house for one of Anita's home-cooked Indian meals. It worked like a dream!

Beyond Geography

One of my early attempts at unifying and aligning the partnership was a project known as the Firm Strategy Initiative. This was not a classic strategy project, which usually just involves a small team going away and thinking about strategic priorities. It was a broad-based, long-term initiative designed to get everyone, especially all the partners, involved in thinking about the firm's strategy and developing initiatives to implement that strategy. Our guiding questions were: To whom should we provide our consulting services? What scope of services should we provide? And what kinds of delivery models and fee arrangements should we employ?

The strategy project was fruitful. Several key new directions emerged, including the establishment of our first virtual office, focused on the area of technology, which we needed to serve better. The dot-com boom was just beginning, and McKinsey was feeling tremendous pressure to improve our technology expertise and capacity, as our clients grappled with the changing landscape and looked to us for help. If we couldn't offer it, there was a new wave of competitors, particularly among the big accounting firms, which were branching out into consulting.

Until now, the firm had always organized its offices by geography; this would be the first time we organized around function as well. A partner named Dolf DiBiasio, who was a good friend of mine, was leading our Stamford office. He was a very successful client guy, and I decided he was the perfect person to lead the new office. I called him up. "Dolf, I want you to say yes."

"What am I saying yes to?" he demanded.

"Say yes, then I'll tell you."

"Yes," he said. So I told him the idea. The business technology office would function like a multilocational office, with its own resources.

"Okay, I'll do it," he confirmed, "but you'll have to give me the protection and support I need if it takes time to build and starts out losing money." I agreed, and we took the idea to the board. It turned out to be a great success and quickly grew to over five hundred professionals. We would go on to create other virtual offices as well, focused on specific functions.

We also turned our attention to global expansion. This was the 1990s, the heyday of globalization, but while the firm was well established in the US and Western Europe, and had some offices scattered around the world, it was not yet truly global. Our clients, meanwhile, were becoming global, and we needed to keep pace. Our new strategy included moving into mainland China, South Africa, and Dubai, and expanding our presence in India.

By the time we formally announced the results of the strategy initiative, many of them were already well underway. But that was the idea—to get people involved and invested in the growth of the firm and to energize and unify the partnership. The culmination of the two-year project was a conference that stands out in my mind for two reasons that have nothing to do with strategy. The first was a deeply sad moment, when I had to announce to the partnership that our colleague Joel Bleeke, who had been a leader of the project, had passed away that very day after a courageous battle with cancer. We were all still reeling from the news when the time came for a big surprise I'd planned. The conference was being held in Florida because a special guest I had invited could not travel any more. An elderly gentleman made his way through the darkened auditorium toward the stage. The people in the front rows recognized him first and rose to their feet. The ovation moved through the room like a wave as more and more people realized that our guest was the ninety-four-year-old Marvin Bower. The applause lasted for ten minutes, and it remains one of the most emotional moments I've ever witnessed in my time at the firm.

The message was clear: McKinsey was looking to the future, but it would never forget its roots. Soon, however, that commitment to balance past and future would be tested like never before, as the firm found itself navigating one of the biggest sea changes the business world had ever seen.

The Internet Revolution

Providing IT systems expertise to our clients was just the first step as the Internet revolution ramped up. Soon, a debate was raging internally about how the firm should position itself in the midst of the frenzy. The traditionalists wanted us to stay in our professional ivory tower, above the fray, while many of the younger partners wanted opportunities to cash in on the riches that seemed readily available. Many good partners left the firm in the late 1990s, particularly in the San Francisco office, where they were lured by the promise of making millions like so many of their friends and colleagues seemed to be doing.

One suggestion that many partners favored was that we should create a venture capital or private equity arm, similar to our competitor's spinoff Bain Capital. I was not keen on the idea, but I commissioned a study to weigh up the proposal, dubbed "Blue Capital" as a nod to our brand color. The issue became extremely divisive on the board and throughout the partnership. Some just felt it was too far from our core business. Others worried we'd be left behind if we didn't take this step. Everyone else was doing it, why shouldn't we? However, there was serious concern that we might create competitors to our own clients and conflict with our values. I was sympathetic to these concerns and was not in favor of the plan. Plus, it raised difficult questions for the partnership. Who would be the shareholders in this venture? If people left the partnership, would they still be owners? Above all, I just felt it was too divisive. The firm was essentially split fifty–fifty.

To my surprise and dismay, the board approved it. That night, I barely slept, thinking over how I could persuade the board to reverse the decision. I had no veto power, but I could appeal to the board to reconsider. I made my argument on the basis that the vote had been so close. For such an important strategic change in direction of the firm, I argued, we should have more than a simple majority. The board agreed, and the idea was scrapped. I think most people were quite relieved.

Another debate sprang up when some partners proposed that we change our fee structure so that we could accept equity rather than cash from some of the new and promising e-commerce start-ups that wanted our service but couldn't afford to pay cash. Again, there were concerns about creating conflicts of interest with our clients if we became part-owners of their upstart competitors. We gave the issue a lot of consideration and in the end developed an innovative approach with limits and appropriate checks and balances, including a committee to approve potential equity clients and apply safeguards. We made sure that while the particular office doing the work got credit for the client, the equity was owned not by the office but by the firm, and it was managed by a completely different team than the client service team.

We also decided to cap the upside. I was concerned that if one of these companies was wildly successful as an accident of the marketplace, several years down the road, we would have difficulties handling an unexpected windfall. Who should benefit? What if the partners who actually did the work bringing in that client had left? This policy came into play with a start-up arm of the Spanish company Telefonica, where we took a 10 percent equity stake but capped it at $10 million. It became worth hundreds of millions, angering some partners who felt we should have been able to profit more. I never regretted the policy, however. The alternative would have been so much more divisive.

Overall, in our experiments with equity payments, I don't think we strayed too far from our core values. Equity never amounted to more than 1 percent of the firm's revenues, and we protected ourselves from potential downsides. There were some, however, who strongly criticized any departure from tradition and felt we had sold out.

Another divisive issue arose when some began to suggest that the firm itself should go public. Booz Allen had done so, along with a number of other boutique firms, including one headed by our former managing director Fred Gluck. It would have been a windfall of cash for the partners, but I was dead against it. The firm didn't need capital. We liquidated the entire firm and distributed everything every year anyway. Why go to the market for money and give up control of our company? We were masters of our own destiny. It would be disastrous, I felt, to cash in for this generation at the expense of the next.

At the partners' conference, I was definitive. "This will never happen under my leadership," I told my several hundred assembled colleagues. "If you decide you want to do this, you should first elect a new leader." Thankfully, they dropped the idea and did not test my resolve, but I have no doubt I would have stood by my words.

These polarizing debates would continue, challenging me again and again to perform a delicate balancing act. Underlying each issue was a central tension: How fast should the firm be growing, and how could it embrace change without compromising its values?

Too Far, Too Fast?

I felt that a certain amount of growth was critical to the vibrancy of any institution. Ideally, I thought we should be growing between 5 and 10 percent each year in size and 15 percent or so in revenue, depending on inflation. But these were just my own thoughts; we never set official targets. That would have contradicted a core value of the firm: *Do right by your clients and results will follow.* I believed in this, but I also believed that to do right by our clients, we needed to expand into new areas, like technology or risk management. We also needed to globalize. In doing that, we grew, and to me that was a natural evolution of the firm. But there were always dissenters who felt we should stay a very small, elitist organization. There had been people who felt this way decades earlier when we were one-tenth the size, and I was sure there would be in decades to come. The definition of "small" just kept changing.

The opponents of growth feared that expansion would inevitably mean a dilution of quality—both of people and of work. Growth tends to mean that the ratio of associates to partners gets stretched to the limit and partners worry that they have less time to serve clients because they're managing and training new recruits. However, the truth was that our most successful offices were those with the highest associate to partner ratios. And the concerns about a decline in quality were not borne out by the evidence, in either client satisfaction or job satisfaction. In fact, the correlation was quite the opposite, which made sense to me, as a growing firm attracted better and more diverse talent.

In truth, at the time, most partners seemed happy about the firm's growth. They enjoyed the higher profile, greater global impact, and the increase in partner compensation that came with it. In the end, during my nine-year tenure as managing director, we more than doubled the size of the staff and tripled our revenue.

Along with the concerns about growth came criticisms that the firm was becoming overly commercial. Certain older partners looked back fondly to earlier days and bemoaned the changing times. What they didn't always take into account, however, was that in those good old days we simply did not have the same stature of clients, nor did we work on cutting-edge problems. I could feel this just by comparing the kinds of issues I worked on in the 1970s and the ones I was working on now. Yes, our profits were growing but that didn't necessarily mean we had become profit-driven. There was a fair amount of revisionist history going on.

I don't mean to imply that there was no profit motive in the firm or that we were unconcerned with financial success. McKinsey charged some of the highest consulting fees out there, and its partners were very well compensated. I appreciated that, as did my colleagues. I also firmly believed it was necessary if we were to stay ahead in the talent game. If our partners were paid only a fraction of the average C-suite executive, what incentive would they have to stay with the firm and not leave for an executive job?

On the whole, I felt that the accusations of over-commercialism during this period, both at the time and in hindsight, were disingenuous and lacking context. Our increased profits, from my perspective, were a natural outcome of doing the best work we could for our clients, during a unique moment in economic history. The firm's overriding creed had always been: *We will be successful if our clients are successful.* From my very first interview, this message had been reinforced. McKinsey consultants are professionals, and they put client interests ahead of the interests of the firm. If we served clients well, we trusted that financial rewards would follow. And rather than measuring our performance by revenue, we measured it by impact—both on our clients and on the firm. Partners were evaluated on the difference they were making to the performance of our clients and the contributions they were making to building the institution. We never had budgets and we never had targets; in fact, some partners were criticized for bringing in too much revenue at the expense of working on the development of the partnership.

If growing revenue had somehow eclipsed client service and become our primary goal, at the expense of our values, I think it would have been evident very quickly in the form of a loss of impact. Instead, the very opposite was happening—McKinsey was increasing its global impact and, wherever I traveled, I felt people's respect for the values the firm represented and their hunger for our expertise.

Breaking Up the Fiefdoms

When my first term came to an end, in 1997, we were riding high, and I was re-elected. With our strategic priorities clear, and having won the confidence of the partners, I decided it was time to turn our attention inward and re-evaluate our governance. The firm's governance systems had not been overhauled in decades. They had been designed for a much smaller and less globalized partnership; were they still appropriate for what the firm had become?

In envisioning this initiative, I had a very specific approach in mind. My idea was not to involve any senior people in the team, but instead to pick twenty young, high-performing directors who I believed were future leaders of the firm. These people, I reasoned, would have a greater stake in the governance system than those within ten years of retiring. They should be the architects of the system that would shape their working environment. This caused some ripples, to say the least. Several senior directors were personally affronted that they had not been included.

I asked the task force to start from first principles and figure out what kind of firm they wanted, what it ought to look like, and how it should be governed. They were to take into account the current realities of the size, scale, and scope of the firm, but also bring fresh eyes to systems that had not been the subject of any serious consideration for decades. Out of their deliberation, several key principles emerged, including the principle of rotation, applied to all elected and appointed roles; a further reinforcement of our move beyond geographic organization into a "three-dimensional" governance structure embracing geography, industry, and business function; an expansion of the board from twenty to thirty to better represent our expanding population of directors, subdivided into four committees, dealing with clients, people, knowledge, and finance; and a new performance measurement system. Many of the principles and practices we established as a result of this process govern the firm to this day, and many of those young directors who led the task force went on to become leaders in the firm.

A Return to New York

My decision to be based in Chicago as managing director turned out to be no big deal. I was constantly traveling anyway, and those times when I was home, modern technology made it possible to do my job without a hitch. My girls were growing up fast, and I spent as much time with them as I possibly could—playing cards, helping with homework, supervising chores. For McKinsey, it was an unusual situation to have a managing director with young children. Most of my predecessors had been old enough when they took office that their children had already grown up and left home. My youngest was only four when I took office.

Because my job required a lot of travel and didn't allow for much vacation, I took my family with me occasionally, determined that they would see the world and grow up to be global citizens. The first couple of times, it was an adventure, but soon we all found it rather exhausting, particularly on long, multi-city trips. I have vivid memories of the six of us, dragging twelve suitcases, trying to squeeze ourselves into two hotel rooms. I'd told the firm that would be enough space for us, not realizing that European hotel rooms don't match American ones for size. But we made the best of it, and I think the girls got valuable exposure to different cultures.

In 1999, in the middle of my second term, I realized that my family was naturally drifting East. Sonu was at Harvard, getting her undergraduate degree. Megha was attending boarding school in New Hampshire and Aditi was about to transition to high school and considering a school in Connecticut. It seemed like the time had finally come for us to return to the East Coast. We packed up our things, sold the house we'd lived in for more than a decade, and moved to a new home in beautiful Westport, Connecticut, overlooking the Long Island Sound.

Recession

In the spring of 2000, as my second term as managing director was coming to an end, the dot-com bubble burst. All the new demand for our services from the tech industry suddenly ground to a halt. Consulting, I learned, is particularly vulnerable to recession because it's a discretionary spend.

Our challenges were exacerbated by the fact that almost every office had over-hired that year, complicated by a long hiring cycle and a belief that the growth would surely continue. In that era of growing demand, no one was worried about having too many new hires; they felt confident they could always be absorbed elsewhere in the firm. The usual acceptance rate for the firm's job offers was about 70 percent, but with the economy shaky, we suddenly got 90 percent, which left us with far more people than we needed when the bubble burst. About 2700 young men and women had come on board and we didn't have enough work to keep them busy. Plus, McKinsey's infamous "up or out" policy had been less effectively implemented during the late 1990s, when the rising tide of the boom made everyone look good.

In the midst of this turmoil, I came up for re-election. Most managing directors are re-elected off the first ballot, as I had been after my first term, but this would turn out to be different. I believe there were several factors at play. On top of the impacts of the recession, there was a large faction of partners who were disgruntled by the governance reforms, in particular those who had lost their board seats as a result of the newly instituted term limits. There were plenty of revisionists who were busy rewriting the story of the last few years through the 20/20 lens of hindsight. I think I was also contending with what I thought of as the "disappointment factor." For every appointment you make, there are certain to be at least four or five people who thought they should have gotten the job. Over a few years, this army of the disgruntled adds up. Plus, the governance project had resulted in some changes to the rules for the managing director election. For all these reasons and more, the first ballot came out with a full slate of seven names, though two of these people, Peter Walker and Dick Ashley, withdrew their names right away, stating that they thought I was doing a good job and they had no interest in replacing me. We went through a few rounds until finally I won. Several people advised me during the process that I should pull out: I clearly didn't have a mandate, they argued. I held my ground.

I wasn't too troubled by this turn of events, for several reasons. First, I felt that it was natural that there were naysayers; after all, I'd been making big changes. Second, I thought we'd created a fair process and it should be allowed to do its work. If I lost, then I would have to step down; if I won, I would serve a third term and then step down when I reached the term limit I had established. I would accept whatever the outcome might be with equanimity, following my creed of karma yoga. Third, I was happy to see seven names on the ballot. That gave me some extremely useful information: it told me who the future leaders of the firm would be. If I got elected, those other six candidates were the people to whom I needed to pay attention. Clearly, they had a lot of support and would be good choices for leadership roles. As always, I refused to relate to them as rivals and thought of them as fellow leaders.

As my third term began, a certain faction of the partners was very concerned about the firm's financials. They saw a simple way to get things back on track: lay off the army of young associates we'd recently hired and back out of some of our promised hires from business schools. "The last thing we need right now is more mouths to feed," they told me.

All around us, our competitors were reneging on offers, but it just felt wrong to me. It's one of McKinsey's guiding principles that people are only asked to leave if they are underperforming or not living by the firm's values. That was not true of most of our new recruits—they'd barely had a chance to prove themselves. Were we going to let short-term economics (and, in some cases, concerns about partner compensation) drive us to fire good people who didn't deserve it? I appealed to my partners on the shareholders' council, which governs personnel issues, to take a longer view and hold firm to our values. Yes, our pay would suffer in the short term, and the balance sheet wouldn't look so good. But we would honor all our promises and stand by our people. The council agreed, and over the next couple of years, while client work was scarce, we created research projects to keep our young associates busy. Total partner compensation went down a bit but the firm remained profitable and there was no financial distress. And when the markets came back, Ian Davis, my successor as managing director, would thank me, because we had the people ready and were the best placed to compete as demand picked up.

During this period, India office manager Ranjit Pandit invited me to visit and participate in a day-long strategy meeting. It was still a young office, and the recession had hit hard. Revenues had dried up. As one partner after another addressed the meeting, I was shocked to hear each of them describe plans to focus on work outside India. They were planning to scatter around the world, effectively declaring the fledgling office a failure. "Why are you being so short-sighted?" I asked them. "This is not the moment to abandon ship. I'll promise you the backing of the firm, even if you don't make money in the short term. I'll make sure you're not passed over for election and so on." The partners rallied, and that meeting became a turning point for the office, which under Ranjit's leadership went on to become very successful.

Turning the Focus Outward

Traditionally, McKinsey had always maintained a low public profile—it was part of the firm's mystique. As leader, in my third term, I felt it was time for a change. We had an opportunity, I felt, to extend our impact beyond the specific clients we served and have a voice in important conversations about the role and responsibility of business in a fast-changing, globalizing world. It was time to get over our reticence about the spotlight. Not everyone agreed with this assessment, but I felt strongly enough to persist. We began to invest time and energy in getting our research showcased at business conferences and seeking out seats in high-level conversations such as the World Economic Forum and similar venues. I joined the WEF board, eventually becoming a friend and strategic advisor to founder Klaus Schwab, and McKinsey was well represented at Davos.

Personally, my focus shifted as well. During my first two terms, it had been natural to give most of my attention to internal issues of strategy, governance, and navigating the turbulent economic conditions. I'd always served clients, of course, and I'd spent a lot of time on other special projects, but as the new millennium got underway, I began to feel a calling to get out of my comfort zone and test my leadership capacity on a bigger stage. I've never been one to settle in a role or a place for too long, and my natural restlessness and drive for personal growth began to turn me toward new challenges. I felt I'd learned so much about how to solve strategic and operational problems in large companies, but I wondered, could McKinsey use its skills to address difficult or intractable societal issues? Could we serve a different kind of organization, like the UN, the Red Cross, or the World Health Organization (WHO), that had global impact?

Energized by this idea, we established what we called the "nonprofit practice," led by Les Silverman. Back in the 1990s, if you mentioned the words "McKinsey" and "pro bono" in the same sentence, you were likely talking about some politically popular but minimally impactful activity like a partner sitting on the board of the local symphony. McKinsey's nonprofit activities, for the most part, were localized and limited to supporting cultural institutions. That was about to change. We'd always had an ethos of service, but it had been focused on our clients. Now, I wanted to expand that service into areas where it was greatly needed. I was determined that part of my legacy as managing director would be a dramatic scaling up of the firm's investment in social issues. I wanted us to contribute our core expertise—management—where it could have maximum impact.

After all, McKinsey was a management laboratory with insight into the best practices of hundreds of corporations. Nonprofits were notorious for lacking the rigor and efficiency of business. In many cases, they had enormous resources and critical missions, but fell short of making the difference that was needed. With our global network of partners and clients, we were perfectly positioned to make our expertise available to organizations that could make great use of it, and enable them to deliver much more effectively on their mandates. To this end, McKinsey began to serve the Gates Foundation, the WHO, the UN, and the US Department of Education. We decided we would accept these assignments independent of the organizations' ability to pay, and we charged only what they could afford, without making any profit.

A Call for Help

On January 26, 2001, I was attending the Davos meeting of the WEF when I received some shocking news. On the 52nd anniversary of establishing the Indian Republic, disaster had struck the state of Gujarat in the form of a massive earthquake, killing close to 20,000 people by some estimates, injuring over one hundred thousand more, and destroying countless homes. It was surreal to be in the pristine beauty of Switzerland, surrounded by the rich and powerful, while watching images on the news of the devastation in the land of my birth. The scale of the destruction was hard to fathom, and I resolved to find a way to help.

I'd just arrived home when my friend Vinod Gupta called and told me that Bill Clinton, fresh out of the White House, was seeking a way to help the earthquake victims. Victor Menezes, vice chairman of Citigroup, was also trying to do something, and I knew many other Indians felt similarly. When I heard that Clinton wanted to meet with leaders of the Indian diaspora to devise a plan, I didn't hesitate. "I'll be there," I told Vinod.

Not only did I attend that meeting, which was held at the Citibank offices in New York, I ended up accompanying the president on a tour of India, including a visit to the affected region. I'd met him once or twice before, but had never spent this kind of time in his company. Although the entire event was rather an over-orchestrated spectacle, it left a lasting impact nonetheless. The devastation was unspeakable, and the response was chaotic and hampered by local government incompetence. We spent time talking to victims in hospitals, including a young boy whose face had been smashed and who had been through several reconstructive surgeries. The president sat with this boy for thirty minutes, and we could all feel his suffering. When we returned to Delhi, his speech to the assembled donors and supporters was all about that single encounter. He described in vivid detail what had happened to the boy and the impact on all of us. There wasn't a dry eye in the room by the time he was done.

As we traveled together over the course of eleven days, the president and I developed a friendship—and a fierce Scrabble and "Oh, Hell!" rivalry ("Oh Hell!" being a card game he loved and taught me how to play). He loved to keep score and would scrawl "Gupta wins again!" on the score sheets, along with his signature, as I won game after game. But he was always up for another. He slept very little, had an extraordinary memory for detail, and carried only two bags, of which one was entirely filled with books. He was a great conversationalist and I saw up-close what made him such an outstanding politician. No matter where we went, even when we stayed in fancy hotels or dined at some of India's best restaurants, I'd always find him talking to the staff in the kitchen or the housekeepers or the organizers behind the scenes at the various events. He sought out the people who were invisible and made them feel heard and valued.

On our return, many of us who'd been involved felt inspired to make this a more permanent fixture, and thus the American India

Foundation (AIF) was born. Victor and I became co-chairs, and our goal was to raise money in America to fund development projects in India. The earthquake reconstruction work in Gujarat was our initial focus but over the course of time we broadened the scope to include more areas of the country and focus on themes like primary education, livelihoods, and health. Over the next few years, the organization grew quite rapidly.

Another initiative of this era was the Pan IIT Alumni association. I'd always stayed closely connected with my own classmates and, as we each built careers in global business, it struck me what a powerful network the IIT alumni were. Interestingly, more than a third of them were working in the US. One day, a group of alumni assembled in my Stamford office, and the Pan IIT Alumni association was launched. We decided to put on a conference in Silicon Valley, and Bill Gates agreed to be the keynote speaker. Around 5000 alumni attended, and a *60 Minutes* special was aired before the conference, bringing the IITs to the attention of the American public in a new way. Today IITs are the most respected and well-represented schools in the leading technology companies, and IITs' growing alumni body stays connected through the association we launched.

As these initiatives took off, I was traveling more and more, and building my global network. I rarely spoke to the press or worried too much about my public profile, but I took great care to cultivate my connections with leaders in business, government, education, and the nonprofit sector. I teamed up with Jeffrey Sachs and Ray Chambers on the Millennium Villages Project to improve lives and livelihoods in rural Africa. Chambers and I also worked on the Malaria No More initiative, founded in 2006, with Peter Chernin. I accepted an invitation to join and eventually chair the advisory board of my alma mater, HBS, soon becoming a personal advisor to Harvard president Larry Summers. I instinctively knew that my network would matter, in ways I might not yet be able to predict. I quickly began to see a virtuous circle developing—my nonprofit work would bring me into contact with other business leaders, who would then become clients for McKinsey, and my client work would connect me to businesses I could then call on to support worthy causes.

I was fifty-four when my third term came to an end. Ian Davis had been elected to succeed me. We had our final board meeting in Stamford, Connecticut, close to my home, followed by a farewell party for all the board members I'd served with during my tenure, including many who'd already retired. It was a wonderful event, made more special by my German colleagues who had decided to surprise me with an elephant, of all things. It was delivered by truck to my daughter's school, just down the road, since that was the only place with space for the truck to park. The schoolchildren looked on in amazement as the enormous creature was unloaded and slowly paraded down the road to my house, where my guests took rides all evening. It was a memorable occasion, even though the elephant completely destroyed my lawn.

11

Let My Country Awake

Education has its only meaning and object in freedom—
freedom from ignorance about the laws of the universe,
and freedom from passion and prejudice in our communication
with the human world.

—Rabindranath Tagore, *Ideals of Education*

In 1971, when I decided to go to business school, there was only one way for an ambitious young Indian to get a world-class education: travel halfway around the world. I often thought back with gratitude to the exceptional educational opportunity I'd been given at Harvard, but I also knew how lucky I'd been to get it, and how hard it had been to leave my family behind. I wished something comparable was available to more young people in my homeland. Around the time I took over as managing director at McKinsey, a vision was beginning to take hold in my mind: *a business school for India.* What if I could rally India's most successful business leaders and educators and inspire them to give back to the next generation?

Although I'd now been living in America for more than two decades, my ties to India were strong. I returned every year, sometimes more than once, visiting my siblings, their families, and my extended family. I donated my time and money to various nonprofits during my visits. Early on, I'd thought that I might eventually do more work in India, but as I became more deeply committed to the firm and more involved in its governance, this idea faded. However, I visited the Delhi office regularly, and I also chaired the US India Business Council. Like my father, I felt it was my calling to serve the land of my birth—and to do so with impact and at scale. In the mid-1990s, it became clear to me that one way I could make a unique contribution was to help give ambitious young Indians a world-class business education. Thus, the idea of the Indian School of Business was born.

"You're crazy!" Anita said, when I told her my idea. "You'll never get something like that off the ground in India. There's just too much red tape, too much corruption." Besides, she added, wasn't the McKinsey managing director job enough for me to take on? I'd been in the role only a couple of years at that point.

She was talking sense, of course, but that didn't mean I would listen. One of my favorite quotes is from Gandhi: "If the cause is right the means will come." It's always been my belief that any project that needs to be done can be done. The school was clearly needed. I just had to figure out how to make it happen. Overconfident I may have been, but it was not entirely unfounded. McKinsey was the biggest recruiter from American business schools, and I sat on the boards of several, including HBS, Kellogg, and MIT. I knew how they operated and what it took to create a successful institution. I hoped I would be able to connect the school I was envisioning with these well-established educational centers. Could it be done? I didn't know, but I was determined to give it a shot. Before long, I'd inspired my McKinsey colleague Anil Kumar to help out, along with my good friend P.C. Chatterjee, founding chairman of the Chatterjee Group. Anil reached out to his Wharton classmate Anil Ambani, son of the legendary Indian businessman and Reliance founder Dhirubhai Ambani, who enthusiastically joined our fledgling team.

Our initial idea was to collaborate with the IIT network, my alma mater, and create a school within IIT Delhi. It made sense to partner with an established institution for numerous reasons, allowing us to take advantage of a reputable brand, infrastructure, and more. The director of IIT Delhi was keen to collaborate. Some IITs had already been experimenting with some business school models, offering a master's in business and creating a department of management, but none of them offered a world-class MBA program. The University of Delhi had an MBA program, established in 1954, and the popular Indian Institutes of Management (IIMs) had been founded in the 1960s. However, none of these institutions were at scale enough to meet the needs of India's new generation of aspiring managers, nor were they truly research-based academic institutions. If Indian businesses were to compete on a global stage, they needed large numbers of highly educated managers and leaders.

However, when we sat down at a meeting to hammer out the details, it soon became clear that the partnership wasn't going to work. Although personally disappointed, the director told us, "Don't do it." The IITs were just too constrained by politics and bureaucracy, he explained. The ministry of education supervised (and often interfered with) their policies regarding recruitment, fees, and more. We were sure we could improve the business education offerings at the IITs, but we were not sure we would have the freedom to create the truly world-class institution we envisioned. I was gravely disappointed. Was this dream going to die before it had even gotten off the ground?

We were walking despondently away from the campus when Anil Ambani spoke up. "Why don't we just do it independently?"

I stopped in my tracks. "Why not?"

The idea was as compelling as it was challenging. Starting from scratch would allow us to do everything exactly the way we wanted it, unconstrained by tradition, politics, or competing agendas. It would also be a tremendous amount of work. But by this point, we were fully invested in the cause. Yes, we were idealistic and more than a little naive. But perhaps, in this instance, that served us well.

Upon returning to the US, I requested a meeting with Don Jacobs, dean of Kellogg. He listened intently to my proposal and then said, "Rajat, if you want to try to do something, I would like to help." His prior experience in supporting schools around the world usually involved already established universities, but he said that if I wanted to put all my energies and capabilities behind a stand-alone school, he would do everything he could to support me. I was honored and encouraged by his words. We were then joined by Dipak Jain, deputy dean and professor of marketing at Kellogg, whom I'd known and advised for a couple of years. He also expressed great enthusiasm for the project and pledged his support. Having helped Kellogg set up a business school with a university in Thailand, he had invaluable on-the-ground experience.

There were three conditions we came to believe were critical for the success of our school. First, it must have a world-class faculty, which would require collaborations with leading global business schools. Second, it would need the support of the local business community, so that they would be prepared to hire our graduates. Third, it must have a self-supporting financial model, in order to remain free from government interference. We knew each of these would be challenging to put in place. The one thing we were not concerned about was attracting outstanding students—India was bursting with bright, educated, ambitious young men and women, and the existing institutions were only meeting a fraction of the demand.

To meet a couple of our objectives at once—getting seed money and building support among the business community—we established an "executive board" and invited a group of India's most respected businessmen, both at home and abroad, to join, with a condition being that they would make an initial donation of at least $1 million. Soon, we had acquired both credibility and cash. In early 1996, we convened our first board meeting at the IIT Delhi campus.

Recruiting faculty turned out to be more of a challenge. It was understandably hard to convince expats who'd built careers abroad to return to their homeland and take a chance on a school that was not even built. After much discussion, we decided to fall back on a visiting faculty model. Professors from other schools could come for six weeks at a time to teach intensive courses. This met with a more favorable response, and we soon had a distinguished lineup. Over time, we hoped to build a local faculty too.

Next, we formed a governing board, and invited members of the global business community to join. We decided that this board would meet only once a year, in either New York or London, so hopefully this would not be too much of a commitment for busy CEOs. I used my connections with companies like Goldman Sachs and Novartis to assemble a very impressive board that lent the school prestige and also opened the door for their companies to recruit at the school.

Our next step was to approach established business schools in addition to Kellogg, looking for collaboration and support. Wharton was enthusiastic, which made sense given that several of their illustrious alumni were on our board. Soon after this, Sumantra Ghoshal, professor at the London School of Business (LSB), asked to join the team and brought LSB on board as a partner. Many Indian-born faculty members at our partner schools agreed to get involved as academic advisors and visiting faculty and to help us develop a curriculum.

My official title was chairman, but I took a very hands-on approach to the role. Every Sunday morning, no matter where I was in the world, I'd dial in to a meeting with the ISB team. McKinsey was extremely supportive of the endeavor, not only allowing me to spend significant time on it, but providing significant pro bono resources, without which ISB would never have gotten off the ground. Particularly critical, in this regard, was McKinsey partner Pramath Sinha, who eventually took on the title of CEO of the ISB initiative, even while continuing to consult at McKinsey.

By early 1998, the pieces were falling into place: we had seed money, reputable partners, and a distinguished faculty. There was just one major element missing: a campus.

In Search of a Home

We knew we wanted the home of our school to have room to expand and the architecture to be iconic. After all, I'd spent two years in Harvard's hallowed halls and cobbled courtyards, and I felt keenly that the physical environment needed to reflect the quality of the education we intended to deliver. I envisioned it lasting hundreds of years, becoming a historic institution like the great universities of the world. Another lesson I'd learned from Harvard was the importance of space. The city-based university has literally no room to expand—a problem I didn't want our school to ever face. Some of our board members thought a hundred acres would be enough, but I wanted several hundred.

Initially, our idea was to build a campus near Mumbai, the commercial capital of India, and we identified a perfect hundred-acre site. Everything looked positive and the sale was all set to be completed, when we got a call from a prominent politician's office asking us to come in for a meeting. Knowing the workings of Indian politics, I was immediately concerned. What could they want? Some of the board members who were familiar with Indian politics shared my misgivings. We were determined that the school would be a meritocracy, with everything completely above board and free from the cronyism that plagued Indian politics. We didn't want to start paying bribes to local officials before we'd even opened our doors. My partners and I knew we could not set a bad precedent. If they proposed anything improper, we decided, we would simply walk out and walk away from the site.

Sure enough, after pleasantries were exchanged at the meeting, they made thinly veiled requests for money, and they also wanted us to reserve a quota of places for students and teachers from the state.

Neither of these was in alignment with our principles or the image we wanted to project, and so we thanked them for their time, told them that we would not be locating our school in their state after all, and walked out. They later called and rescinded their demands, but we stood firm. We didn't want to get deeply invested in a state that operated this way. Instead, we created a competition between states to bid for the campus, and that was how we found ourselves, one humid summer day in 1998, standing on a beautiful hilltop outside the city of Hyderabad, strewn with large boulders. There was no infrastructure out there, not even a road, but the local government was promising to build one and to ensure that utilities were in place.

In the end, the decision was not difficult: the Hyderabad proposal stood head and shoulders above those we'd received from other states. It turned out that the recently elected chief minister of Andhra Pradesh, Chandrababu Naidu, was on a mission to modernize his state and turn Hyderabad into a high-tech powerhouse to rival Bengaluru. He saw the school as a great asset in that regard and pulled out all the stops to be the winning bid.

The only hesitations were related to the fact that while Hyderabad was an up-and-coming city, it was not Delhi or Mumbai, or even Kolkata or Chennai. But we decided to take a chance on it, and it was a decision we never regretted.

When it came to fundraising for the building of the campus, the generosity continued. Adi Godrej continued to be a champion of the project, and he and his wife, Parmeshwar, opened their home in Mumbai as a hub for fundraising events. And I continued to tap my network. I remember the day I asked Daniel Vasella, CEO of Novartis and one of our early board members, for his support.

"How much money do you need?" he inquired.

I wasn't quite prepared for that question, but I told him I thought $1 million would be good. He said he would think about it. A couple of weeks later, I received a check for $2 million. Dan's accompanying note said, "You'll need more money than you think!" Hank Paulson from Goldman Sachs was another very generous donor, along with several Silicon Valley and Indian business leaders.

Unfortunately, before we'd collected on much of our promised funding, the tech bubble burst. Some of our Silicon Valley supporters were unable to make good on their pledges, and our construction project was on shaky ground for a while. Eventually, we had to take a bank loan to complete the work. I worried that the confidence we'd built in our initiative would take a hit, and we'd have trouble attracting faculty and students if we appeared financially unstable. The press didn't help, giving us low odds of success.

Meanwhile, we faced another hurdle: the All India Council for Technical Education (AICTE), which was part of the ministry of education, made it clear they disapproved of our independence. When we requested for forms to apply for our accreditation as a university, they refused to even send them. We already had reservations about being under their regulatory regime and their attitude only confirmed my misgivings. The board debated the issue at length. We had our hearts set on granting MBAs, which we could not do without accreditation. On the other hand, there was nothing to stop us issuing diplomas with the signatures of the deans of Kellogg and Wharton alongside that of our own dean. Perhaps this would be enough to get our students hired while retaining our independence?

In March of 2001, we received a formal notice from AICTE declaring that we had no authorization to start a school and announcing their intention to shut us down. This was the first of many such letters over the years.

To shore ourselves up against such attacks, we took a proactive approach to getting political support at the highest levels. Our reasoning was that if we had powerful champions and a high public profile, there would be a backlash against any attempts to shut us down. We already had a supporter in Chandrababu Naidu, and to solidify that relationship we invited him to do the groundbreaking, as well as to speak at our inauguration. Other politicians who were invited to the school over the years included prime ministers Atal Bihari Vajpayee and Manmohan Singh, and education minister Kapil Sibal, who came despite strong objections from the bureaucrats. Later, President George W. Bush chose ISB as the only private institution he visited on his trip to India in 2006. His roundtable discussion with students was nationally televised. All of this visibility protected ISB, although to this day its legal status remains tenuous.

I pressed ahead with the next critical piece: the search for a dean. I had hoped that Dipak Jain from Kellogg would take on the role, and initially he agreed to a co-deanship, but then Don Jacobs was taken ill, and Dipak stepped into his shoes at Kellogg, eventually being tapped to succeed Don. He felt terrible letting us down, but it was not an opportunity he could pass up. I was happy for him, but disappointed for ISB. Sumantra Ghoshal had offered to take on the role of dean, working with Dipak, if he could divide his time between ISB and London. His name would give us the credibility we were seeking, even if his part-time status wasn't ideal. However, just months before our planned opening, he too withdrew, saying he felt his skills were unsuited to being an administrator. Nothing we said would convince him.

There simply wasn't time to find another reputable academic ready to make the move. With that off the table, there was clearly one man who knew ISB better than anyone: my McKinsey partner Pramath Sinha, who'd been acting as CEO. Pramath had a PhD from the University of Pennsylvania and was at heart an academic. I sat down one day with him and his wife. "Look, Pramath, I think at this stage you have to do it."

Pramath looked surprised, but understood that he was the only logical choice. "You'll have to convince my wife, though," he told us. In the end, she agreed, and I persuaded Pramath to take a one-year leave of absence from the firm, just until we could find a replacement. He would be well supported by deputy deans Savita Mahajan and Ajit Rangnekar, and I breathed a sigh of relief. At least we would not be opening without a dean.

We might, however, be opening without a roof. Construction was moving with typical Indian slowness, hampered by heavy monsoon rains. We had broken ground at the end of 1999, and our opening had been moved from its initial date of summer 2000 to June 2001. Still, it was an ambitious timeline; when I visited toward the end of 2000, I was alarmed by how far behind schedule we were. Would we be forced to compromise on the vision of a world-class facility in order not to miss our deadline? I sent a strongly worded letter to the head of the architectural firm, and the board decided to push back the opening one more month, to July 1. Then it was just a race against time, but the team pulled out all the stops.

This was just the first of many twists and turns in the ISB story. At every step, we were told it couldn't be done, and we surprised our critics with creative and counterintuitive solutions. People said it could never be done in India, but we found ways to bypass the bureaucracy and stay independent. They said we couldn't run a business school primarily with visiting faculty, but we made it work, attracting the cream of the world's business talent to teach our students. They said it would be impossible for us to attain university status, but we proved we could be successful without it. They said our fees were too high and we could never compete with the government-funded IIMs, but we came up with an innovative system of student loans to make it work. They said our executive education program, critical to the school's cash flow, would fail after 9/11, but we launched it successfully and it soon became the biggest in the country. They said our one-year MBA program would be viewed as second-rate, but in the spring of 2001 we received more than 1100 applications and admitted our first 128 students.

On July 1, we opened our doors. Thanks to the enormous efforts of a veritable army of workers and volunteers, we were ready—or at least ready enough. There was still scaffolding in the atrium where we held the ceremony, which had to be artfully disguised. But the campus was stunning, with its striking pink stone buildings, its clean modern lines with subtle nods to the area's Mughal architectural heritage, and its vivid green lawns. Inside, the facilities and technology were state of the art.

Once the school was open, our principles continued to be tested. Our admission system was "needs-blind," meaning no one had to disclose their ability to pay on their application. We would accept people on their merit and then provide them with scholarships and loans if needed. We worked with the banks to set up student loans that would accept our diploma certificates as collateral, removing that burden from students' parents. We refused to allow interference in the admissions process from any of our board members or donors seeking special dispensation for their friends and family members.

This was important to me. I'd been on the boards of many educational institutions over the years and had often been asked to intercede on behalf of a friend or family member's son or daughter seeking admission. Similarly, I'd often been asked to help with job applications. I'd thought long and hard about how to approach such moments. I believed in meritocracy and didn't want anyone to get ahead simply based on their connections. However, I also didn't like to deny people my support. One such case that I'll never forget involved my younger brother's son. After graduating Princeton, where he'd been accepted without any help from me, he wanted to work in the Teach for America program. I happened to know the founder, and my brother asked me to write to her in support of his son's application. I did so.

A week later, I got a call from my nephew, who was irate!

"Uncle, I want you to retract the email. I don't want an unfair leg up."

His father clearly had not consulted him before making the request.

"I appreciate how you feel," I told him. "But read the letter first."

I'd thought carefully about how to write it, acknowledging my bias as his uncle, listing the qualities I thought he would bring to the program and expressing my respect for and trust in the admissions process, regardless of the outcome. After reading the letter, he felt differently and decided to let it stand. The same thinking informed the rules we created around the ISB admissions process. Friends and relatives could write letters of recommendation, but, regardless, their family members would go through the same process as everyone else and be considered on their own merits.

I personally followed this protocol when another of my nephews applied to ISB and was rejected. Both he and his mother were heartbroken and implored me to intercede. I'd been a mentor to the boy, helping him choose a career path, so, understandably, he was very hurt when I refused to use my influence on his behalf. I felt bad for him. I felt responsible for him and his brother. Plus, I knew what rejection felt like. I remembered how it had felt when McKinsey turned me down and how grateful I had been when Walter Salmon stepped in and got me a second chance. But I couldn't compromise ISB's commitment to meritocracy. I called and explained to him why this was important to me and why I couldn't break the rule even for someone I loved. I was disappointed for him, but secretly I was proud of the school. In rejecting a founder's family member, our system had passed a significant test and not succumbed to nepotism. He later forgave his uncle when I helped him apply to the prestigious Kellogg school at Northwestern University, and he went on to become a successful entrepreneur.

On June 23, 2002, I was proud to step up to the lectern and deliver the convocation speech for our very first graduating class. Looking out over the sea of faces, I saw India's future. I wished we had more diversity of international students, and more women, but we were off to a great start. Almost all of that first graduating class had job placements with great companies, at home or abroad. Pramath and I, along with a few others, had worked every weekend for months on this—calling companies, persuading them to come and interview our graduates. It was all worth it for that moment.

As the school became established and continued to grow, there was always a tension between the board's desire to scale fast and the faculty's preference for a smaller cohort and a slower pace of growth. With so many results-oriented businessmen involved, the board won out, and

ISB grew from 128 students in the first batch to 560 within five years. At its ten-year anniversary, it boasted more than five thousand alumni, and today that number has passed ten thousand. ISB graduates more than eleven hundred students every year. A second campus has been established in the northern city of Mohali—largely funded through the generosity of four friends, Sunil Mittal, Sunil Munjal, Mickey Punj, and Analjit Singh—and the school continues to thrive.

In 2008, only seven years after we had opened our doors, to everyone's surprise, ISB made the prestigious *Financial Times* ranking of the top 20 business schools in the world. I was honored, but not sure we deserved it—yet. Had our brand gotten ahead of our reality? We had not yet attracted the foreign students we wanted, nor established a large permanent faculty. I told everyone we needed to work hard to catch up with our brand. But I was proud of the achievement. I knew that the quality of our students, their placement record with blue chip companies, and the quality of the curriculum were all deserving of the honor. ISB would remain on the list for many years to come and still features today.

Another more personal moment of satisfaction came in 2006, when I invited the Indian business titan Ratan Tata to be our fifth convocation speaker. Tata had been an early supporter but had withdrawn from the board. The reason he gave, at the time, was that he felt our priorities were wrong: we should not have been spending so much money on a fancy campus when India was such a poor country. However, when Tata gave his convocation speech, he graciously acknowledged that he had been wrong about the campus. Looking around at the beautiful, state-of-the-art facilities, he said he now understood why we'd insisted on doing it this way.

There were many moments in the journey when I wondered if we'd bitten off too much, but we were determined to follow through on our vision. ISB is one of my proudest achievements, and one of the aspects of it that means the most to me is that it doesn't bear my name or any other person's name. Before ISB, most philanthropic endeavors in India were old-fashioned, funded by and named after wealthy or influential individuals. ISB was different. It's not "my" school or any of its funders'; it's India's school, built by a group of dedicated people who love their country and want to contribute to its future. This was my intention from the beginning—that India's business leaders and the Indian diaspora would feel a collective ownership of their business school and support it with their time, their money, and their recruitment efforts. ISB demonstrated to the Indian private sector that it could play a catalytic role in shaping society.

It demonstrated something to me as well: how much human beings with disparate interests and backgrounds can achieve when they unite for an unselfish purpose. ISB would become a template for many institutions I and others would build in the years to come: unique, multi-stakeholder coalitions, marrying the public and private sector, often bringing unlikely partners to the same table, held together by a common vision.

12

Transition

Man's abiding happiness is not in getting anything but in giving himself up to what is greater than himself, to ideas which are larger than his individual life, the idea of his country, of humanity, of God.

—Rabindranath Tagore, *Sadhana*

Fall 2003

"Take a new job," Anita suggested. "Maybe it's time for a change. Become a CEO or do something completely different."

I was fifty-four years old. Staring out of my front window at the elephant tracks still visible on my once-pristine lawn, I was reminded every day that my time as managing director had come to an end and I needed to decide what was next. I was ready to move on—the job had been physically and emotionally demanding, and I'd given it my all. Retirement was the last thing on my mind, as my wife well knew, but I think she hoped I might at least slow down a little.

I thought seriously about her suggestion. Was it time for a change? I didn't feel ready to leave McKinsey. For some reason, the idea that I would spend my entire career in one institution appealed to me. The new managing director, Ian Davis, was a friend, but I was careful not to get in his way or offer advice unless asked. I'd been in his shoes once, and I knew how important it is for a new leader to establish his own independent leadership style and authority. I decided to try to carve out a different kind of role for myself within the firm: something no former managing director had ever done. I'd remove myself from governance responsibilities and focus my attention on bringing in new clients. As a managing director emeritus, I'd be available to represent the firm on the global stage as needed, and I'd also expand my philanthropic activities, with McKinsey's blessing, and have a greater impact on the global problems I cared about.

I tapped my vast network and continued to introduce major clients to the firm. Interestingly, I think the freedom of my new position made me even more effective. I could focus on building relationships, without the urgency to close the deal. Sometimes the secret to client development is simply patience. A case in point was Lee Scott, CEO of Walmart. The retail giant was flying high in the early years of the new millennium and made it clear it had no use for consultants. McKinsey had been trying to develop them as a client for some time, but to no avail. I met Lee when he joined the board of Tsinghua University School of Economics and Management, and we shared a long, slow car-ride to dinner in Beijing's terrible traffic. At the end of our wide-ranging and fascinating conversation, I proposed to Lee that I visit him in Bentonville, the Arkansas headquarters of Walmart, so that we could continue.

"Okay, you can come," he said, "but don't expect any work from us. We don't use consultants."

Undeterred, I made the trip and we met for an hour. At the end, I asked him if our conversation had been of value to him, and he acknowledged that it had. "So we should do it again," I said, and three months later I returned. This went on for three years, with nothing to show for the time and travel other than a growing trust with Lee. And then finally, one day, he called me with an assignment. That was the beginning of the firm's extensive work with Walmart.

Most companies, especially large, complex ones, are going to need help sooner or later. But they'll call a consultant when *they* are ready, not when you're ready. The key is to be the first person they think of when they decide to make that call. I achieved this by focusing on providing value in my relationships—contributing to their thinking without any immediate expectation of return.

This approach was also effective with P&G CEO A.G. Lafley. A humble and understated guy, he was famous for not using consultants. I liked him immediately and suggested I come and meet with him, which I did, several times, over a couple of years. It might have looked like it was going nowhere, and then one day, just before Thanksgiving in 2005, he called me out of the blue while I was at lunch with a friend in Manhattan. "I'm at the Waldorf. Can you come and see me?" When I arrived, he explained that James Kilts, CEO of Gillette, had proposed a merger. He wanted me to form a team to help evaluate the deal, on a very tight deadline. We did so, and recommended that they go ahead. But when Lafley and Kilts met to negotiate, things turned sour. They couldn't agree on price, and as everyone left for their Christmas vacations, they had to disclose that the discussions had failed and the deal was off.

On January 1, I got a call from Lafley. "I should have done the deal," he said.

I told him I agreed, and I thought he shouldn't make too much of the price. "If you believe in the technology, and it's a strategic fit, you won't care if you pay a few dollars more a share."

"You're right, we should do it," he said. "But I can't call Jim."

"Why not?" I asked. But he just reiterated, "I can't. But I want you to call and reopen discussions."

I met Kilts, who had been a client in my Chicago days, for lunch, and quickly learned that he was not at all happy with how things had unfolded. He had told Lafley the price was non-negotiable, and was not happy that Lafley had tried to negotiate anyway. But he, too, conceded that the deal still made strategic sense, so he tasked me with setting up a meeting, with the condition that price would not be discussed. They sat down, one on one, on Martin Luther King Day, out of the spotlight of staff, lawyers, and the media, in a small office in Rye, New York, and did the deal. P&G became a significant client of the firm, and I would eventually be invited to serve on their board.

Because I was still one of the most productive directors in the firm, as well as being a former managing director, McKinsey was willing to give me a lot of freedom to focus on the causes I cared about as well, along with an incredible platform from which to do so. This was a major benefit of staying with the firm—one that I would never have gotten if I'd left to take a CEO job. I began to spend about fifty percent of my time on social issues.

Over the past few years, I'd been increasingly active in the world of global philanthropy, through McKinsey's not-for-profit practice. One of my favorites was the Gates Foundation. I'd first met the foundation's president, Patty Stonesifer, at a gathering of philanthropists in 2001. In those days, the foundation was just getting going with a handful of staff, and Patty asked me to come and speak to her about organizational development. We formed a strong friendship, and a few years later McKinsey did an assignment with the foundation, now much bigger, to identify areas that the foundation could focus on, particularly related to AIDS prevention. Eventually, Bill invited me to chair the advisory board for the foundation.

Another Side of Kolkata

"It's *here*?"

One minute, we had been walking through a familiar Kolkata neighborhood. The next minute, we had turned a corner and stepped right into the infamous red-light district, Sonagachi. I was shocked. I'd visited Kolkata many times as a child and teenager—accompanying my uncle to the street markets early in the mornings—but I'd had no idea this place existed. Later, as an adult, I heard about it, but I'd imagined some shadowy den of iniquity on the fringes of the city, not this centrally located network of clean, narrow streets, with its neat rows of little one-room shacks. Another thing that surprised me, although in retrospect it should not have, given the reason for our visit, was the number of young children running around.

My guide on this particular occasion, in 2003, was Ashok Alexander, a former McKinsey senior partner who'd joined the Gates Foundation to run the AIDS prevention program that had been launched following our recommendations. The disease was spreading in India, often transmitted from sex workers to men who went back to their villages and infected their wives. The project, known as Avahan, was designed to focus on high-risk groups—organized brothels, truck stop sex workers, and so on—and encourage condom use and other safe sex practices. Gates invited me to be its chair, working closely with Ashok as well as Helene Gayle and Patty Stonesifer, which was why I found myself strolling the streets of a part of my hometown in which I had never expected to set foot.

We spent a whole day in Sonagachi, talking with the residents about their practices and the manner in which they were treated by their clients. These women knew the dangers of AIDS and wanted to protect themselves, but one of the biggest issues that quickly became clear was that there were economic incentives working against safety. Customers were willing to pay more for sex without condoms. There were also varying levels of understanding when it came to the dangers of AIDS.

Interestingly, Sonagachi was one of the few brothels that were unionized, so we encouraged them to unite around a policy of condom use. The response was positive. In general, we found the women we approached to be receptive and pragmatic, much more so than many people in government who still clung to denial, refusing to believe that casual sex was so prevalent in their country. AIDS prevention is a challenge anywhere in the world, but India presented some particular cultural barriers. People believed that an AIDS epidemic could never happen in a religious country like India. They saw it as a Western disease, connected to lifestyles and values India didn't condone. Sure, it was spreading in Africa, but that was Africa. Indians were convinced of their superior morals and, in some cases, willfully blind to the reality. Our work required a delicate navigation of these attitudes and a lot of education. In the beginning, we tried hard to get accurate statistics about the prevalence of the disease. At a certain point, however, I realized that it didn't really matter. "Let's just run the program," I said. Our energy was better spent on intervention than on cultural disputes.

A New Challenge

"You can't do anything in health without the support of the government," Bill Gates told me emphatically. "I'll give you $15 million, but first you need to get the government on board."

"Yes, yes," I assured him. "They have already promised their support."

This was not entirely true. What Prime Minister Manmohan Singh had actually told me was, "Okay, we'll support it, but first show us that you can raise money from the private sector."

It was a couple of years after the AIDS project, and I was raising funds for a new and ambitious venture: creating a public health foundation for India. I knew that I needed both the government and the private sector on board. Hence, I found myself performing a delicate dance between Bill Gates and Prime Minister Singh, assuring each that the other was committed when in fact neither wanted to be first, even though both were enthusiastic.

The idea for the foundation had first come from Barry Bloom, dean of the Harvard T.H. Chan School of Public Health. He had invited me to breakfast one day in 2002, shortly after I returned from the first ISB graduation, the culmination of so many years of hard work. Glowing with pride, I told Barry about the event and was surprised by his response.

Vith my parents and sisters at our Delhi home

Top left: Posing for a picture aged three
Top right: With my siblings including my younger brother
Bottom: At the inauguration of the student activity center at IIT

Facing page, top: "Posh Puja" ceremony in the Kashmiri tradition at our wedding
Bottom: With Anita during my early days as managing director at a McKinsey conference in South Africa

Above: Marvin Bower dressed as Santa at my Scandinavian farewell party

Facing page, top: All my McKinsey partners from Scandinavia with Marvin Bower
Bottom: Vacationing with my four girls in Colorado when I learned of my election to managing director of McKinsey in March 1994

Funnel Cakes
7UP
OPEN
WELRY IN THIS SH
is made in
VERTON COLORADO

Top: At the ISB board meeting with the founding board members
Bottom: Meeting Premier Zhu Rongji of China

Facing page, top: With President Bush at the Oval Office being recognized for my work in global health
Middle: Playing Scrabble with President Clinton on our travels in India
Bottom: Fireside chat with Bill Gates at the first Pan IIT conference

Top: In discussion with Secretary General of the United Nations Kofi Anan regarding management reforms at the UN
Middle: At the launch of the Public Health Foundation of India with Prime Minister Manmohan Singh, Professor Amartya Sen, Kapil Sibal, education minister, and Anbumani Ramadoss, health and family welfare minister
Bottom: In discussion with Speaker Nancy Pelosi at our home in Westport

Top left: Speaking at the UN General Assembly session for heads of state which s held every five years

Top right: With Prime Minister Manmohan Singh after his speech to McKinsey partners

Bottom: With my German partners on McKinsey's board who brought along an elephant o my retirement party

Extended family get-together for Thanksgiving

Top: With Deepali at her graduation from Brown in the middle of my trial

Bottom: The graduation I had to miss. Aditi with Sonu and Anita at Harvard Business School

Top: My IIT friends at our annual get-together

Bottom: Meera and Nisa spending time with me the day before I went to prison

Top: Most of my immediate family visiting me in prison
Bottom: Meera and Nisa visiting me at what they thought was a private camp

Top: The bridge foursome that played every day

Bottom: My first steps of freedom outside the prison after serving my sentence

Facing page, top left: With my brother, who visited frequently

Top right: With Pramath Sinha, who also visited me frequently from India

Bottom left: My walking outfit in winter with two neck warmers, two hats and my MP3 player

Bottom right: Walking in deep snow with my bunk-mate

Top: My four girls celebrating Megha's birthday after my release

Bottom, left: With Lekha, born after my release, enjoying a walk on the beach

Bottom right: Dancing with Riya, my youngest granddaughter, at Aditi's wedding

"A business school? That's easy."

Easy? I would hardly describe it that way. "If you want to *really* make an impact in India," he continued, "start schools of public health." He explained that he'd recently visited my homeland as part of a WHO meeting on leprosy and had been horrified by what he saw. "India has many good doctors," he said, "but you can't expect the state of the country's health to improve through simply treating people once they get sick. It's a poor nation with too many people and there simply aren't enough resources. India needs preventative care and the promotion of health, so people don't get sick in the first place. You have to reduce the disease burden, not just treat the diseases." With his background, he knew how much change was possible and resolved to make it a priority to find a way to help. Hearing about my success with ISB, he decided to issue me a challenge.

Barry's comments got me thinking, and I realized he was right. However, as I told him at the time, I had little prior experience in public health. He suggested that I put together a concept proposal, and I convinced McKinsey to do a study on the state of public health in India. We convened a three-day conference to discuss the findings, inviting all key stakeholders.

The results of the study were not encouraging. The need for a world-class public health institution was clear, but most public health institutions struggle to get adequate funding and this one seemed doomed to the same fate. By now, however, the idea was lodged in my mind. *Any project that needs to be done can be done.* We had proven this to be true with ISB. Everyone told us it couldn't be done, but we did it anyway. Why couldn't the same be true of this? The key was to figure out *how*. In a series of conversations with multiple stakeholders—NGOs, the ministry of health, and private businesses—we conceived of a novel plan: a public–private partnership that would be jointly funded by the private sector, the government, and foundations/NGOs. One school was not enough to truly move the dial. Instead, we would create a foundation that could start a network of schools and research institutions. Once the plan had taken shape, we set out to build a coalition of support among policy-makers, businesspeople, health advocates, academics, donors, and global luminaries. I spent a lot of time in India during this period, working on the ground to keep everyone aligned behind the vision. The support of Montek Singh Ahluwalia, head of the Planning Commission, was critical. The team from McKinsey India provided invaluable help, particularly a young associate by the name of Prashanth Vasu and partner Gautam Kumra, whose hard work and enthusiasm was central to the foundation's success.

Unlike ISB, which stayed completely independent of politics, the public health foundation needed political support, hence my fundraising challenge. Eventually, I managed to convince both Bill Gates and Prime Minister Singh to follow through on matching pledges, and I secured an additional $20 million from Indian business leaders.

In 2006, the Public Health Foundation of India was officially launched, with Prime Minister Manmohan Singh and Nobel laureate Amartya Sen as keynote speakers. The goal of the institution was to build large-scale capacity for public health education, research, and advocacy in India. I recruited the celebrated cardiologist Dr. Srinath Reddy, the prime minister's personal physician, to run it. Suddenly, on the day before the inauguration, we realized we still had no logo. Dr. Reddy, who turned out to be a man of many talents, sat down and sketched a beautiful image of a seed blooming into a flower, accompanied by the words "knowledge to action," which PHFI uses to this day. I consider recruiting him to be my greatest contribution to PHFI. A passionate evangelist for public health in India, he is largely responsible for the foundation's dramatic growth and success.

As we had done with ISB, we initiated a competition between states to provide land for schools, and five campuses were created. Today, the foundation has a threefold objective. First, it conducts fact-based research on public health issues and seeks to influence public health policy; second, it trains public health professionals, offering degrees in public health, epidemiology, health management, and so on; and third, it conducts training programs for health workers. It has been a huge success. I served as chairman for the first five years, forging a strong bond with Dr. Reddy, and continue to be involved to this day.

Based on the success of PHFI, I was invited by Prime Minister Manmohan Singh to begin a similar initiative on urbanization, working with Kamal Nath, the minister for urban development. India was rapidly urbanizing, having recently crossed the 50 percent threshold; however, it was woefully unprepared in every way—from infrastructure to finances to governance. The government provided 200 crore rupees of seed funding with the condition of matching funds from the private sector. However, before the Urban Development Institute could be fully operational, I would be forced to withdraw because of my legal issues, the government would change, and people and priorities would shift.

A Global Cause Meets a Personal Passion

One of the most ambitious projects I was involved with was the Global Fund to Fight AIDS, Tuberculosis and Malaria. Founded in 2002, it was an initiative of Kofi Annan and the United Nations, but it was envisioned as being quite different from the UN in its structure. The fund was a public–private partnership, bringing together representatives of governments, foundations, and the private sector to pool resources and attack the three biggest killers in the world besides chronic diseases like heart disease and diabetes. It would soon become the world's largest health fund, disbursing $3 billion a year.

I was invited to join the board soon after the fund's inception, as a representative of the private sector. I was still managing director of the firm at the time, but my third term was coming to an end, so I felt I would soon have more time to commit to such initiatives. The Global Fund was appealing both in its scope and its structure. I was drawn to its ambitious goals and potential impact, and I had always felt that public–private partnerships had the best chance to effect change.

I also had personal reasons for wanting to do my part in the fight against AIDS, malaria, and tuberculosis. Each of those three diseases had touched my life in a very direct way. My father had almost died from tuberculosis in a British prison, and it was that episode that weakened his system and led to his premature passing. I'd suffered from malaria myself as a child in India, as had almost everyone I knew back then. I'd also nursed Anita's younger brother, Arvind, who was like a son to us, through the disease. I'll never forget rushing him to hospital with a 106-degree fever racking his twelve-year-old body. Thankfully, he was visiting us in the US at the time and we had access to the best modern medical care. I couldn't help but think of the millions in India who suffered from and succumbed to malaria without those luxuries. As for AIDS, I'd lost a dear friend to its ravages. David Manly, my can-mate at Harvard who had taken me into his family for every holiday and gotten me my first job, was diagnosed with HIV and died in the mid-1980s. He never even saw his fortieth birthday. The Global Fund had lofty targets of saving millions of lives. Thousands of people died every day from these diseases, and our goal was to halve that number. But I meant it when I told the board that even if we could save just one person, it would be enough to persuade me to get involved. That one person would be someone's parent, someone's child, someone's best friend.

The Global Fund's board had a unique multi-stakeholder structure with representatives from "donor countries," "recipient countries," communities living with the diseases, foundations, NGOs, and the private sector, which was the seat I filled. I was present at the first board meeting, and we commissioned a team from McKinsey to help the fund set up its organizational structure, key processes, and so on.

The first task we faced was to appoint an executive director, and I was on the search committee. This was when I got a taste of how challenging it might be to work with all these government representatives. There was plenty of UN-style political maneuvering at work from the beginning, with countries wanting their people in key positions. I felt it was important to resist this and put a meritocratic stamp on the organization from day one. At the board meeting where the executive director role was to be decided, the search committee presented our candidates in order of preference. At the top of our list was Richard Feacham, dean of the London School of Hygiene and Tropical Medicine, who had done extensive work in public health and was head and shoulders above the other candidates when it came to being qualified for the job.

Another candidate who was much lower in the evaluation of the search committee was a former American ambassador in Africa. The US representative on the board was Tommy Thompson, secretary of health and human services under George W. Bush, and he was determined to appoint this guy and had been lobbying on the sidelines of the board meeting. As the US was the largest donor country to the fund, he clearly felt their choice should have greater weight. He made an impassioned speech in favor of the ambassador, even though campaigning was not allowed in the process, and even implied that his country's continuing support was contingent on the fund choosing his candidate.

Looking round the room, I wondered if anyone would stand up to Thompson. I quickly realized that every other board member was representing either a government or an organization, and they were hesitating to take a strong position without approval. I was the only one in the room who was not answerable to any specific entity; I simply represented the business world as a broad sector. So I took a deep breath and stood up to respond. I reminded him that the search committee had conducted an exhaustive interview and screening process and his attempt to override our strong recommendation was out of line. The board as a whole was free to reject our recommendation, but he had no authority to simply elect someone else, without having done the work and gone through the search committee.

There was a stunned silence. No one expected me to take on a US cabinet member in such an impassioned manner. But to me, the risk of his displeasure was much less potentially damaging than the risk of sitting back and letting him foist a less-than-qualified candidate on the board. At the next break, Thompson left the meeting and didn't come back. Richard Feacham was elected, and the Global Fund began its operations. Our choice would prove to be a wise one, as Richard did a great job and I came to think of him as a close friend and partner in shaping the fund.

When the role of chairman came up for re-election, I suggested to the other board members that we ask Tommy Thompson. He still seemed to bear a grudge over the executive director issue, and I thought maybe this would help. "He'll never say yes," people told me. "He's a sitting cabinet member." But I thought it was worth a try. When I made the proposal to Thompson, he seemed surprised that this overture was coming from me, after our previous clash. I explained that I thought it would be good for the fund and demonstrate the US commitment to the cause. I also knew him to be an extremely capable politician. "Besides," I told him, "you'll get to learn something new. You've always spent time in the US but this is a much more global institution and you'll get a window into the world's health." He was intrigued. "But they'll never elect me," he said, aware that there was some anti-US feeling on the board. I suggested that I would work on his behalf to warm up the board members. In the end, he stood for election, was chosen unanimously, and became a very good chairman.

Despite a few bumps in the road, the Global Fund began to do very good work and win praise as one of the most innovative health funds in the world. In 2007, the chairmanship was up for change, and, to my surprise, many wanted me to stand for election. It was quite an unusual step to invite the private sector representative to chair an organization of this nature, given that we were by far the smallest contributor compared to the various governments and foundations. I told my supporters I would stand but I would not campaign. The last thing I wanted was to feel indebted to the agenda of some particular government, so I refused to play politics. Everyone else jockeyed for position, but, in the end, I was unanimously elected chair.

Now that I'd been given the role, I decided to make the most of it and do as much as I could during my term to create change and increase the fund's impact. I had proven my commitment and value to the board over the past five years, attending every meeting, and now I would test the limits of my support.

One of the first changes I made was a cultural one. The board meetings were very formal, with members addressed by the name of the group they represented: "France," "United States," "Uganda," and so on. I was tired of being addressed as "Private Sector" and felt that this group of people needed to roll up their sleeves and get to know each other. We spent too much time on procedural work and not enough talking about the actual issues on the ground. The fund had a mandate to save lives, and we needed to ensure that this got the majority of our attention, not diplomatic procedure and politics. I told the board we would be shifting from process to substance, and that each board meeting henceforth would include a substantive discussion about how to defeat each of the three diseases. I also had new name cards printed with people's actual names on them.

Interestingly, I quickly found that my experience leading McKinsey was extremely relevant here, although the institutions were very different. I'd become skilled in the art of persuasion—pulling the noodle rather than fruitlessly attempting to push—and this would come in useful now as I took on the leadership of an unwieldy group of politicians, civil servants, philanthropists, and activists and attempted to align them behind the mission of the fund.

Shortly after I became chairman and made my acceptance speech, I was approached by a young woman in her mid-twenties named Naina Dhingra. I had met her a couple of times, as she'd once worked at the Global Fund and later interacted with us as an AIDS advocate. "You should hire me as your staff," she told me.

I laughed. I'd chaired plenty of boards and had never needed a staff to help me. I listened to her pitch and was very impressed with both her credentials and her commitment to the cause, but I remained unconvinced. However, as my Global Fund chairmanship got underway, I quickly realized that this was a more demanding role than any I'd previously held. I called Naina and told her she was right, and she became an invaluable full-time staff member, tirelessly supporting my Global Fund work.

I was a very active chairman and led by example, making field visits to our various recipient countries and going out to the villages and the slums to meet the targets of our initiatives and to see our programs in action. Between these visits, Naina would organize dinners with the most influential people in each country, and some very innovative ideas came out of those discussions, along with lasting connections. On one particularly memorable trip, Naina and I traveled to Ethiopia to meet the health minister, Tedros Adhanom Ghebreyesus, who personally drove us on field visits to the villages where his initiatives were proving to be very effective. I was so impressed by his work that I recommended him to succeed me as chairman, and he would eventually go on to become head of the WHO.

Most importantly, during my chairmanship I changed the way the fund functioned with regard to its core mission. Up till then, we had relied on the various governments to come up with proposals, and our job had been to allocate funds in a fairly passive manner. I felt, however, that with the amount of money we were responsible for—several billion dollars a year—we needed to see ourselves as a financing institution and to view our allocations through the lens of an investment strategy. "We owe the world some clear, holistic impact in the fight against AIDS, TB, and malaria," I told the board. "Diseases don't respect borders, so we need to look beyond individual countries in our thinking." I proposed that we needed to identify the macro impact we wanted to have and then work backwards, thinking creatively about which strategies worked best and where our funding dollars would have maximum impact. Rather than limiting our efforts to country-focused initiatives, we asked representatives for each disease to come up with proposals for broader solutions.

I had a particular interest in tackling malaria. After all, malaria was easily preventable—much more so than AIDS or TB. But it did not have the lobbying power of the AIDS groups, and efforts in the field were uncoordinated and ineffective. I was connected with two very passionate and powerful advocates for malaria prevention: the celebrated economist Jeffrey Sachs and the humanitarian and UN special envoy Ray Chambers. Jeff and Ray saw an opportunity to make a huge impact in the fight against this deadly disease, at relatively low cost. The most effective weapons in this battle were simple mosquito nets, sprayed with insecticide. Indoor spraying was also effective, and there were new medications called ACTs, which were not yet widely available. If we could get all the various malaria groups to join forces and focus on getting these things to the people in the hardest hit areas, which were mostly in Africa, we could save millions of lives. The Global Fund partnered with their organization, Malaria No More, as well as the World Bank, UNICEF, and the UN, in an ambitious drive to cut malaria deaths by half. The task force, launched in 2008 and driven largely by Suprotik Basu, a young executive from the World Bank, and Melanie Renshaw, from UNICEF, was charged to come up with effective national plans. It would go on to successfully save around half a million lives a year.

As chairman, I tried to be outwardly focused, but some internal politics were inevitable. The biggest battle I fought was to extract the Global Fund from the WHO, which had provided a lot of support over the years but was also trying to impose its personnel policies on us. The WHO was notorious for protecting its employees no matter what, making it impossible to have a true meritocracy. This approach was at odds with the business-minded outlook I was trying to foster, so I decided to get us out. This met with opposition from all sides. Most people in the fund came from the UN community of civil servants, and they had never worked outside the multilaterals. Over time, however, people came to appreciate their liberation from the WHO's red tape.

I also found myself embroiled in politics of a different kind, when I inadvertently challenged the Chinese government. The Global Fund had a practice of rotating our board meetings between member countries. Hosting a meeting carried some prestige, and many countries invited us to come, including China. We scheduled a meeting in China, but then discovered that there was one problem: China had terribly restrictive policies around AIDS, particularly when it came to getting visas. The AIDS activists were adamant—we could not hold a meeting in a country that would not allow our constituents, including some of our board members, to enter. I remembered how, in my early days at McKinsey, Mike Murray had pulled out of a lucrative South African assignment rather than allow me, a young associate, to face discrimination from apartheid. There was no question in my mind what the right course of action here was, even though it was politically difficult. We informed the Chinese government that we would be changing the location of our meeting unless their visa policies were amended.

Not surprisingly, this caused some upsets. Who were we to be dictating policy to the Chinese government? We were ready to simply move the meeting, but to my great satisfaction, the government relented and changed the visa requirements, allowing us to hold a very successful meeting in China. While there, we made sure to meet with members of the gay community, who were the targets of very intense discrimination, and find ways to ensure that our AIDS funding would reach them.

Every three years, the Global Fund has what's known as a "replenishment round," where it raises money from the donor countries. The chairman is very involved in lobbying politicians and presides over the fundraising conference. When my turn came, the conference was held in Berlin, and I convinced Kofi Annan to co-chair with Angela Merkel. The process was quite a political education, as I met with dozens of senators and congressman to make my case. In the end, we were very successful, exceeding all expectations and raising over $12 billion to fund the coming three years' work.

A Noble Calling

I loved working with the Global Fund and consider it one of the most treasured aspects of my life experience. How often does one get the opportunity to shape an organization with such extensive resources and such global reach? I felt similarly about my work with the UN, as special management advisor to Kofi Annan. I was glad to be able to bring my business experience and knowledge to the nonprofit world, where such thinking is sorely needed. Indeed, this was the theme of my remarks when I was invited to address the UN General Assembly in 2005 and 2010. I was very honored and a little overwhelmed to step up to the podium where just a few hours earlier the US president had spoken, and I hoped that the assembled heads of state would take away an expanded sense of what's possible when business, government, and civil society all combine their skill sets and perspectives.

There is so much need in the world, at every level, from the immediate and local to the systemic, long term, and far-reaching. Personally, I've always felt that the way I can contribute is by tackling problems that many feel are too big and won't be solved within a single lifetime. I knew that to do this, my colleagues and I needed to build institutions that would outlast us. My experience at McKinsey, as well as in building ISB, had given me a particular ability to manage multiple constituencies with very different objectives and bring them together for a common cause. This work wasn't an afterthought or a side note to my career: it felt like the continuation of my life's work. For Bengalis, social justice is a way of life, a proud tradition that we don't see as acts of charity but as a noble calling.

At the end of 2006, I announced my intention to retire from McKinsey at the end of the following year. Hank Paulson, who was then at the helm of Goldman Sachs, not yet having left to become treasury secretary, was encouraging me to join the Goldman board, and directors were not allowed to join corporate boards until their final year with the firm. So I decided to retire one year short of the official retirement age. At the end of 2007, aged fifty-nine, my long career with the firm came to an end.

The directors' conference that year was held in India, and it turned into a moving retirement party, complete with a Bollywood-themed celebration and a speech from the prime minister—the first time a sitting head of state had ever addressed the firm. He recognized the contributions I had made to India's development and said he had come to honor me. It was an emotional moment for me. I'd been with the firm thirty-five years, my entire career and most of my adult life. I couldn't imagine not being with the firm. In fact, I wasn't leaving entirely—they would provide me with an office and a secretary, and I would maintain a consulting role and continue to introduce and serve clients. I would always be a McKinsey guy. As the firm's leader, I had shaped it in ways that I could only hope would last after I had moved on. As a human being, it had shaped me indelibly.

Part III

Trial

Therefore rise up, Arjuna, resolved to fight!
Having made yourself alike in pain and pleasure,
profit and loss, victory and defeat,
engage in this great battle . . .

—Bhagavad Gita, 2:37–38

13

Testimony

He who is too busy doing good finds no time to be good.

—Rabindranath Tagore, *Stray Birds,* 184

May 2012, New York City

Sixteen seconds.

"It looks bad," my lawyer told me. "You hung up from the Goldman board meeting in which you learned about the Buffett investment, and sixteen seconds later you called Rajaratnam. He immediately bought Goldman stock. The next day, he told one of his traders that he received a call right before the markets closed, telling him something good might happen to Goldman."

I was sitting in a small office, high above Sixth Avenue, with several members of my legal team. After a long and depressing winter, spring had finally come, but I had no time to enjoy the gentle sunshine and the new life that was bursting forth in my beloved garden at home. I was spending every day at the law offices, preparing to testify at my upcoming trial. I was worried we'd left the preparation too late—it was only when I decided to take over an empty office and show up every day that the lawyers finally responded to my requests to rehearse. One of the legal team, Robin Wilcox, would play the role of the prosecutor and grill me on the events leading up to my arrest, sometimes with an audience for added effect.

These practice sessions were a strange and awkward affair for me. I'd given countless speeches over the course of my career—addressing students, business leaders, humanitarians, even the UN General Assembly—and I was fully confident of my ability to speak clearly and persuasively. I had been unafraid to step on to the biggest of stages, always trusting my insight and instinct. But I didn't like having other people telling me what I should and should not say. My lawyers stopped me constantly, adjusting and fine-tuning my story based on a multitude of possible reactions from judge and jury. I appreciated their thoroughness, but all this second-guessing made me feel disconnected from the simple truth. Unlike most business leaders, I'd never used a speechwriter; instead, I simply wrote what was authentic to me. Often, I would start with a favorite poem, but I couldn't see the judge being very receptive to me quoting stanzas from Robert Frost, Rabindranath Tagore, or the Bhagavad Gita on the witness stand. Frost would have been appropriate here though, I mused: I would indeed be taking "the road less traveled" by taking the stand in my own defense.

One point we returned to, again and again, was the sixteen-second gap. I understood that it looked bad. Clearly the prosecution was counting on the jury thinking so too. The truth was that the government had only a meager collection of circumstantial evidence for their claims against me, but a good storyteller could make it look criminal. Predictably, Preet Bharara's PR machine had played up the September 2008 Buffett investment in their press release following my indictment, commenting that the speed at which I ended one call and placed the next made "starkly evident" my eagerness to "lavish" inside information on my so-called good friend, "so quickly it could be termed instant messaging."[1]

How was I supposed to convincingly counter this narrative? At face value, the government's highlighting of the sixteen-second gap seemed reasonable. Why would anyone jump off of one call and on to another with barely enough time to catch a breath unless he had something of great urgency to communicate? The thing is, it actually wasn't that unusual for me at all, as anyone who knows me would immediately tell you. My life was so tightly scheduled that I'd gotten into the habit of using any break between meetings, however brief, to return phone calls. My family constantly upbraided me for my habit of picking up the phone the moment a conversation paused or a meal was over. No matter how disciplined I was, it was a challenge to keep up with the demands of my philanthropic work, my investment ventures, and my board roles. If there was a precious window in my schedule, the first thing I'd do was get my secretary on the phone and ask her to place the first call on my list. It's also not surprising that the first name on my call list during the summer and fall of 2008 was often Raj Rajaratnam—after all, one of the most important things on my mind at that time was figuring out what happened to my $10 million investment in the Voyager fund.

That was the real story behind many of the events referenced in the charges. It was the story of a ridiculously busy, overstretched man trying to manage his personal financial affairs while also guiding numerous major companies and nonprofits, at home and abroad, during one of the most volatile periods in our economy's history. But how was I to tell that story in such a way that it eclipsed the more dramatic and sensational spin the government was putting on it? This was the challenge facing my legal team and me as we prepared for my trial in early 2012.

Gary was outspoken about the weakness of the government's case: "In all my years in court, never have I seen a case with so little evidence. It's just a bunch of vague mumbo-jumbo! Where are the financial benefits? Where are the trades? Where is the profit-sharing agreement? And where is the motive? They don't have a case. This isn't evidence—it's just circumstance and hearsay."

"But what's our strategy?" I kept asking. "I know I didn't do what they're accusing me of doing, but I don't see how we can prove a negative. As thin as it is, the government has a story that sounds believable. And I can't offer any concrete evidence that proves I didn't do something."

The lawyers kept reminding me that the burden of proof rested on the government. Let them prove it, they'd counseled. Our job is to show the jury that they simply don't have the evidence. To emphasize his point, Gary would tell me that I didn't even have to put on a defense if I didn't want to. I understood this. Their arguments made sense—in a world where I truly was innocent until proven guilty. But I felt like I'd already been judged. I couldn't just sit back and hope we could introduce enough reasonable doubt that it would become clear the government didn't have a case. For months now I'd said nothing while my name and reputation were destroyed. I needed to tell my story, and I needed to tell it well.

The charges against me were one count of conspiracy to commit securities fraud and five counts of securities fraud. These counts referred to four incidents of alleged tipping: March 12, 2007; September 23, 2008; October 23, 2008; and January 29, 2009.* The prosecution had constructed a narrative around each, connecting dots from information discussed during a board meeting I had just attended, to call logs or calendar entries showing I'd called or met with Rajaratnam, to trades

* The charges against me when I was arrested in October 2011 related only to two incidents, September 23, 2008, and October 23, 2008. However, the prosecutor had spun several "counts" out of each. We challenged this "surplusage" of charges in a pretrial motion. The government then filed a superseding indictment in January 2012, which added two new charges, March 7, 2007, and January 29, 2009. The 2007 charge was the thinnest of all, with not even a phone record as evidence, but it was important for the prosecutor to try to extend the date range back to a time before my conflict with Rajaratnam over Voyager.

made by Rajaratnam or his traders shortly thereafter, and, in some cases, to recorded conversations between Rajaratnam and his traders.

The truth was, I didn't remember the precise content of any of the phone calls or conversations that were listed in the charges. They were just a handful among thousands, and none of them had been remarkable enough to stick in my mind four years later. The prosecutors were declaring that they showed a "pattern," yet they were cherry-picking just a few instances that fit the pattern they wanted to show. If there were a pattern, it was a much less nefarious one: a pattern of me diligently trying, again and again, over a period of several months, to get information out of Rajaratnam about my Voyager investment, during one of the busiest times in my career.

My task, as I prepared for the trial, was to piece together the events and the context surrounding each of the alleged incidents, in order to offer an alternative—more truthful—story to the damning tale the indictment had spun. I had to take myself back to a life that already seemed so far away—a time when every day was filled from dawn to dusk with purposeful activity. A time when I was living a life of my choosing, not playing an unchosen role in someone else's story.

Sitting on my desk, a printed stack of my calendars from 2007, 2008, and 2009 served as a painful reminder of that life that had been taken from me. Meetings, dinners, assignments, conferences, speaking engagements, board activities, fundraisers—these were not just appointments that filled my days, they were the very fabric of the life I'd worked so hard to create.

Had I been too busy? In retrospect, yes. My family had certainly thought so, and Anita had repeatedly appealed to me to cut back and learn to say no. She'd believed that after I retired from McKinsey, I would scale down my activities and spend more time at home. I did just the opposite—saying yes to more board seats, philanthropic causes, and speaking engagements. I was still following the "law" that there is no such thing as too much work or too little time. But I'd also been doing what I loved, having an impact on companies I respected and causes that mattered to me. As we prepared my defense and rehearsed my testimony, using the calendars to jog my memory, I was transported back to those days.

The Office

The story I planned to tell in court began in March 2007, shortly after I had announced my intention to retire from McKinsey by the end of the year. I was fifty-eight years old, but I wasn't ready to hang up my suit and stay home. And one of the new ventures I was excited to have more time for was a new investment venture I'd launched the previous year: New Silk Route (NSR). The private equity world appealed to me, as it seemed a natural extension of my career as a consultant, investing in companies and helping them grow. Plus, it was an efficient way to make money, given that I already knew so many people in business and had access to capital. I saw it as a good way to earn an income while leaving much of my time free for my family and for my philanthropic activities.

The purpose of NSR was to invest in India. My partners in the venture included an old friend named Parag Saxena, former Goldman Asia chairman Mark Schwartz, and Raj Rajaratnam, with whom I was still on good terms at that point.

Rajaratnam's relationship to NSR was somewhat ambivalent. Initially, the plan had been for NSR to have a dual strategy: part hedge fund, part private equity. Parag would run the private equity arm, while Rajaratnam ran the hedge fund. Mark would be COO, and I would be chairman of both. However, once we started raising money, it became clear that investors didn't like the dual strategy. Raj, meanwhile, was getting a taste for the international markets and wondering if he could do better on his own. He thought the hedge fund part was more valuable and came up with the idea of creating a Galleon International brand, independent of NSR. Eventually, that's what happened. NSR focused on private equity, and what had been the hedge fund arm became

Galleon International. There was some initial discussion of a 15 percent cross-ownership between the funds, and the possibility was raised that I might serve as chairman of Galleon International. Rajaratnam never seemed committed to this path, however, and nothing came of it. Later, wiretapped calls would reveal his preference for keeping Galleon International for himself. The two funds went their separate ways. In early 2007, however, we were still figuring it all out, and Rajaratnam had generously given us an office in the Madison Avenue building that housed the Galleon hedge fund.

On Monday, March 12, I had a busy schedule, as usual. I left my home in Westport before dawn and drove into the city. After a couple of early appointments, I had a Goldman board meeting, via phone, scheduled for 11:30. My previous meeting ran late, so at 11:37 I rushed into the NSR office and dialed in.

This was the first incident referenced in a substantive count in the indictment (Count 2; Count 1 was the general "conspiracy" charge). The board meeting included a quarterly earnings report that was better than expected. Twenty-five minutes later, Rajaratnam apparently told his traders to buy 350,000 shares of Goldman stock, which jumped in value the following day when the earnings were announced, allowing him to sell at a significant profit.

What made the government believe that I was the source of Raj's information? Principally, the fact that I called in to the Goldman board meeting from the Galleon building. It was another of those facts that looked bad, but in reality had quite a simple, non-conspiratorial explanation. That I made a call from that line was an unremarkable occurrence, given that NSR operated out of that office. On the day in question, my calendar showed that the Goldman meeting was at 11:30 and I had an NSR partner meeting at noon, so it would have been impossible for me to participate in both had I not been in one place. Did I run down the hallway after the meeting to tell Raj about Goldman's earnings? No. But it was too easy for the prosecutor to plant that image in the public imagination.

In reality, the Goldman board meeting probably fell to the back of my mind as I hurried through an afternoon of NSR-related meetings and then headed to JFK to catch a flight to Seattle, where I was scheduled to spend several days working with the Gates Foundation.

A Busy Summer

It was about a year later that things started to fray in my relationship with Raj. By the spring of 2008, I had officially left McKinsey, although I continued to provide consulting services to the firm, introducing clients and advising partners. It was in April that year that Ravi Trehan first brought to my attention the fact that Rajaratnam had withdrawn money from the Voyager fund without informing me or giving me my pro rata distribution. This was worrying, but I wanted to be sure, so I requested paperwork. Curiously, I had not been receiving monthly statements for some time. The fund, however, was doing well, according to Raj, so I was not too worried. I was always inclined to give people the benefit of the doubt, so I hoped he would provide a good explanation. After all, why would he be lying about money and trying to avoid paying me a few million? He was worth billions. It seemed illogical, and at this point I still trusted him and took his stellar Wall Street reputation at face value.

Soon, however, I would have another reason for needing documentation related to Voyager. My bankers at JP Morgan had requested some documentation in connection with the annual renewal of my line of credit. Specifically, they needed to see things like the fund's offering memo, partnership agreement, and the net asset value of my investment. I had none of this information, so I requested all of these from Raj in the early summer of 2008.

It was an extremely busy summer. Besides Goldman, I'd joined several other corporate boards by that point, one of which was P&G, a company I'd gotten to know when I introduced them as a client to McKinsey a couple of years earlier. I had great respect for P&G's CEO,

A.G. Lafley, and enjoyed serving on their board. One of the matters we discussed at the board meeting in the summer of 2008 was the proposed sale of the coffee company Folgers to Smucker's. This was another incident mentioned in the indictment—not as a specific count of insider trading, but as an "overt act" demonstrating a conspiracy. The prosecutors alleged that I had told Rajaratnam about this impending deal, and he'd told a colleague.

Even by the prosecution's standards, the evidence around this claim was so close to nonexistent that I think they couldn't justify a substantive charge. All they had was a call record showing that a call was made from an unassigned phone line at McKinsey to Rajaratnam's assistant's line, and a Galleon trader saying he'd heard from Raj's brother that he'd gotten a tip from an unknown source about the deal, which was surely hearsay. But since it was mentioned in the indictment, it would come up in court and I needed to be prepared to defend it. I didn't see that this would be too difficult: phone records clearly showed that at the exact time when the prosecutor was alleging that I had called Rajaratnam from the unassigned line at McKinsey, I was in fact on another call on my assigned private line, which lasted several minutes

In truth, during the summer of 2008 I did not give much attention to the outcome of the Smucker's deal, and I certainly didn't tell Raj about it. It would not have been hard for him to get wind of the deal, however. There were several leaks in the press and much speculation by analysts in the preceding weeks. This was not surprising, given that there were dozens of people involved in the process.

As for me, I had other things on my mind. My work with the Global Fund was extremely consuming, as Ray Chambers, Jeffrey Sachs, and I were rolling out our ambitious malaria initiative. Our goal was to raise $1.8 billion from a consortium of donors to fund the rollout of bed nets and medication to hundreds of thousands of people in Africa. We had already spoken to our people on the ground and told them to plan for the biggest push against the disease that had ever happened—but we hadn't secured the funding. I felt that we needed our partners to be ready to go before I approached the funders, but it was a risky strategy. I didn't want to leave them high and dry if the money didn't come through.

Closer to home, I had another consuming event: Sonu was getting married—the first of my daughters to tie the knot. Her fiancé, Meka, was Nigerian, and we were planning a full-scale cultural mash-up of a wedding at our home in Connecticut at the end of June, with several hundred guests attending.

I was also weighing up a job offer. The private equity firm KKR & Co. had invited me to take up a senior advisor role. I was leaning toward accepting; I felt ready for a new challenge, and this was something I could balance with my philanthropic work. There was just one issue: Goldman Sachs was objecting, claiming it would create a conflict of interest with my seat on the board. Personally, I didn't see why I couldn't have accepted this role and continued my Goldman directorship. Plenty of other directors had close ties to various private equity firms. But Blankfein was adamant. So I found myself with a difficult decision to make, one that weighed on my mind and took up a fair amount of my attention that summer.

I continued a punishing travel schedule. That month, it had included a trip to Stockholm to attend the ICC World Council Meeting and meet with Marcus Wallenberg about his proposal to put me forward for the ICC chairmanship; a trip to Geneva immediately after Sonu's wedding, to attend a Global Humanitarian Forum meeting hosted by Kofi Annan; a day in London; and a Goldman Sachs board meeting in St Petersburg, Russia. Goldman held one board meeting a year offsite, and it was customary for spouses to be invited along, so Anita accompanied me on the trip.

July 4 weekend I stayed home, catching up on various matters. On Monday, when my assistant returned to the office, she noticed that Rajaratnam had finally sent the audited 2007 financial statements for Voyager. These didn't help with JP Morgan, but at least they might shed light on the redemptions. Knowing I was trying to take a few days off, she forwarded them directly to Greg Orman, my financial advisor, a former McKinsey analyst who'd become a trusted friend and had taken it upon himself to help me better manage my affairs and learn to say no to poor investments in my friends' businesses. There, in the fine print, was evidence of the $23 million withdrawal Ravi had noticed, plus over $25 million in commissions. When Greg showed me this, my heart sank. I hadn't wanted to believe it, but here it was in black and white. Not only had Rajaratnam made redemptions without telling me or giving me my share and taken commissions that had not been agreed upon, he had also substantially multiplied the leverage risk of the fund by depleting the equity.

"We should talk to a lawyer," Greg said, and I reluctantly agreed. I hated to escalate this kind of situation, but it seemed necessary. My travel schedule picked up again, however, leaving me little time to even digest the information I'd received, let alone take action. To be honest, I think I was happy to have an excuse to at least postpone, if not avoid, the confrontation. *If you have ten problems, ignore them—nine will go away.* That had always been my policy and for the most part it had worked well. But Rajaratnam would prove to be number ten, and I would pay dearly for my procrastination in dealing with him.

In the weeks that followed, I attended meetings in Boston, Chicago, San Antonio, Dallas, Bucharest, and New York before taking Anita and Kushy to London for a brief vacation. During this time, my bankers at JP Morgan continued to request the Voyager documents, emailing and calling my assistant daily. She emailed a colleague of Ravi's who I'd suggested might be able to help, as well as my accountant. None of these avenues proved fruitful, so I told her that I'd raise the matter personally with Rajaratnam when I arrived back in New York on July 28. We were scheduled to meet about NSR, so I knew I'd have an opportunity. I still needed to confront him about the redemptions as well.

After the meeting ended, I pulled Raj aside and reminded him about the documents, but he was evasive. "Let's talk tomorrow," he said, "I have to run. But I want to talk to you about Goldman as well." He was meeting with Goldman president Gary Cohn later that week, he said, and he wanted me to brief him about some relevant matters and give him some talking points.

An Ill-Judged Conversation

The next day, Tuesday, July 29, I had a rare day at home in Westport. I was glad to have a moment to catch my breath before leaving the next day for another trip, this time to Washington, DC, with Ray Chambers, for the signing of President Bush's historic PEPFAR bill for AIDS relief, at which the president was to honor me for my work with the Global Fund. Of course, my calendar was still busy, with a breakfast with a local congressman, a doctor's appointment, a contractor coming to fix numerous issues at the house, and several calls. One of these was to Rajaratnam.

That call was the only conversation between us that was recorded during the government's exhaustive wiretapping of Rajaratnam's phones. It was the call that was played at Rajaratnam's trial, the call that cost me my relationship with McKinsey.

One detail about that call that no one paid attention to was the short discussion that followed our conversation about Goldman's possible purchase of a commercial bank. It related to the Voyager fund and the statements I'd been requesting. Raj promised he'd get someone in his office to send me the balances, noting that the fund was "slightly down" as of the end of June. That didn't concern me too much. At this point I just wanted to get my bank the documents they needed. I put off challenging Raj about the redemptions; it didn't seem like the right moment. Our conversation continued, turning to Anil and the now-infamous million-dollar payment.

Finally, before we hung up, I asked him again what he thought about the KKR position. He had told me he knew the principals well and had even claimed they'd tried to buy Galleon (a claim I would later learn was untrue). I was eager to hear his thoughts on the wisdom of taking the job, since I still hadn't made a final decision. "I'd do it in a heartbeat," he replied. When I listened back to the tape, years later, that comment jumped out at me. Raj knew that taking the KKR job would mean resigning from Goldman, yet he encouraged me to do it—a fact that did not fit well with the prosecutor's claims that I was his source at Goldman. Surely, if that had been the case, he'd have been encouraging me to keep my board seat, with its access to valuable secrets?

Raj's guy never did get me those Voyager documents. I was starting to get irritated—by this, and even more so by the unexplained redemptions. It felt like he was stalling, and I couldn't understand why.

In August, we had the final closing of the NSR fund after a very successful fundraising campaign. By this point, the hedge fund arm had become Galleon International and NSR was independent of Galleon, although Rajaratnam remained a passive investor. Our offices had moved out of the Galleon building. The talk of cross-ownership never came to anything, and nor did my proposed chairmanship.

I disappeared into another series of international trips, this time including an international AIDS conference in Mexico City; a WEF board meeting in Geneva; and a brief trip to India for an ISB board meeting, a Genpact leadership strategy workshop, and various other meetings and speaking engagements. A highlight of this marathon was a board meeting at Tsinghua University School of Economics and Management, China, which happily coincided with the Beijing Olympics. Anita and I enjoyed the chance to cheer on the athletes from both our home country and our adopted one.

It was during that trip to China that the KKR issue came to a head. Blankfein, who was also on the business school's board, was adamant that I could not do both. Finally, during a board dinner with our spouses, he leaned across Anita, who was sitting between us, and told me loudly, "It's one or the other: Goldman or KKR. You have to choose."

At some point between these trips, Renee informed me that we'd received a letter from Rajaratnam, dated August 4, stating my balance in Voyager as of the end of 2007, and describing the fund as "relatively unchanged before any expenses." She forwarded this to the bankers at JP Morgan, but it was not enough to satisfy their requirements. They continued to press Renee for documents, including information about the fund's investment strategy, liquidity, and redemption provisions. Soon afterwards, Rajaratnam had his guy George Lau write up another letter, which still did not contain the necessary information. I met with him in person a couple of days later, reiterating our requests more forcefully, but he continued to stall. (Interestingly, in a wiretapped conversation between Rajaratnam and Anil Kumar the following day, which we'd found among the evidence, they both commented that I seemed upset at the meeting—hardly surprising, given my suspicions about Rajaratnam and his frustrating evasiveness. They also gossiped rather nastily about my financial ambitions and my overstretched schedule—it was not a conversation that would support the idea that we were "co-conspirators.") Later that same day, I had lunch with Rajaratnam (he described it to Kumar as "a nice long chat"). I don't remember the details, but perhaps he reassured me that he'd take care of my requests. I continued my travels, arriving home just in time to accompany Kushy on a visit to Brown University in Providence, Rhode Island.

The Road Not Taken

After much thought, on long flights, I had come to a decision on KKR: I would accept the position. Since Blankfein was resolute in his ultimatum, I told him I would be resigning from the Goldman board. At the board meeting on Tuesday, September 9, 2008, he made a somewhat awkward speech thanking me for my service. The board members clapped politely as I opened the box he'd presented to me and held up a pair of gold cufflinks, which reflected the lights from the chandelier overhead. My time as a Goldman director was over—or so I thought.

The next day, I flew to London for a series of meetings, and then on to Paris for an ICC board meeting, where I received an urgent message to call John Bryan. Lehman Brothers, he told me, was on the brink of bankruptcy. Everyone in the industry was panicking, wondering how they would be affected and who would be next. My board resignation had not yet been publicly announced. Now, as every bank scrambled to maintain an appearance of stability, Bryan appealed to my sense of service to Goldman and my long-standing relationship with him.

"Don't resign just yet," he requested. "It will look bad for the bank. We need to maintain a united front."

I felt torn. Clearly Blankfein did not want me on the board; he'd made that more than clear. Anita was outraged when she heard about the request.

"Don't you dare!" she exclaimed. "You don't owe them anything! Why should you do this for them now, when they treated you so unfairly and weren't willing to accommodate your career choices?"

I appreciated her perspective, and I knew she'd never liked Blankfein, but I did feel a sense of duty to the bank. Perhaps it was because of my relationship with Hank and John Bryan—I felt I owed them my loyalty in this precarious moment. I didn't really feel I owed Blankfein anything, but perhaps, I thought, acceding to this request would improve our relationship. So I withdrew my resignation, though I didn't dare tell my wife right away. Standing by Goldman in their hour of need seemed like the right thing to do. I never imagined that they would not do the same when my hour came. And I had no premonition, on that day, that I would pay such a high price for my loyalty. Had fate not intervened in the form of the Lehman collapse, I would have walked away from Goldman with my cufflinks in my pocket and my entire life would have looked different. That road not taken would haunt me for years to come.

The Lehman bankruptcy hit the headlines on September 15,

2008, sending the global economy into a tailspin. It also had personal implications. Lehman was the prime broker for the Voyager fund. Unfortunately, I had no time to call Raj and try to find out what this meant, nor to chase up the information that JP Morgan were still requesting. I met with my banker that afternoon, and she insisted that we could not move forward without the Voyager papers. I encouraged her to contact Raj's team directly, and assured her that I would increase my efforts as well. First, however, I had to fly to Dallas for a two-day board meeting with AMR Corporation (the parent company of American Airlines) and then make a thirty-six-hour trip to Frankfurt, Germany, for a Genpact meeting. I was growing increasingly anxious about Voyager and concerned by Rajaratnam's elusiveness. What was he hiding? Why were his associates so cagey in response to my bankers' requests? Why wouldn't he provide the information we needed? It had been more than two months now since we first requested documents that should have been easily provided. Several emails the next day still elicited little response.

Saturday, September 20, was Sonu's thirtieth birthday, and Anita's birthday was the next day. The entire family came home for the weekend for a double celebration, along with many of Sonu's friends. It should have been a happy time, but the pall of the financial crisis hung heavy, as did my concerns. At dinner on Friday night, talk quickly turned to the recent Lehman bankruptcy. One of Sonu's friends had worked for Lehman and was now out of a job. They all wanted reassurance that things were going to get better, and I did my best to explain that all markets have their ups and downs.

The other issue weighing on my mind that weekend was our malaria initiative. I'd finally begun fundraising, but so far only the Global Fund's $1.2 billion was confirmed. We still needed $600 million, and we had only a few days until the launch. It would be up to me to find a way to close the gap, and there couldn't have been a more difficult time to be asking people for money.

Thanks to her job in the financial industry, Sonu knew better than her sisters what was going on in the markets and the possible implications. She also knew me too well to be fooled by my attempts at a positive outlook. After breakfast the next morning, she motioned to me to come into the library, where we could talk without burdening her mother.

"What's happening, Baba? It's not like you to be so upset, even when things are difficult. Is there something more going on?"

I told her about Voyager. "I'm worried that Raj isn't being straight with me. He took out that money without giving me my share, and I've been trying to get some basic information for months, and he's just giving me the runaround. He keeps saying the fund is doing okay, but now, with this Lehman thing, I'm really worried. Lehman was our prime broker."

We discussed the matter for a few more minutes, and I resolved to renew my efforts to get information out of Raj on Monday. "Now, let's try to put it aside," I told Sonu. "It's your birthday, and I don't want Anita to be worried. Let's celebrate."

The Buffett Investment

On Monday morning, September 22, I asked Renee to call Caryn, Raj's assistant, first thing. She explained, once again, which documents we were looking for and asked Caryn to pursue the matter directly with Raj. At the same time, my bankers and my accountant were emailing various people at Galleon. I had to attend a Goldman Sachs Foundation lunch in the city, followed by a dentist appointment, but, as soon as I got out, I asked Renee to try calling Raj directly. She left messages at his office and on his cell, one of which would be intercepted by the government's wiretap. Raj did not return my calls, but I couldn't spend more time on it that day—I needed to secure the funding for the malaria project. We were launching in just two days, at the annual Clinton Global Initiative conference. I called my friend Bob Zoellick, who was president of the World Bank and was still on the fence about joining our consortium of funders. "I know you support a lot of projects," I told him, "but this one is different. It's a once-in-a-lifetime opportunity to make a massive difference." Just twenty-four hours before the launch, Zoellick came through with a commitment of several hundred million. The Gates Foundation also donated generously.

September 23 was tightly scheduled, even by my standards. Studying my calendar as I sipped my morning coffee, I felt intense frustration that I still needed to pursue the Voyager matter, on a day when my first call started at 8 a.m. and my last meeting finished at 10 p.m. I was still finalizing the malaria funding and preparing for our big launch the next day. There were no gaps in the calendar whatsoever, other than my drive to the city and a fifteen-minute break between a meeting that finished at 3:15 and a call starting at 3:30. Perhaps then I can go to the bathroom, I thought to myself. Then I received a message from my secretary that Goldman was calling an emergency board session for that afternoon. It would begin at 3:15.

It was not unusual for board meetings to be scheduled at short notice during those volatile weeks, with the entire financial industry on edge. A few days earlier, on the heels of the Lehman bankruptcy, the Federal Reserve had bailed out AIG (which effectively amounted to a Goldman bailout, since Goldman was one of AIG's biggest creditors). Paulson and Bernanke were proposing more bailouts, and everyone was wondering which banking giant would be next to fall. The Goldman board had been meeting every few days as we tried to help steer the bank through the crisis. I asked my secretary to cancel my 3:30 meeting with the president of Muhammad Yunus's nonprofit, Grameen America. I'd been looking forward to learning more about Professor Yunus's agenda, but it would have to wait; Goldman took priority.

I hurried through my morning appointments in Connecticut and then resumed my efforts to call Raj during my drive to the city. Call records show that I spoke to him that morning, and I most likely asked him, once again, to please send the documents. He promised he would get them to me by end of day. Arriving in the city, I went straight into a series of appointments, including a meeting with a young entrepreneur and IIT alumnus, Sandeep Tyagi, who was seeking an investment, and a discussion about a proposed business school following the ISB model, which I unfortunately had to cut short to make the Goldman call. I dialed in to the board meeting at 3:15, ready to deal with whatever new crisis the bank was facing that day.

On this particular day, however, the news was surprisingly positive: the legendary Warren Buffett had agreed to make an investment of $5 billion. It was a game-changing move by the Berkshire Hathaway chairman, one that amounted to a massive vote of confidence in Goldman while other financial institutions were flailing. As a board member, I was made privy to the inner workings of this hastily made deal, which had been set in motion just the previous day by the Goldman banker Byron Trott, a trusted confidant of Buffett's. There was no doubt that Buffett was getting extremely favorable terms, but in that climate it was still a blessing. The board unanimously approved the deal, and I hung up the phone at 3:54, with a full six minutes before my next meeting. So of course, I called Renee.

"Did Raj send the Voyager documents?"

"No," she said. "And Jeffrey from JP Morgan just emailed me yet again asking what's happening." Aaron, my accountant, had also been copied on the email and had said he'd follow up right away. But we'd been down that road several times before, so I didn't hold out much hope he'd be successful. I looked at my watch. I still had five minutes before my next meeting. I told Renee, "Get me Raj."

This event was the subject of Counts 3 and 4 in the charges. The prosecutor's story was that on that call, I told Rajaratnam about the deal, still secret, and he immediately ran out on to the trading floor, shouting, "Buy Goldman Sachs!" The only evidence supporting this story, besides the testimony of Galleon traders that they'd gotten the instruction, was the speed with which I called Rajaratnam and a vague remark that he made to a colleague the next day, caught on a wiretap: "I heard that something good might happen to Goldman."

In reality, I don't know if I even spoke to Raj. According to the logs, the call lasted less than a minute, which leads me to think that, at most, he just got on the line and told Renee or me, "I'm working on it, I'll get them to you soon." There was simply no time for his secretary to go find him and for us to have a conversation of any significance. It's quite possible I didn't even speak to him at all—his secretary may have come back and told Renee he was unavailable. She had no particular memory of the incident, which is hardly surprising, since this was just one of dozens of unsuccessful attempts she'd made to call Raj on my behalf during those months. Call logs show a couple of other attempts to call his cell phone immediately afterwards, lasting just seconds—all of which confirms my conclusion that this was just another failed attempt to reach him. They also showed that my next call was to Ravi Trehan, lasting a couple of minutes, during which I probably expressed my frustration at still not being able to get the Voyager documents from Rajaratnam. It's worth noting that Ravi also ran an investment firm, Broad Street Capital, yet he made no Goldman trades that day—another fact that called into question the notion that I was hurrying to tip my friends about the Buffett investment.

The government's story seemed to deliberately gloss over the specifics of the series of calls, instead focusing on the sixteen-second gap and spinning a story about my haste to get to Raj before the markets closed. The indictment also seemed to overlook the critical fact that many of these calls in which I was allegedly passing tips were calls placed by Renee, who often listened in to note important follow-up tasks or appointments. This would hardly make sense if I were engaged in illegal activity. Lastly, it omitted to consider that Goldman's stock price had started going up at 1 p.m. that day—the moment the special board meeting was scheduled—indicating that word had already gotten out that "something good" was going to be announced.

Frustrated, I moved on to my next few appointments. Ina Moroz, a McKinsey associate from Paris, was waiting outside the office for my next meeting. I hadn't even closed the door, she remembered later, although she didn't hear the content of my call with Raj. Next was a meeting with the World Bank's head of malaria and Ray Chambers in preparation for the malaria project's launch, followed by a meeting with a Nigerian advisor for the Millennium Development Goals, and a dinner honoring Ethiopian Health Minister Tedros Adhanom Ghebreyesus, a key partner in our malaria efforts. Thoughts of Buffett's billions and Rajaratnam's evasiveness were soon far from my mind as the conversation turned to a project that could save hundreds of thousands if not millions of lives.

By 6:00 p.m., the Berkshire Hathaway investment in Goldman Sachs had become public, grabbing headlines in every major news outlet. Blankfein was quoted claiming that the deal was "a strong validation of our client franchise and future prospects."[2] The press seemed to agree, with the *New York Times* reporter Richard Beales observing that "the sight of one of the world's canniest investors taking out his checkbook has given a lift to other financial stocks." The bank, he concluded, had "snatched from the jaws of defeat something that can be passed off as victory."[3]

In a car between appointments, I checked in with Renee: still no statements. Irritated, I made one more attempt to contact Rajaratnam. It was 6:15 p.m., and he'd already left his office, so I called his cell phone directly, but got only his voicemail. I left a message, which would later become part of the evidence at my trial. In the prosecutor's tale, the friendly tone of my message was further proof of the conspiracy he was trying to conjure up. What he seemed to be overlooking was that in my message I said to Raj that I was "calling to catch up"—a strange thing to say if I had, as they were alleging, spoken to him only hours earlier.

I stayed in the city that night, as the next day I was attending the Clinton Global Initiative conference and launching the malaria project with Ray Chambers and Bill Gates. I was also scheduled to speak at an AIF summit at New York University, lead a workshop and chair a panel at the ICC World Business and Development Awards, as well as take half a dozen phone meetings. Looking back at my calendar, I can't imagine how I did it all. Meanwhile, the emails between my assistant, my accountant, my bankers, and Raj's people continued. I spent three more appointment-packed days in New York before heading home to pack for a much-needed vacation with Anita in Colorado.

Upon our return, I barely had time to unpack and repack before I was on a flight to San Francisco for an AIF gala, followed by a trip to Geneva for a Global Fund board retreat. I arrived home on Thursday, October 9, just in time for an HBS advisory board meeting in Boston, followed by a P&G board meeting in Cincinnati.

On October 16, I had one day at home, and among the many pressing things I needed to catch up on was a meeting with Greg Orman, my financial advisor. It was around this time, possibly in that meeting, that I finally learned the truth about Voyager.

It was worse than I'd feared. Left more vulnerable by Raj's large withdrawal, the highly leveraged fund had gone to zero following the Lehman collapse. My equity was lost—all $10 million. Raj hadn't lost a penny, having taken out his initial investment and more before the crash. Later, when we gained access to the wiretaps, they would shed light on what was going on behind the scenes. Rajaratnam was caught on tape several times during September discussing Lehman's desire to terminate the Voyager facility, the search for a new broker, the pressure on the fund following the Lehman bankruptcy, and the possibility that the fund would be shut down before the end of the year. In an October 2 conversation, which we'd stumbled upon while combing through the wiretaps, he flat out admits to one of his employees that he'd lied to me about the fund's success and never told me about the redemptions. "It's part of the game," he says, dismissively. "Look, when you take leverage—you know. . . . I hope Rajat is a big boy. . . . I didn't tell him that I took that equity out, right?" He also suggests that they make up a story to keep me from getting too upset, telling me they were making a claim against Lehman to try to recoup the funds or negotiate with banks for a reduced payment. None of this would suggest that he considered me a valuable source, indeed, quite the opposite. He was cavalier about losing my money and seemed perfectly happy to lie to me.

Even before I knew this backstory, I was furious. The loss of the money upset me, but it was Raj's duplicity that really hurt. Ten million dollars was a large sum, for sure, but everyone was losing money in those days, and Voyager had been a risky investment in the first place, so if I'd lost the money fair and square, I'd have been philosophical about it. What upset me was that Raj's actions had increased the risk, without my knowledge, and I'd paid the price. I'd wanted to give him the benefit of the doubt, hoping there was a reasonable explanation for all this. Now it was clear why he had so intently avoided all the calls, emails, and requests for information over the past months. He'd been stalling, knowing that the fund was in trouble but hoping he could find a way to hide it from me. I held him accountable for the loss and became even more determined to file a lawsuit against him. All of this was going through my mind during the period in which the government alleged I was tipping him—how could that possibly make sense?

Our relationship was strained, to put it mildly, but Raj tried to placate me, suggesting, as he'd planned with his colleague, that he could make a deal with the banks to recoup our money.

"All the banks are taking haircuts on loans right now," he declared, with his usual swagger. "I'll get our equity back."

I hoped he was right. My financial advisors confirmed that the banks were making such deals, so perhaps Rajaratnam could pull it off. I decided to hold off on my plans to sue in case we could resolve things. I still believed that he might have the money and decide to give me my share as he should have done in the first place. I'd never sued anyone in my entire career, and I didn't know where to start. Plus, I had no time to deal with it now; the next day I was flying to

Florence, Italy, for a McKinsey Global Banking CEO Roundtable, and then on to Barcelona, for the firm's annual directors' conference.

Throughout these weeks, I, like everyone in business, followed the news closely as the economy struggled to right itself. Goldman, buoyed up by Buffett's billions, was doing better than some, but still flailing. On October 3, President Bush had signed off on the Troubled Asset Relief Program (TARP), authorizing $700 billion in bailouts. The stock market responded with its worst week in seventy-five years. More bailouts followed. The markets continued to churn. On October 23, 2008, I was flying back to New York from Barcelona, planning to make a brief stop at home before heading to Rhode Island for a Brown University parents' weekend with my youngest daughter. Upon landing, I picked up a copy of the *Wall Street Journal* and read a report that, according to an "unnamed source," Goldman Sachs was planning to lay off 10 percent of its staff.[4] So I was not at all surprised when I checked in with my secretary and heard that Blankfein had called a last-minute board meeting later that afternoon to discuss this unfortunate situation.

When the meeting ended, no doubt I called Renee and asked her to go over the call list. I'd have been eager to deal with important matters before jet lag kicked in and reluctant to have them bleed over into my weekend with Kushy. Once again, Rajaratnam was number one—having just returned from several weeks away I wanted to know what was happening in his conversations with the banks regarding Voyager.

I don't remember the exact conversation, but the general theme of our communications during that period was me pressing for a resolution but trying to be courteous, not wanting to alienate him, and him asking me to be patient, insisting he was working on it. The morning after that particular call, however, he dumped a large amount of Goldman stock, avoiding significant losses. Once again, he was caught on a wiretap bragging to a colleague that he'd heard from somebody on the board that Goldman was losing $2 a share and he was "gonna whack it." This incident constituted Count 5 of the charges against me, with the prosecutor alleging that I was that "someone" who had hurried to pass on valuable secrets.

Raj didn't get that information from me. In fact, the board had not even discussed earnings on the call. It had been a last-minute "posting call" to discuss the impending layoffs and deal with the fallout from the *Wall Street Journal* leak. Besides, the number Raj quoted was not even accurate—we would later learn that, according to the profit and loss (P&L) statements from October 22, Goldman was losing $1.75 per share. No one rounds up those kinds of numbers.

There were no minutes from the call, so I had no way to prove this other than the statements of other board members, who did not seem to recall the details. In his SEC deposition, Blankfein had been hopelessly vague about this call, but had tried to claim that it was customary for him to always discuss earnings. Either way, in this instance, Rajaratnam didn't need an insider at all to have known that dumping the stock was a wise move—the leak about the 10 percent staff cut had made that clear. For the prosecutor, however, it was enough of a fit for the narrative he was trying to build.

I met with Rajaratnam once more at the end of October, trying to ascertain whether he really was working out a deal or just stalling again. A few days later, I left for an extended trip to India, with the Voyager matter still unresolved.

Thanksgiving that year was another gloomy gathering. By this point, the whole family knew about the Voyager situation. A more personal sadness also tinged that particular holiday every year—the absence of my nephew Sanjoy, known as Partho, Didi's only son. He had been like a brother to my girls and he and Sonu had made it something of a tradition to cook Thanksgiving dinner together. In 2002, Partho had succumbed to an acute form of leukemia, aged only twenty-six. We could never celebrate Thanksgiving without feeling his loss anew.

My sixtieth birthday came soon after, on December 2, but none of us really felt like celebrating. The rest of the year was an endless list of meetings, much of which has blurred in my mind. One event that stands out, however, was a Goldman board meeting in early December where we learned that the bank was losing close to $5 a share. This was a much greater loss than the October loss that I was being charged with tipping Rajaratnam about. Surely if there were a "pattern," as the prosecutor alleged, I would have made sure to give Raj a heads-up about this event? But there were no calls, meetings, or any other communication between us. At this point, I wanted nothing to do with Rajaratnam. I wished I could just forget about him altogether, but I still hoped to get my money out somehow, and I was still considering suing.

No amount of busyness could shake the dark cloud that seemed to hang over me. It wasn't just the money; it was the sense of having been taken advantage of. This may seem strange to say, but I really had not believed that this would happen to me. In retrospect, I can see that McKinsey, where I had spent my entire career, was an unusually principled, high-minded environment, and I had been to some degree sheltered from the more cutthroat corners of the business world. Of course, I knew that there were all kinds of people in business, and things went on that weren't always above board, but to be honest, I rarely encountered any of that personally. I had built a career on being trusting, open, generous, and believing the best of people. My wife, my daughters, and many of my friends had warned me, teased me, and at times despaired for me, but it had always worked out. Now, Rajaratnam's actions shook me more deeply than I could have predicted because they seemed to strike at the essence of my worldview. Suddenly I was awash in self-recrimination about being too trusting and too busy to keep closer tabs on my investment. Perhaps, too, I was feeling a premonition of what was to come.

It was in this melancholy state of mind that I sat down to lunch with an old friend early in January 2009. I'd known Ajit Jain since he joined McKinsey in 1980. He'd left some years later to work for Warren Buffett's Berkshire Hathaway, and was now Buffett's right-hand man.

We'd always stayed in touch and saw each other regularly, but I had not confided in him about my troubles with Voyager. Only a few close friends knew what was going on. That day, however, I could think of little else, and when Ajit gently inquired as to what was weighing on me, I told him the whole sorry tale. He expressed his shock and sympathy, and I felt a little better, at least temporarily.

Later that month, I flew to Saudi Arabia for a speaking engagement in Riyadh, and then on to Switzerland to attend the WEF meeting in Davos. I always enjoyed the conference and had played a key role in shaping the organization through many years on the board. On Thursday, January 29, I called in to a P&G audit committee meeting during which a decline in sales growth was discussed. Later that day, I received a message to call Rajaratnam. I was still holding out hope that his discussions with the bank might bear fruit and thought that maybe this would be the good news I was waiting for. But all he had to tell me was that it had come to nothing. The money was gone.

Soon afterwards, Galleon shorted about 180,000 P&G shares, making more than half a million dollars in profit. Again, the government alleged that I was the source of this information, which I was not. This incident was the subject of Count 6, the final charge.

After that call, it was clear that Rajaratnam had no intention of making things right. Up to this point, I had not challenged him about the redemptions and commissions, afraid of antagonizing him further and jeopardizing my fragile hope that he might find a way to recoup my capital. But now that hope was gone, so I confronted him. He was defensive, insisting he'd had a right to take his money out. Legally, he did, but to not inform me or give me the opportunity to do the same was clearly not in the spirit of the agreement. I was still considering suing and even discussed it with Greg Orman and an attorney sometime in January. But I couldn't seem to find the energy to fight. Since I'd resigned myself to the fact that the money was gone, the best I could do was learn from my mistakes and be more cautious in the future about who I trusted. Rajaratnam, I resolved, would never be a part of any business I was involved with. Our story had come to an end—or so I thought. Nine months later, he would be thrust back into my daily awareness with the news of his arrest and everything that followed.

Unprepared

As my court date drew close, I told this story to my lawyers again and again, trying to recall as much detail as possible, as well as to contextualize the events within the realities of my life. With the trial just days away, I sat in the office poring over my calendars late into the night. It was emotionally exhausting work—I couldn't help but second-guess the decisions I'd made and inwardly berate myself for being so trusting. I was also losing faith in the system, losing confidence that I would be given a truly fair trial. But I tried to put aside my feelings and imagine how my story would sound to a jury hearing it for the first time. Surely when they heard about the incidents in context, the government's allegations would appear in a whole new light.

On the Friday before my trial, I was still preparing, worried we'd left it too late or hadn't done enough. But there was little point in dwelling on that now. I would try to put it all out of my head and enjoy a last quiet weekend with my family. Before I could go home, however, there was one last thing I needed to do.

Alone in my temporary office at the law firm, I got out my computer and created a new email message. In the address field, I entered the names of all my family, friends, and colleagues—dozens and dozens of people who I knew would be thinking about Monday's trial, studying every news report, and wondering how I was doing. Looking at their names brought up a surge of emotion. These people were what mattered to me—not money, not acclaim, not attaining some elite status, as the prosecutor was trying to suggest. My battered reputation was not an abstract idea to me—it was contained in these relationships that I'd built so carefully, over decades. Thanks to the damage already done, there were countless names I could no longer include on my list of friends.

I knew that my real friends would stand by me, no matter what. So many of them had called, written, or visited since the charges, assuring me of their continuing support. Some had even created a website where those who knew me could write their testimonies to my good character, in an attempt to counteract the negative portrait painted by the media. My former McKinsey colleague Atul Kanagat, who managed the site, had assembled an amazing list of contributors. Every one of these people I was proud to call my friend, and it was all of them that I felt I should write to on the eve of my trial.

"As I sit here reflecting on the last year," I typed, "I am filled with emotions. The overwhelming one is God is putting me through a test, and my duty is to do the very best I can and be prepared to accept whatever outcomes. I know I have done nothing wrong and expect to be fully vindicated."

14

A Cropped Portrait

That side of our existence whose direction is towards the infinite seeks not wealth, but freedom and joy. There the reign of necessity ceases, and there our function is not to get but to be.

—Rabindranath Tagore, *Sadhana*

New York City, May 21, 2012

"Gupta Cannot Take a Mother Teresa Defense."

I've shared headlines with many noble human beings in the course of my long career in business and philanthropy, but never before had my name been paired with Kolkata's saintly nun. And yet on the eve of my trial, her name was on everyone's lips along with mine, thanks to a colorful analogy used by Judge Rakoff during a hearing just a few days earlier.

"If Mother Teresa were charged with bank robbery, the jury would still have to determine whether or not she committed a bank robbery," he'd declared, as part of a warning to my lawyers against overemphasizing or even discussing my philanthropic work. I certainly didn't consider myself a Mother Teresa, but this move to curb any mention of my decades of engagement in humanitarian causes was frustrating, to say the least. Gary argued vigorously that it was unfair, that if the government was seeking to paint me as greed-driven, I should be allowed to correct that perception with the references to reality of how I've spent much of my time and energy. Rakoff, however, was not just unmoved but sarcastic in his comments.

This was not the only significant pretrial ruling that went against us. Rakoff had also denied our motion to declare the wiretaps inadmissible. In particular, we were referring to the two recordings in which Rajaratnam tells one of his traders that he received information about Goldman from an unnamed source. We argued that these constituted hearsay and were therefore inadmissible. As Gary had pointed out to the judge, there was a high risk that jurors would give undue weight to these audios, although in fact they contained no actual evidence against me, because compared to the vague and circumstantial nature of the rest of the evidence, these calls seemed more concrete.

Rakoff, however, ruled that the tapes were exempt from the bar on hearsay evidence because they were in "furtherance of a conspiracy." This seemed to me to be an absurd contortion of the law. It was a circular argument: the government wanted to use the tapes as evidence to prove the charge of conspiracy, but they were already assuming the conspiracy existed in order to allow the evidence! This just added to my sense that I was being judged guilty before I had been tried. But it appeared that even the most logical arguments would not persuade the judge.

Day one of my trial dawned in fittingly somber fashion. At our New York apartment, where we'd be based for the next few weeks, I dressed in my best suit, the same one I'd have worn if preparing for an important consulting assignment. For a moment, the familiar ritual of choosing shirt and tie, belt and shoes lulled me into a sense of normalcy. But the look on Anita's face as she handed me my tea snapped me back to reality.

Robin arrived to pick me up promptly at 8 a.m., and we drove across to the east side to pick up Gary, before heading downtown to the courthouse. We didn't say much, as the city streets crawled by. Even Gary's jocular manner seemed muted. By the time we arrived, the heavens had opened. The downpour did not deter the press, however, who huddled beneath umbrellas as they surged around my car, thrusting microphones and cameras in my face. Using my own umbrella as a shield, I hurried into the courthouse, glad that Anita and the girls had traveled separately and were already seated inside, in the second row. As my lawyers guided me to our place in the front row, I noticed many other familiar faces. My old IIT friend Rajiv Johri caught my eye across the room and smiled his encouragement. I was touched to see Sonu's husband, Meka, and Megha's partner, George, among the packed crowd, along with many other family members and friends.

Gary had told me that Rakoff had a reputation for being quick with the jury selection process, and this trial was no exception. By 2 p.m. it was decided. My fate would be in the hands of four men and eight women, including a nurse, a schoolteacher, a retired librarian, a youth advocate, and a beauty consultant. It would be up to these people to decide whether I was a scheming, greedy, envious man who traded corporate secrets for access to a billionaire's circle, or an honest, trustworthy, but overstretched man who made a poor choice of business associate and was guilty of nothing more than bad timing. My greatest concern was how few among the twelve had experience or understanding of the worlds of business and finance. There was only one executive, from a nonprofit. Would they be able to follow the complex discussions of securities law, trading processes, business deals, and more?

As opening arguments commenced, Reed Brodsky, the lead prosecutor, took to the floor and told his version of the story. I'd become familiar with Brodsky through a couple of the pretrial hearings I'd attended, and I didn't particularly like him. He was a brash, street-fighter type who had fought every one of our pretrial motions with great vigor. There was clearly no love lost between him and Gary. His opening was well prepared and confident, painting the case as a classic insider trading scheme in which rich and powerful men—sophisticated, highly accomplished graduates of elite, prestigious business schools—teamed up to cheat ordinary, hard-working investors. He even claimed that my intent was to allow my friends to make money off of the financial crisis—an argument clearly designed to gain the jury's sympathy and paint me as a Wall Street villain. As expected, he concentrated on the September 23, 2008, incident following the Warren Buffett investment, playing up the drama of those months and my privileged position as "the ultimate corporate insider." He also sought to reinforce his claims of a "pattern" with rhetorical tricks, repeating the same phrases to describe each incident so that they echoed through the courtroom with cumulative impact.

As for Voyager, he spun it as a joint venture in which Rajaratnam and I were "flying high and making huge profits" from 2007 to 2008. He acknowledged the fund's collapse that fall, but in a strange twist that made no sense, he seemed to claim that my alleged tipping was part of an attempt to get Rajaratnam to repay my $10 million.

Before Gary could take his turn, the issue of mentioning my charitable work was discussed again, outside the presence of the jury. Brodsky wanted to ensure that Gary wouldn't be referencing my "humanitarian character" in his opening remarks.

"Your Honor, just to be clear, he won't mention AIDS, malaria, or tuberculosis."

Rakoff appeared to find this funny, replying, "Or the bubonic plague."

I personally didn't think it was a joking matter—not the diseases themselves, nor this bizarre ruling that prevented my lawyers from mentioning the role I'd played in the fight to eradicate them. There I was sitting with my life's work and reputation on the line and the judge was making fun of a serious legal discussion. I was further irritated when Gary chimed in, "Or even scurvy." I'm sure his intention in continuing the joke was to stay on good terms with Judge Rakoff, but it rankled nonetheless.

"We Don't Guess People Into Guilt"

Gary was energetic and passionate in his opening remarks, highlighting the absurdity of the idea that "in the twilight of an illustrious life" I would "decide knowingly, willingly, deliberately to suddenly one day become a criminal, and do it for no benefit." It was, he pointed out, "a very strange insider trading case because the evidence will show that Rajat Gupta did no trading." To drive the point home, he explained: I'd never sold a single share of stock in any of the companies involved. I'd never taken any payment. He highlighted the profound absence of real, hard evidence, despite the confidence with which Brodsky described the conversations he imagined had occurred. The prosecution's claims, he declared, were based entirely on speculation and guesswork: "We don't guess people into guilt in America."

I wished I could believe that were true. But guesswork had already cost me my reputation, my career, and my ability to serve. Gary's avowal of the presumption of innocence and the greatness of our justice system rang hollow to my ears. Yes, in theory, it was up to the government to meet what he called the "awesome burden of proof beyond a reasonable doubt," but I couldn't trust that this was really how it worked. I needed to tell a better story.

At the heart of Gary's statement was an argument he'd made to me since the beginning of the case: to prove insider trading, the prosecution needed to show evidence of three things: one, that I provided information to Rajaratnam; two, that I did so expecting him to trade on it, as part of an explicit quid pro quo agreement; and three, that I received some benefit in return. This last point was critical in my case. While there is no statutory definition of insider trading, the "controlling decision" referred to by most judges comes from a 1983 Supreme Court case, *Dirks* v. *S.E.C.*,* which established

* Dirks was a whistle-blower who disclosed inside information in order to expose a fraud, but was charged with insider trading because some of the investors he warned subsequently sold their stock, avoiding significant losses. The Supreme Court decision

that to prove a tipper guilty of insider trading "the test is whether the insider personally will benefit, directly or indirectly, from his disclosure. Absent some personal gain, there has been no breach of duty to stockholders."[1]

According to the indictment, I had "benefited and hoped to benefit from [my] friendship and business relationship with Rajaratnam in various ways, some of which were financial." Yet no evidence had been provided for this hopelessly vague claim. Of course, there was none, because it didn't happen.

In contrast, every other individual who had been charged with tipping Rajaratnam had a clear quid pro quo in place and received personal monetary benefit. Anil Kumar made $2 million–$3 million, channeled into the infamous Swiss bank account in the name of his maid. Former Intel executive Rajiv Goel received $600,000—enough to buy a home and to provide care for his ailing father. Rajaratnam also earned $700,000–$800,000 on Goel's behalf in Goel's personal account. Intel-marketer-turned-stock-analyst Roomy Khan got tips from Rajaratnam, which she traded on very profitably herself, making approximately $1.5 million. She claims he offered her money to stay at Intel and feed him information. Danielle Chiesi's hedge fund made at least $1.7 million trading on illegal information, much of which she received from Rajaratnam. Adam Smith and Michael Cardillo, both Galleon traders, no doubt saw Raj's gratitude reflected in their salaries and bonuses. I received nothing because, unlike those individuals, I was never one of Raj's insiders.

Gary explained this definition to the jury, highlighting the fact that not only had I made no money, I'd lost $10 million. He also pointed out that during the time in which the alleged incidents occurred, Rajaratnam was a respected figure on Wall Street and a highly valued customer at Goldman, with multiple relationships at the bank who

---

to acquit Dirks established that to prove a tipper guilty of insider trading there must be a demonstrable benefit.

could have been his "inside sources"—a point that would be crucial to our defense strategy. And he gave a brief sketch of my life history and career. The prosecution was presenting a "cropped picture" of me, he argued, that he intended to correct. However, with Rakoff's restrictions, he was barely able to expand the frame even a little.

As Gary's remarks drew to a close, I felt a little more hopeful. He was convincing, and although opening statements are not considered evidence, they provide critical framing. Perhaps we could indeed shake the "frail edifice" of the government case, as Gary described it. Perhaps the truth would prevail. "Rajat Gupta is not afraid of the truth!" Gary declared to the jury. "We are only afraid of confusion and misunderstanding." Unfortunately, confusion and misunderstanding would turn out to be at the heart of the government's strategy.

The next morning, they called their first witness: Caryn Eisenberg, Rajaratnam's executive assistant. She took the stand clutching a red notebook, which she told the jury was where she had kept her list of her boss's most important callers. He had given her several names, she said, and instructed her that if any of these people called, she was to interrupt him, no matter what he was doing. My name was on the list, along with two names that would be familiar to anyone who had followed Rajaratnam's trial: Anil Kumar and Rajiv Goel. Also named were my NSR cofounder Parag Saxena and a hedge fund investor, Stanley Druckenmiller.

It was a good story, the red notebook with the secret VIP list. I could see how it must look to the jury. I made a mental note to talk to my lawyers about contextualizing this detail during my testimony, wondering how I could do so without sounding self-important. It was yet another of those simple facts that could be made to look suspicious but was quite ordinary in my life. I was probably on dozens of such lists—I was a very busy, influential, and connected person, and taking my calls would have been a priority for many of my business associates and colleagues. But the jury wouldn't know this—to them it no doubt sounded highly conspiratorial. The list also served to imply guilt by association. Kumar and Goel had pleaded guilty to insider trading, and there was my name alongside theirs in the red notebook.

Unsurprisingly, in questioning Eisenberg, the prosecutor zeroed in on September 23, 2008, the day of the Buffett investment. It was another good story—the call Eisenberg said she received right before close of markets from someone on the list needing to urgently speak to her boss. Strangely, despite the shortness of the list, she wasn't able to positively identify the caller, but she'd clearly been coached to say the right things to imply it was me. My lawyers objected numerous times to the leading questions from the prosecutor, but most of her testimony was allowed to stand, including the observation that after getting off the phone and instructing one of his traders to buy Goldman, Rajaratnam was "smiling more."

During cross-examination, David Frankel, one of my legal team, was able to highlight some inconsistencies in Eisenberg's story. We knew from seeing transcripts of interviews she had done with Rajaratnam's lawyers before his trial that her story had changed quite a few times. Her memory of September 23 and 24, 2008, had not always been as clear as she was now claiming that it was—for example, she'd originally claimed that she arrived in the office early on the 24th and everyone was gossiping about the Buffett deal, but later, after her memory was jogged, she said she'd come in late after a doctor's appointment. David also focused on a remark she'd made indicating that sometimes when I called, Rajaratnam told her to pretend he wasn't available and even "snuck out of the building" to avoid me. An instant message conversation between Eisenberg and another of Rajaratnam's assistants, which we offered in evidence, confirmed this. "Raj made me lie to Gupta. He doesn't want to see him," she had written.

This seemed to be at odds with the picture the prosecution was trying to paint, in which Raj waited eagerly for my tips. In reality, I'm sure he often avoided my calls, particularly once the Voyager situation became contentious and he was trying to stall me. Furthermore, I may have been on his VIP list, but I was not one of his trusted inner circle. I was never invited on the special trips he planned for some of his most important business connections, as Eisenberg confirmed during cross-examination. Most importantly, David brought out the fact that Rajaratnam had several close connections at Goldman and that one of those was also on the VIP list: a Goldman account executive named David Loeb.

Mr. X

Loeb had come to our attention a few months earlier, although at first we only knew him as Mr. X. Under US law, the government had been required to share with us all the evidence they had generated during discovery. They did so with a vengeance—dumping a total of 3.2 million pages of documents on us, with no guidance as to what might actually be relevant. As my legal team combed through the mountains of paper, they stumbled upon something potentially critical: evidence that Rajaratnam had an alternative insider at Goldman. The documents seemed to suggest that the government actually had wiretap recordings of this person tipping Rajaratnam about stocks.

When my lawyers told me what they'd found, I felt vindicated. From the beginning, I'd tried to explain that I was not Raj's only Goldman connection; he had many friends on the inside who could have been feeding him information. What wasn't clear to us was whether the government even knew what they had on this individual, who we had begun referring to as Mr. X. Why weren't they pursuing charges against him?

Immediately, we filed a motion demanding that the government provide us with any evidence they possessed that someone at Goldman or P&G was illegally tipping Rajaratnam, about any companies. The Mr. X discussion took center stage at one of the pretrial hearings, with Brodsky claiming that all such evidence was among the papers he'd already given us. Without a name, however, the search was daunting.

Eventually Brodsky conceded that he would give us the name, allowing us to search the electronic database of discovery.

We learned Loeb's identity in February, and sure enough there were actual wiretap recordings of him giving Rajaratnam tips about stocks including Apple and Intel: much stronger evidence than the thin circumstantial case they'd built against me. Why wasn't it being considered that he could be Raj's Goldman source? Shortly afterwards, the government announced it was investigating Loeb, along with two other Goldman executives, for insider trading. Would they even have pursued that investigation had we not brought the evidence to their attention? Or were they just intent on pinning the crimes on me, given my higher profile? (As it turned out, Loeb was never charged with any crime. How was this possible, when the evidence was so clear? I couldn't help but wonder, was it some kind of exchange for Goldman's testimony against me?)

We intended to call Loeb as a witness, suggesting to the jury that there was a credible alternative source for Rajaratnam's information. I was glad David had managed to introduce his name into the conversation on day one.

Trial by Boredom

Over the next few days, the prosecution continued to build their dramatic narrative around the Buffett investment. They called a brash young Indian trader, Ananth Muniyappa, who claimed to have been one of those ordered to buy Goldman stock that afternoon in September 2008. They called Byron Trott, the smooth-talking Goldman executive who'd orchestrated the Buffett deal, and had him tell the story of how it came about, in the midst of a climate of "complete chaos and fear," as he described it. They went to great lengths to establish the high degree of secrecy surrounding the deal, although we had documentation we planned to use that clearly showed Goldman stock beginning to go up the moment the emergency board meeting was announced. It could not have been quite as secret as they were trying to claim.

Despite these attempts to add drama, the government's case was characterized by a mountain of mind-numbing minutiae. Indeed, it seemed that their strategy was to deliberately overwhelm the jury with detail, often in the form of stacks of documents that were then projected on to the big screen, page after page, while witnesses were asked to read sentences aloud and explain their meaning. An FBI agent explained wiretap protocol in such exhaustive detail that the judge applauded the jury for not having fallen asleep, even though they "had every reason to do so." A McKinsey IT security manager spent hours testifying about long lists of phone numbers and the names to which each was assigned, until the judge inquired of the prosecutor, "How much more of this are you going to ask the jury to endure?" A Galleon employee was called to comment on the office floor plans. The guy who installed the Galleon swipe card system was asked to describe how it worked. I remember actual file cabinets full of papers being wheeled in on trolleys, jurors' eyes glazing over as they were subjected to hour upon hour of calendar pages, phone records, emails, and meeting minutes from board meetings that were often unrelated to the incidents that were under consideration. Reporting on the case, *New York* magazine observed, "If dullness were a crime, the proceedings in courtroom 14B at the Southern District Court on Pearl Street would be a graver offense than the actual matter at hand . . ."[2]

These tactics served, over and over again, to muddy and confuse what was in fact quite a simple picture. They gave the impression that the government's case was exhaustively researched and backed by reams of evidence, when in fact there was very little there. The jurors, none of whom were well-versed in business or finance, looked by turns bemused and bored. They may not have been falling asleep, but how could they possibly be asked to retain and contextualize the volume of detail they were being asked to consider? Even the judge acknowledged that the prosecutor was naive in thinking the jury would be able to "peruse carefully a thousand documents" and requested that he "sharpen up" his presentation. The fear Gary had referenced in his opening, of confusion and misinformation, was looking increasingly justified. Clarity seemed unlikely to prevail in this courtroom.

Adding to my concern were the countless hard-fought legal battles that took place outside of the presence of the jury—before each day's proceedings began, before and after breaks, after the jury were dismissed in the evenings, and at numerous sidebars throughout each day. Lawyers conferred over every other question, making progress excruciatingly slow. Sometimes it seemed that more time was spent in colloquy than in examination. Objection after objection was voiced, sustained, or overruled. It was a revelation to me how much of a trial comes down to disputes over what is and is not allowed to be said: what evidence is admitted, which witnesses can be called, what questions can be asked, what form those questions can take, what words may or may not be used. The rules of evidence, I was learning, were very specific, yet there were numerous exceptions that could be invoked. The hearsay rule was particularly tricky, and almost never seemed to go in our favor. All these decisions, made by the judge alone, shape the narrative that the jury hears. I came to believe that many cases must be won or lost at the sidebar.

I wondered how it must appear to the jurors. It certainly bore little resemblance to the courtrooms portrayed in the movies, with lawyers making eloquent speeches and rapid-firing questions at witnesses. I imagined it was like trying to watch a movie being made by two competing directors at the same time. The actors would begin a scene, but every two minutes one or other of the directors would yell "Cut!" and everyone would go off into a huddle on the side. The jurors never saw the material that ended up on the cutting-room floor, nor did they have a script to refer to. They were expected to piece together the narrative from the disjointed collage of half-finished scenes that was presented to them. In their place, I thought, I'd find it near impossible to follow the storyline, much less interpret it accurately.

Each day, as I sat in the courtroom with my lawyers, my wife and four daughters would take their seats behind me. There was only one day when those seats were not filled: on Thursday, May 24, Aditi graduated from HBS. I had been unable to convince the judge to allow me to attend. The day I told her I couldn't be there, she'd assured me that she would be fine, but I could hear the tears she was holding back as she hurriedly got off the phone. Her empty place, along with her mother's and Sonu's, reminded me all day that I was missing what should have been one of my proudest days. I could not help but remember Sonu's graduation some years earlier—a joyful return to my alma mater, where I was well known and respected among the faculty and students. How would it be today? I wondered. Would Anita, Sonu, and Aditi be subjected to gossip and awkward looks? What were they supposed to say to all the people who knew me and knew why I was absent? I'd asked Aditi once if my legal problems had affected her at school, and she quickly told me no. Only later would I learn that she had been subjected to many humiliations because of my case—articles about me had been left anonymously in her locker, scathing emails were circulated calling for my resignation from the HBS board, and well-meaning professors suggested she take a year or two off until it all died down. She'd even been forced to sit through a class taught by Preet Bharara himself. I didn't know all this on the day of her graduation, but I had no doubt it must have been excruciating for her and was touched by her courage. I wished I could have been there with her to hold my head high and remind people that I had not been found guilty of any crime.

Most of that day's evidence dragged on like the preceding days'. The former CFO of Smucker's testified about the Folgers Coffee deal. The government was trying to highlight how secret the deal had been, but on cross-examination the witness had to admit that in fact there had been numerous leaks to the press and dozens of people had been involved in the deal-making process, including teams from both companies, several law firms, several banks, and other advisors. As the afternoon drew to a close, the government called their next witness, Goldman director Bill George. Originally, they had been planning to call my friend John Bryan, but a few weeks before the trial, they had announced a substitution, claiming that Bryan did not remember the board meeting in question. Clearly, the prosecutor wanted someone from Goldman to testify about the events of October 23, 2008, and specifically to say that he remembered the board being told that Goldman was going to lose $2 a share. This would validate Rajaratnam's wiretapped conversation in which he claimed to have heard that figure from someone on the board. Since there were no minutes from the meeting, they were relying on witness testimony. I appreciated that John had not wanted to testify against me, but I wished he had been willing to tell the jury what actually happened at the meeting rather than simply claiming forgetfulness.

I knew Bill, but not as well as John. He didn't want to look at me as he took the stand. While unable to say that the board had been told any specific amount for Goldman's share price, he did say that he remembered the bank was going to lose money, for the first time in its history. "Of course they were going to lose money!" I thought to myself, frustrated. "We were in the middle of the worst financial crisis in decades, and it had been all over the papers that they were laying off 10 percent of their staff that day!" Those layoffs had been the only thing discussed in the board meeting, but any investor off the street could have figured out from that article that Goldman's share prices were about to take a dive.

George also testified about the events of June and July 2008, in relation to the July 29 call when I had inappropriately confirmed to Rajaratnam that Goldman was considering buying a commercial bank. The government wanted him to testify that this information was considered confidential, which he did. On cross-examination, however, my lawyers were able to demonstrate that numerous analysts and news outlets had been speculating about the possibility for weeks before that call. The ideas I'd shared with Raj, while inappropriate, were certainly far from secret.

The government followed George with Michael Cardillo, a former Galleon-trader-turned-government-cooperator whose six charges of securities fraud had been reduced to one when he agreed to plead guilty, and who was still awaiting sentencing. Clearly, he'd made a deal and would have said just about anything on the witness stand. He testified about the January 2009 incident involving P&G's declining sales, as well as the Folgers–Smucker's deal, but much of what he had to say was blatant hearsay—third-hand reports from unnamed sources with nothing to corroborate them, not even phone records. We tried to get Cardillo's testimony barred, but Rakoff once again ruled against us, using the same frustratingly circular "conspiracy" argument he'd used to allow the wiretaps. At least Gary had a chance to discredit him during cross-examination, highlighting his obvious incentives for testifying in return for a reduced sentence. He did a good job of poking holes in his carefully rehearsed tale and shining a light on the general culture of exaggeration and one-upmanship that characterized trading at Galleon.

We were one week into the trial, but already it felt like an eternity. Every evening, after a long day in the courthouse, I'd been rehearsing for my testimony. Although by this point I should have been ready, I felt unprepared. When I finally got back to the apartment each night, I'd be exhausted but often too anxious to sleep. The girls came most evenings, along with my brother, Anjan, and his wife, Mala, and my sister Kumkum and her husband, Mrinal. Didi was the only one of my siblings unable to be there—her husband, Prabir, was seriously sick and could not travel. We would sit together, trying not to talk or think about the trial. I refused to read the papers, but Megha told me that they seemed only to be confirming the prosecutor's false story—leaving out anything that supported my case.

In an attempt to take everyone's mind off of our troubles, I found myself telling stories about my parents, and my father in particular. Although my daughters knew the basic facts about their grandparents, I'd never really told them the stories my father had told me. Now, I talked about his passion for independence, his time in jail, his suffering at the hands of the British. I reflected on his great love for my mother, and his refusal to marry her until India was free and he was no longer risking imprisonment or worse. I told them how he almost died from tuberculosis, and how his life was saved by his classmate-turned-warden. I even told the story of his death.

It comforted me a little to speak of my father and helped put my predicament in perspective. He had endured much worse than I was facing, yet he retained his dignity, his faith in humanity, and his equanimity. I did not know why fate had dealt me such a harsh blow at this stage of my life, after being so generous for so long, but I'd do my best to meet it in a way that would have made my father proud. I wished he could have known his granddaughters, the four young women listening with rapt attention to the stories of his life in a New York City apartment, half a world away from Kolkata.

The Memorial Day weekend should have been a respite, but even as I proudly watched my youngest daughter graduate from Brown University, I was silently undergoing cross-examination in my head. I did my best to be present for Kushy, but I could tell that she, like all of us, was too worried to enjoy the day. I was almost anxious to get back to the court—I just wanted to get this ordeal over as fast as possible.

A Job that Was Never Mine

During the second week, after Cardillo completed his testimony and several more witnesses were called to comment on reams of documents, the government called a man I had briefly been acquainted with, a Galleon marketing director by the name of Ayad Alhadi. Raj had hired him in early 2008 when the former NSR hedge fund arm was in the process of becoming Galleon International. In those days, we'd still been unclear about the relationship between the two funds, and discussion of a 15 percent cross-ownership was ongoing, as well as a potential role for me as chairman of both. So when Raj asked me to join Alhadi for some fundraising meetings in the Middle East, I was happy to help. My name and stature in the global business community would give investors confidence, he explained. I had a couple of planning meetings with Alhadi and then made a stop on my way to India to accompany him to investor meetings in Abu Dhabi and Dubai in March and April of 2008.

Once it became clear, by late that summer, that the Galleon International cross-ownership and chairmanship were not going to come to anything, I stopped helping Alhadi fundraise. It had never been a formal role, and I never received any financial compensation, but the prosecutor was intent on blurring that picture. If he could convince the jury that I'd worked for Raj, he could make a stronger argument that Galleon's success was my success, and hence I had benefited from Raj's illegal trades.

Alhadi played his part in court, testifying that when we met, I'd been introduced to him as "the new chairman of Galleon International." It was infuriating. There were no contracts, no employment records, no payments, no evidence whatsoever to support the claim that I'd held this job, yet this guy was allowed to just tell the jury I had.

A battle was brewing as the second week came to a close: on Friday, the prosecutor was planning to call Heather Webster, a JP Morgan private banker who had advised my family and me during 2008. She had met with me at my home in April of 2008 to discuss my financial status and my estate planning. During the meeting, she had taken handwritten notes, which the prosecutor planned to introduce as evidence. In an after-hours conference, my lawyers fought to have her notes barred, arguing that they were not verbatim statements and would be misleading. In particular, we were concerned about the fact that she had jotted down a summary of my personal financial assets, and one line of her notes read: "Chairman, Galleon International, $1.3bn, owns 15% of it. Invests in long/short equity in Asia, entitled to performance fees."

Given the timing of that meeting, I'm sure I told her the Galleon role was a possibility, since at the time I believed it was. This meeting had taken place just weeks after my trip to the Middle East with Alhadi. But she had noted it as if it were already a fact, and she had no independent memory of the content of the discussion. The fact was, I never worked for Raj, nor did I own 15 percent of Galleon International. But the prosecutor planned to use Heather's notes to claim I did, and therefore further bolster the shaky benefit argument that they had begun to build with Alhadi's testimony.

While the government was arguing for the notes to be admitted, they wanted only the part that supported their story. On the next page were notes from our estate planning discussion, where Heather had written that I planned to give away 80 percent of my wealth to charity during my lifetime. These notes, Brodsky argued, were "potentially prejudicial and confusing," and he could not risk bringing them before the jury.

We didn't see how they could have it both ways. If they wanted to include the notes, they should include all of it. At least then we'd have an opportunity to counter the narrative of my greed. As Gary argued to the judge, my intention to give away my money was "thoroughly inconsistent with the notion that [I] would be doing an insider trading scheme for money." But in yet another baffling move against us, on the morning when Heather was due to take the stand, Rakoff decided to allow the Galleon notes, but barred the section on my plans for charitable giving.

It was a moment that seemed to sum up the trial. I couldn't believe it. What could possibly be the logic behind this double standard that on the one hand declared her inaccurate notes to be admissible evidence and on the other made an exception for one part that was both accurate and extremely relevant to my defense? If Heather was being deemed a credible witness, then didn't the jury deserve to hear that I had told her I planned to give away so much of my money—a fact that flew in the face of the whole thrust of the prosecutor's characterization of me? How was this not relevant, when the charges against me hinged on accusations of greed? Not wanting anyone to see the despair that I'm sure was written on my face, I clasped my head in my hands.

Anita was more demonstrative in her disgust, getting up and marching out of the courtroom. She did not return till after Heather's testimony was completed, but she didn't miss anything; the prosecutor got exactly what he wanted, and the most we could do on cross-examination was to highlight the incomplete and potentially inaccurate nature of the notes, and the complete absence of supporting memories. The one small advantage to having Heather on the stand was that it gave my lawyers a chance to offer in evidence the numerous emails from the summer and fall of 2008 that showed my frustrating quest to get information out of Raj about Voyager. As my personal banker, Heather had been privy to much of this, and we were able to elicit testimony that supported the story I'd be telling when I took the stand.

Well-Prepared Witnesses with Little to Say

Anita returned to the courtroom just in time for a new source of disgust: my former colleague Anil Kumar was taking the stand. She knew, like few others, the extent to which I'd gone out of my way to help Anil advance his career at the firm and support his family. She had graciously welcomed him and his wife to our home on a number of occasions. Now, he was repaying that generosity by testifying against me, even though he had no direct knowledge of the case. Indeed, my lawyers had tried hard to argue that he should not be called as a witness at all. Nowhere was he named as a co-conspirator, yet the prosecutor intended to elicit a description of Anil's crimes, including tips he'd given to Rajaratnam and his elaborate offshore payment arrangement.

Gary accused Brodsky of trying to retry the Rajaratnam case in the midst of my trial, since Anil had nothing to contribute to the evidence other than an implication of guilt by association. We also objected to a line of questioning that intended to claim that Anil violated McKinsey policy by "moonlighting" for Raj and that I was aware he was doing it, showing my disregard for the rules. In fact, McKinsey had no formal policy on that front, and I was unaware of the true nature of his arrangement with Raj, despite whatever impression the July 29 tape might have given. At least the judge agreed with us on blocking that particular line of questioning, but the rest of Anil's testimony was allowed to proceed. As he made his way to the witness stand, head bowed in an exaggerated show of deference to judge and jury, I turned and caught my wife's eye. She just shook her head.

Anil testified at length, although he had little of substance to say. Unlike the halting progress of the trial thus far, his testimony stood out for its full-sentence, even full-paragraph, answers, with relatively few interruptions from counsel. Listening to him spout off his rehearsed statements and play expert educator to the jury was its own kind of torture. His manner was obsequious and strangely childlike for a fifty-three-year-old self-confessed criminal—every answer was followed by "sir," he apologized repeatedly, and several times he referred to his crimes in terms reminiscent of a contrite schoolboy. "I had an understanding with Mr. Rajaratnam that I was doing bad things," he confessed, looking pained. As I was seated right in front of him, he had to try hard not to catch my eye, but he successfully managed to do so, even during sidebars.

The main thrust of the prosecutor's questions for Anil, as far as I could see, besides highlighting his guilt in order to tarnish me, was an attempt to pin the timing of my dispute with Rajaratnam at a much later date than when it actually occurred. Anil told the jury that he had heard about the Voyager losses in mid to late October 2008, which was indeed the time I'd learned the fund had gone to zero, but many months after my dispute with Raj over the redemptions had begun. Anil, however, claimed that I had discovered the redemptions only in early 2009 and had showed him the evidence at that time. This was simply untrue, and Anil had no basis for saying it, having never been involved with the issues surrounding the funds.

As I listened to Anil, my frustration with Ravi Trehan bubbled up for the hundredth time. He was the one person who could have credibly corrected this false narrative, since he had been the one who discovered the redemptions in early 2008 and brought them to my attention, and I'd had numerous conversations with him about my troubles contacting Raj, including the one on September 23, the day of the Buffett investment. Early on, he'd talked to my lawyers and confirmed the timeline, but recently, he'd simply stopped returning my lawyers' calls. I knew that somehow they'd gotten to him. The government even had his name on their list as a potential witness for the prosecution. If he'd been willing to take the stand in my defense, I'd have been less concerned by the stories Anil was telling. After all, the jury knew Anil was a collaborator, and my lawyers made sure to emphasize that during cross-examination, highlighting the fact that he'd had numerous meetings with the prosecutor to prepare, pointing out that his sentencing had been postponed until after my trial. (Later that summer, he would be given a noncustodial sentence of probation in recognition of what prosecutors described as his "extraordinary" cooperation.) There were numerous inconsistencies between Anil's current testimony and his previous depositions, as our cross-examination revealed. Surely the jury could not see him as a credible witness. But without Ravi I worried Anil's testimony would carry undue weight. And if Ravi testified for the prosecution, what might they have told him to say?

We were about to enter the trial's third week, and the government still had a long list of witnesses to call. The judge had promised the jury we'd be done in four weeks, but clearly most of that time would be used by the prosecution. After all, they still had their star witness to call, Lloyd Blankfein, and the judge had a prior engagement on Tuesday, so the court would not sit that day.

Arriving to great media fanfare on Monday afternoon, Blankfein seemed to enjoy the attention of the hushed courtroom and the deference of judge and counsel. Like Anil, he carefully avoided meeting my eyes.

As soon as Blankfein began to speak, it was clear that he'd been prepared. Very well prepared. (Some months later, when I saw the legal bills, for which I was deemed liable, my suspicions that he had been coached extensively in preparation for his testimony would be confirmed. While some such preparation is common and accepted practice, day after day spent with numerous very expensive lawyers seemed excessive.) Blankfein had nothing of substance to say, since he didn't remember any of the events in question. So how was the government to get him to confirm their story about the board meeting? To get around his complete lack of memories, the prosecutor carefully elicited testimony as to what his general practices and routines were with regard to things like informing board members about the bank's financial performance. For example, they wanted to show that I'd been given confidential information about the bank's earnings on various occasions, most notably in the October 23 call. Blankfein did not remember if he had done this, so he simply answered each question with a variation on "it was my general practice." After several objections, Gary, visibly frustrated, requested a sidebar.

"This man has no recollection of these things!" he exclaimed. "I can say that with greater certainty than I would in the normal course because we took his deposition."

I remembered that deposition all too well. It had taken place about three months earlier, in connection with the SEC case, and Gary had suggested that I sit in—he thought that my presence might soften the Goldman chief up a little and appeal to his humanity. That didn't play out so well, and I simply spent an acutely uncomfortable nine-plus hours listening to my former colleague verbally stumble around, contradict himself again and again, and essentially demonstrate that he had no clear memory of any of the events in question. Clearly that hadn't changed. He still had nothing to say, but now his expression of that nothing was polished and precise. Damn, I thought. We'd made an error of judgment in deposing him—we'd given the prosecution a preview of all the areas where they'd need to rehearse.

Gary persisted with the judge. "His memory is so bad he can't remember a specific thing about anything! This is taking habit evidence and really trying to substitute it for a witness who has absolutely no recollection of any of these matters, and yet it would be conveyed to the jury as if this guy actually remembers something."

Rakoff, however, after examining the witness himself for a few moments, ruled that "custom and practice" was admissible evidence. Blankfein was allowed to testify that it was his "practice" to always inform board members of the bank's estimated P&L, as well as projections as to where it was trending. He was also allowed to testify that it was his "practice" to "estimate off the estimate" or round numbers. These were both critical points with respect to the October 23 call. First, I knew he had not talked about earnings; the call had been about the leaked *Wall Street Journal* article about the layoffs. But if he maintained that it was his practice to always talk about earnings, and there were no minutes of the meeting, how could we disprove that? Second, the rounding of numbers mattered because the actual P&L from the previous day, October 22, was $1.75 per share. However, in the wiretapped call on October 24, Rajaratnam boasted he had heard Goldman was going to lose $2 a share. In my experience, those kinds of numbers would never be rounded up or down in board meetings—if we'd been told about earnings at all, it would have been the precise figure. But the government's story relied on that $2 per share detail. They had not been able to get this number out of Bill George, who had only testified that he remembered the bank was losing money. But they clearly hoped to get around that by having Blankfein testify that rounding up was his "practice."

Besides these legal contortions, which Rakoff kept allowing, there was another frustrating aspect of Blankfein's testimony. The prosecutor asked him about my 2008 job offer from KKR and even went so far as to ask about my expected compensation—something we had never discussed and that was certainly not relevant to the case at hand. Before my lawyers could object, he casually answered, "Five," meaning five million. My jaw dropped. Not only was it an incorrect figure, but it served to cement the image of me as financially motivated. The belated objection was sustained, but the damage was done. On cross-examination, Gary sought to reframe my withdrawn resignation as an expression of loyalty to the bank, but I worried that the exaggerated figure would stick in the jury's minds.

As the long day came to an end, the judge reminded the jury that tomorrow, Tuesday, would be a day off and that Blankfein's testimony would continue on Thursday morning to accommodate his commitment to attend his daughter's high school graduation on Wednesday. This rankled a little, as I remembered Aditi's missed graduation during the first week of the trial. While he celebrated his daughter, we sat through a day of testimony that the judge described as "excruciating"—a Galleon analyst who identified emails and phone numbers; McKinsey's associate general counsel, who had assisted in document production to the USAO; a Goldman technology forensics officer; and a guy from the FBI who had prepared the government's summary charts. Along with each witness came yet another flood of documents. The only positive that stood out for me was that in cross-examining the Galleon analyst we were able to bring into evidence the statements from the Voyager fund. What we'd discovered was that Rajaratnam kept two sets of books—one showing his redemptions and the other set showing no record of them.

In cross-examining Blankfein on Thursday morning, Gary made a point to emphasize the Goldman chief's lack of specific memories of any of the events in question. He was also able to show documentary evidence that much of the information that was being touted as confidential—for example, Goldman's consideration of buying a commercial bank in the summer of 2008—was in fact discussed by the bank with industry analysts and reported on in the media.

Then he zeroed in on the October 23, 2008, incident. He showed the jury the front-page *Wall Street Journal* article from that day reporting that Goldman was about to lay off 10 percent of its workforce. He showed email evidence that the board meeting had been called that very morning, right after the publication of the article.

Blankfein, incredibly, claimed not to remember the *Wall Street Journal* article. I found this hard to believe. Those layoffs had affected more than three thousand people, and those people had not been informed that they were about to lose their jobs until they read it in the papers. Such a corporate faux pas should have made a much greater impression in a CEO's memory than a couple of dollars' movement in the stock price. Yet when Gary inquired about it, Blankfein had no answer. We played a voicemail announcement that he had issued to the firm that day in response to the article, expressing his regret about the leak, and at least he had to admit that this was the kind of information he would have wanted to bring to the attention of his board, especially given that just a week earlier he had told the board the bank was looking to increase its staff (a fact he also claimed not to remember).

Gary also sought to highlight for the jury that Goldman had received TARP funding from the government during the financial crisis, a fact that should have raised eyebrows regarding their impartiality. And he drew attention to the unusual degree of preparation Blankfein had received, which had included officials from the USAO not only sitting in but taking the lead when he testified at the SEC—a highly unusual practice. Even the judge acknowledged this, ruling in our favor for once that we could continue that line of questioning as relevant to bias.

At one point, when Blankfein was talking about making calls to board members, Gary saw an opportunity he couldn't resist.

"Sometimes, in light of your job, you find yourself going from one meeting to another?" he asked.

"Yes," Blankfein replied.

"And while you're in meetings, you often get phone calls, right?"

"Yes."

After carefully laying his foundation, Gary went for the punchline: "So like many busy executives, when you finish a meeting, you often try to use that time to return your phone calls the minute you walk out of a meeting, right?" When Blankfein replied affirmatively, Gary added one last question: "Those phone calls don't necessarily have anything to do with anything that was discussed in the meeting you were just in, correct?"

"Yes," Blankfein replied. Gary turned back to look at me, an expression of triumph on his face. I nodded and attempted a small smile, but I was under no illusions that scoring this small point would count for much in the midst of a testimony that for the most part had played according to the prosecutor's plan.

Privately, I wondered what had incentivized Blankfein to dedicate so much time to the case. I knew him well enough to believe that there must have been something in it for him or for the bank. In the years to come, as Goldman remained seemingly untouchable amid the ongoing recriminations following the financial crisis, my questions only persisted.

By the time the government finally rested its case, on Friday, June 8, 2012, my morale had weakened considerably. What I had sat through was not just three weeks of testimony—it was the grand finale of a several-year campaign to blacken my character and rewrite history. Its momentum felt inexorable. While my defense team had occasionally scored a point or raised questions about the credibility of a witness, overall we seemed powerless to slow the tide. It was going to be up to me to tell the real story and convince the jury I was telling the truth. No one else could tell it for me.

15

Unsung

The song that I came to sing remains unsung to this day.
I have spent my days in stringing and in unstringing my instrument.
The time has not come true, the words have not been rightly set;
only there is the agony of wishing in my heart.

—Rabindranath Tagore, *Gitanjali*, 13

New York City, June 8, 2012

"Why would I give up the chance to defend myself? I'm the only one who can tell my story."

It was Friday night, after the prosecution had rested its case, and my lawyers had spent the past few hours trying to convince me that I should not take the witness stand on Monday as I had planned. I knew they had reservations, but I'd thought it was decided.

Gary patiently explained his concerns again. Most people in my position didn't testify because it's too risky. The prosecutor would like nothing more than to get a chance to cross-examine me. I could open myself up to lines of questioning that I didn't know how to handle. I might incriminate myself without even knowing it. If I testified and the jury found me guilty anyway, I might get a much longer sentence.

I understood the danger but felt confident that I could handle whatever questions the prosecutor would have. And in my mind, the risks were outweighed by the potential benefit. I knew I was a persuasive speaker, and I was confident in my story. No one else could explain to the jury why the prosecutor's carefully constructed narrative made no sense. Yes, I knew that my taking the stand would shift the focus of the trial. The case would come down to whether or not the jury believed me, rather than whether or not the prosecution had provided adequate proof of guilt. But having just sat through three weeks of prosecutorial storytelling, I was more convinced than ever that the true burden rested on me. I needed to tell a better story.

The judge and the prosecutor were asking for a firm decision by the following day. Gary had told them it was "highly likely" I would take the stand, but, in fact, he still hoped to change my mind. When I remained adamant, he had suggested we call my wife and daughters and get them to weigh in. I'd already had this conversation with all of them, numerous times, so I didn't see how that would change anything. They had all told me their feelings on the matter, but they knew it was ultimately a decision I had to make. But finally, I suggested to Gary, "You call and speak to them. Don't tell them I'm here. Maybe they will say more, or I will hear them differently if they are talking to someone else."

"It's too risky." Anita's voice cracked with emotion. "I just don't want to see him put himself through that. Who knows what they'll throw at him during cross-examination, or how they'll try to drag his name through the mud. They've done enough harm already. Besides, it's too late for it to make a difference now. And if he testifies and loses, the sentence will be harsher." She paused, silent for a moment. "He always thinks it will be different for him. He really thinks that just because he's telling the truth, the jury will believe him. You'd think he would have learned by now that people believe what they want to believe!"

As I listened, silently, I looked around Gary's office. It was a modest office for someone of his stature, but the view was iconic: the Chrysler

Building on one side, the Empire State on the other. One wall was covered with framed courtroom sketches from the firm's biggest cases. Would a scene from my trial be up there one day? I wondered. I tried to focus on the dilemma at hand as if for the first time. Anita's instincts had been accurate so many times. She'd been right about Goldman, right about Rajaratnam, right about Anil. I hadn't listened to her then, and look where I had ended up. Was I making a similar mistake? I could hear the fear in her voice, and I hated to be the cause of it.

Sonu, who had been the most involved in the legal process, understood my desire to tell my story, but, as a law school graduate herself, she also respected the good sense of the lawyers' advice. My eldest daughter has one of the clearest minds I've ever encountered, with a keen sense of how to balance risk and caution. Her wise counsel had helped me make many important decisions over the years. If she was leaning against it, perhaps I should listen. Megha, too, was hesitant, the lawyers' caution clearly swaying her. My younger daughters were not on the call, and I was glad they weren't put in this difficult position. Ultimately, it was my choice to make. But the decision I made would affect all of them.

I'd never been one to shy away from risk or succumb to fear. I'd trusted my own instincts, and, for the most part, they'd served me well. But not always, I reminded myself. I'd made serious mistakes in trusting people like Rajaratnam and Anil. I'd believed that things would work out for the best, that people would do the right thing. And they didn't. Was I making the same error in taking the stand? Was I being naive in thinking that truth would be heard? If there was any lesson to be learned from the events of the past two years, it was that justice did not always prevail. Maybe the defensive stance that my lawyers and family were advocating was a sensible one.

I felt more conflicted than I had over any decision in my life to that point. Throughout this process, I'd been sure of my intention to testify, despite my lawyers' and my family's reservations. But now I was questioning my own certainty, and my usually optimistic outlook was beaten down by three long weeks in court. I'd always been the strategist, the chess player with his eye on the long game, the one to whom business titans and world leaders turned when they needed a clear-eyed view. Now, my vision had narrowed to the step in front of me. I could no longer see the way forward. A passage from the Bhagavad Gita came to mind, where Arjuna, the warrior, is desperately torn over the decision to engage in a great battle. "My will is paralyzed, and I am utterly confused," he says, imploring his charioteer and teacher, Lord Krishna, "Tell me which is the better path for me?"[1] I wished there were a wise teacher to whom I could turn for advice in this moment.

After my lawyers hung up the phone and said goodnight, I lingered in the office, hoping some clarity would come. Finally, still tormented by indecision, I got in my car to drive home. As the brightly lit city streets gave way to the darkened hills of Connecticut, a strange sense of resignation came over me. I was tired and defeated. I did not have the energy or confidence in myself to go against the advice of my lawyers, my wife, and my daughters. By the time I pulled into the driveway, my decision was made, although it did not feel like I was the one who had made it. I would not take the stand.

Regret

To this day, that decision is my greatest regret. Without my testimony, our defense was considerably diminished. After all, how can you demonstrate that you did not do something? How can you prove a negative? We were overly reliant on character witnesses, and the judge had severely curtailed the number we could call and curbed what they could say. He even ruled that my lawyers could not use the term "integrity" in examining character witnesses, because it was "too vague." Perhaps, in this case, he was right, I mused. Integrity was a virtue that I'd striven for my whole life, but what did it really mean? Did it demonstrate integrity to miss the fact that one's business associates were involved in illegal activity? Could one be said to have integrity if one was too busy to pay close enough attention to critical financial details and ended up being cheated? I had lived a full life and tried to do good in the world, but I had not always achieved balance or integration between my many commitments.

I felt honored by the presence of the witnesses we did call and appreciative of their unshaken faith in my honesty and their willingness to state it in public. At least one of them, I knew, had been pressured not to take the stand. Pramath Sinha, ISB's first dean, had received an unexpected and intimidating call from an FBI detective one day during the trial. He was asked a series of interrogative questions, including queries about whether he had been involved with Rajaratnam or used his office. Shaken, he hung up the phone only to find a series of missed calls from his niece, who told him the FBI had called her home and spoken to his elderly mother, who had been extremely confused. When my lawyers heard this story, they confirmed that such incidents were all too common.

Ajit Jain testified via video, telling the jury about the lunch we'd had together in January 2009 when I'd told him about the Voyager situation and how Raj had "swindled or cheated" me. It had stood out in his memory because I was clearly so agitated and it was unusual for me to talk to him about my investments. His testimony powerfully supported the argument that I was furious at Rajaratnam for his duplicity regarding the Voyager investment. Moreover, the idea that I would discuss my relationship with Rajaratnam with a senior Berkshire Hathaway executive if I had, as alleged, been involved in an insider trading transaction relating to Berkshire's investment in Goldman Sachs was entirely nonsensical. I knew that the lawyers at Berkshire Hathaway had strongly discouraged Ajit from testifying, so it meant a lot to me that he went ahead. Barry Bloom, former dean of the Harvard School of Public Health; Richard Feacham, founding director of the Global Fund; Ashok Alexander, another McKinsey partner who had served with me on the Avahan board and worked for the Gates Foundation;

and Anil Sood, my old friend from elementary school who worked at the World Bank—each of these men had taken time out of their busy schedules to testify in my defense and I was deeply grateful.

Again and again, the prosecutor sought to ensure that not one disease would be mentioned, which was absurd, since global health was the context in which several of these witnesses knew me. Indeed, those who'd worked with me at the Global Fund could not even state the organization's name without mentioning three diseases. As a result of the numerous constraints, each of these illustrious people was given only a few minutes on the stand—a travesty in my mind, when hours and hours had been dedicated to the testimony of those with nothing more to offer than the authentication of phone numbers and trading records. But such was the judge's ruling.

Character aside, my defense depended on two essential points: the timing of the Voyager dispute, which undermined the idea that I would be doing Raj any favors; and the Loeb evidence, showing that Raj had an alternative Goldman source who had been caught tipping him on several occasions about other companies. We needed at least one of these arguments to plant reasonable doubt in the minds of the jurors.

The problem was, we had very little evidence to show for the Voyager dispute. Ravi, the one person who could have corroborated the story, including the critical details of timing, had let me down. We couldn't risk subpoenaing him, because he'd clearly switched his loyalties and we couldn't trust him to simply tell the truth. At least he had not ended up testifying for the prosecution, but that was cold comfort. My lawyers decided against calling Renee, my secretary, because she did not have specific memories of the incidents in question, and she was clearly terrified at the thought of being subjected to cross-examination. We had been hoping to call the lawyer with whom I'd discussed possibly suing Rajaratnam in 2008, but the judge ruled against it on a technicality. That just left Greg Orman, my financial advisor. His testimony could offer validation of my claim that the Voyager dispute had begun in mid-2008, although he had not been as close to the situation as Ravi. During cross-examinations, we'd managed to bring into evidence much of the email correspondence relating to JP Morgan's document requests, as well as the dual statements, and we intended to play the October 2, 2008, wiretapped call between Rajaratnam and his lieutenant Sanjay Santhanam, in which Rajaratnam says, "I hope Rajat is a big boy," and admits, "I didn't tell him I took that equity out." But we needed an authoritative voice to counter the government witnesses who had set the date in 2009. After much discussion, we'd decided that Sonu would take the stand and testify as to the conversation we'd had about Rajaratnam's duplicity on her birthday in September 2008. The lawyers had been hesitant, but she'd insisted she wanted to do it. Would it be enough? I didn't know.

I was a little more hopeful about the Loeb defense—if the judge allowed it to go ahead. We intended to play the two wiretapped conversations between Loeb and Rajaratnam, as well as show numerous emails in which Loeb was trying to get Raj to call him urgently. We also had evidence of Loeb's ongoing relationship with Adam Smith, the Galleon trader who had pleaded guilty to insider trading and testified at the Rajaratnam trial. Smith had been Loeb's principal contact. We had subpoenaed Loeb to appear as a witness. However, Brodsky, predictably, was trying to bar the Loeb tapes and other evidence. The judge had yet to rule on the matter.

Meanwhile, we called a handful of other witnesses. Richard Schutte, the former Galleon COO, testified about the legitimate sources of information that influenced how Galleon made investment decisions, and we showed documents that included advice to buy Goldman based on analyst predictions. Schutte's testimony also highlighted the close relationship between Galleon and Goldman and the amount Galleon was paying Goldman annually—revenue that we knew had a bearing on Loeb's compensation. Schutte also testified that he had been involved in almost every personnel decision at Galleon during the time in question, and to his knowledge I had never been chairman of Galleon International.

Suprotik Basu, the young executive from the World Bank who'd been Ray Chambers's right-hand man, was our next witness. He had been present during many of my meetings on September 23, 2008, since he and I had been working intensely on the malaria initiative. While he had not been in the room when I was on the Goldman board call or when I called Raj, we had hoped he could testify to the more important matters that were occupying my attention that day. However, he would have to do so without mentioning malaria too often. He at least was able to confirm my phone habits: "My picture of him is with an earpiece in his ear constantly, doing different phone calls between meetings."

A strange mix of pride and shame overwhelmed me as Sonu took the witness stand, so poised and articulate. I was grateful she'd been willing to do this, but it should have been me up there, not her. My eldest daughter has tremendous courage and integrity, and I often think of her as my moral compass. I had not been joking when I told the several hundred assembled guests at her wedding that when faced with difficult decisions, I often ask myself, what would Sonu do? But now she was doing the thing I had chosen not to do. Of course, it was not exactly equivalent—her testimony carried far less risk. Nevertheless, as I listened to her answering the prosecutor's questions, for the hundredth time that day I doubted my decision not to take the stand.

Sonu recounted the weekend of her thirtieth birthday, a few days before the Buffett deal in September 2008, when she came home to find me distraught over the revelation of Rajaratnam's duplicity and I told her the whole story in detail, sitting in the library. Her testimony about this helped to establish the critical dates, but I was not sure it would be enough. Would the jury believe her over Anil? In his cross-examination, Brodsky asked only two questions.

"Ma'am, do you love your father?"

"Yes, I do," Sonu replied.

"You would do what you could to help your father?"

"I would do many things to help my father," she replied, her composure unruffled. "I would not lie, though, on the stand."

After Sonu's testimony was adjourned for the night, the battle over the Loeb evidence came to a head. I was not present for this conference—feeling helpless and exhausted, I waived my right to appear and went home to be with my family. I was losing the will to fight—and what could I do anyway but sit silently while every door to the truth was closed in front of us? In my absence, one more was slammed shut: in a final blow to our already weakened defenses, the judge made a ruling that we could not present the Loeb evidence, dismissing it as "replete with inadmissible hearsay" and likely to "create endless confusion on the part of the jury."

Sonu completed her testimony, though severely curtailed by the prosecutor's multiple objections, and we called our final character witness, Todd Summers, who had worked with me at the Global Fund. He was followed by James Roth, a client relations guy from Goldman Sachs, who briefly testified about how he prepared Goldman president Gary Cohn for his meeting with Rajaratnam in the summer of 2008, and finally we called an associate from the law firm who had assisted in preparing our summary charts and would testify to their accuracy and the methodology used to prepare them. At this point, it all felt like an afterthought—a pointless prolonging of our severely truncated case. We had no more substantive witnesses to call. My lawyers had decided not to call Greg Orman, feeling that we'd already brought into evidence all the information he would have testified to, and it wasn't worth giving the prosecution the opportunity to cross-examine him. The last defense exhibit was the tape of Rajaratnam telling his lieutenant, "I hope Rajat is a big boy," and admitting he never told me he took money out of Voyager. And then we were done. The defense rested its case—which to me barely felt like a defense at all.

I sat there, numb. Could this really be it? I felt these disjointed fragments weren't enough. I wanted to leap up and tell the judge I'd changed my mind, I wanted to tell my story. How could the jury be expected to construct a convincing alternative to the government's narrative from a couple of guys talking about yet more trading records and phone numbers, my daughter recounting one conversation, and a handful of people testifying that they knew me to be honest but had no direct knowledge of the events in the case? But it was too late. The jury was excused, and the judge suggested that after a short break the lawyers could raise their objections to the instructions he intended to give to the jury the next day.

I'd had enough. I simply didn't have it in me to sit through any more arguments over the finer points of the law. "Can I leave?" I asked Gary. After one look at my face, he nodded. "I'll ask the judge to excuse you."

The following day was dedicated to the summations, or closing arguments. They did indeed seem to sum up the whole trial, not just in content but in spirit. Mr. Tarlowe, speaking for the government, was eloquent and impassioned. He told their version of the story with great dramatic flair, evoking the chaos of the financial crisis, the now-familiar story of the Buffett deal, and so on. Accompanying his speech were dozens of detailed charts in which they displayed the cherry-picked selection of calls, trading records, emails, and so on that they claimed revealed a "pattern." We had argued for the inadmissibility of these charts on multiple grounds, but the judge had allowed them in. Tarlowe asserted that the only reason I received no payment for my alleged tips was that Galleon lost money that year, and my compensation for the chairman job (which I never held) was tied to the fund's performance.

It was a good story. Not a true story, but a convincing one nonetheless. When our turn came, Gary reiterated many of the themes from his opening statements, referencing the trial evidence supporting those themes: the lack of hard evidence, the complete absence of trading or financial benefit on my part, my attempted resignation from the Goldman board, and of course the Voyager dispute. He accused the government of having resorted to "one of the oldest prosecutorial tricks"—rolling out a parade of witnesses to "bamboozle people into thinking something was proven when it wasn't"—and appealed to the jury not to be fooled. But without me telling a cohesive alternative story, could the jury really be expected to see the prosecutor's case for the smoke and mirrors it was?

I found that even I couldn't follow the narrative—and I had lived it. I had a sense, that day, of being almost outside of myself, observing the proceedings in the courtroom from a great distance. It was like a dream in which I could see events happening but was powerless to act or contribute in any way. I could barely hear Gary's words, or those of Brodsky as he got up to give his rebuttal—until one phrase, toward the end of Brodsky's speech, cut through my trance-like state.

"To believe the defense team, you have to believe that Mr. Gupta is one of the unluckiest men in the world. You have to believe he is a victim of these incredible incriminating circumstances happening to him again and again." He went on, elaborating on his theme, but I was stuck on the phrase. The unluckiest man in the world? It certainly felt that way. Was it bad luck? Or was it simply my destiny? It was too late to take the stand and attempt to make sense of it to the jury. But how was I to make sense of it all to myself?

The next day, the judge charged the jury, and deliberations began. Now, all we could do was wait. It was Megha's thirtieth birthday, and though none of us felt like celebrating, I insisted we go to a restaurant for dinner. I tried to focus my attention on my daughter, recalling how proud I was of her independent spirit, her creativity, and her dedication to making a career as an artist, despite numerous setbacks. But the look on her face made it difficult to forget. "Don't worry, Baba," she said, but clearly she was not taking her own advice. "I'll be alright, baby," I told her. "Are you alright?" Megha and I have a close bond that goes back to her earliest days. Anita always says that our second daughter, who was a colicky baby, preferred me to comfort her, and I was very successful in calming her. I wished I could do so now.

There was nothing to be gained from sitting around the apartment thinking about the outcome of the trial. *Do your best and don't be attached to the outcome of your actions.* Never in my life had my father's creed been put to a greater test. Could I remain unattached to the outcome of this trial, when it meant so much for my family and my future? Could I maintain the equanimity of the karma yogi as twelve strangers decided my fate? Could I let go of the feeling that I had been treated unfairly? And above all, could I put down my regrets? This last one was the hardest. After all, it is one thing to be detached from outcomes when one knows one has done the right thing to the fullest of one's abilities. But I could not silence the voice in my head that told me I hadn't done everything I could have done. I hadn't taken the stand. Maybe it would not have changed the ultimate outcome of the trial, whatever it would be, but at least it would have allowed me to feel spiritually at peace.

The Verdict

"The jury has reached a verdict."

Word spread fast through the cafeteria on the second floor of the courthouse. I was playing cards with two of my daughters and looked up in surprise. No one had expected it to come so quickly. How could they possibly have weighed up the enormous volume of evidence in such a short time? The jury at Rajaratnam's trial had taken two weeks to reach a verdict, and they'd had concrete evidence to consider! I instinctively felt that this didn't bode well, but I tried to keep those fears to myself. Carefully, I gathered up the cards and put them in their box. I looked around for Sonu, who had gone to catch up on some work, anticipating a much longer jury deliberation. She was nowhere to be seen. We all stood up, silent, and I hugged each of the girls. The crowd parted and people stepped back to allow my family to take the elevator alone. For thirty seconds, it was just us, sealed off from the world. I asked my daughters, "Are you okay?" What was unsaid, but understood, was that if they were okay, I would be okay.

We took our seats in silence, and Sonu came hurrying in—she'd been in a Starbucks down the street and noticed that the gathered throng of journalists at the next table had suddenly got up to leave, indicating that something was happening back at the courthouse. One of them told her there was a verdict. We all stood as the jury filed in. I noticed immediately that they were not looking at me, another worrying sign. As we waited for the verdict to be read, I glanced back and saw that the girls were sitting two on either side of their mother, as if to protect her. My overwhelming feeling was pain at having let them down. The events of the past few weeks swam before my eyes. All the rulings that went against us, the truncated defense, the choice to stay silent and not take the stand. It was too late now—none of it mattered. It was done. The jury foreman stood, and the courtroom fell silent.

"Has the jury reached a verdict?"

The foreman replied that they had, and the clerk read aloud the first of the substantive counts (Count 2), relating to March 2007. "Guilty or not guilty?"

"Not guilty."

For a moment, there was pure relief. I heard Anita gasp behind me, but before I could even turn to her, my hopes were dashed by a string of "guilty" verdicts on Counts 3, 4, and 5, as well as Count 1, the conspiracy charge. I was acquitted on Count 6 as well (the one relating to the 2009 P&G earnings), but this was small comfort. The repeated word "guilty" mingled with the loud sobs of my youngest daughter, and all I could think of was my family. I went to them and gathered them all into a long hug. The courtroom fell silent. When I looked up, I saw tears in the eyes of many of the jurors. I believe they did not want to find me guilty; they simply had not been given a good enough reason not to.

16

360°

All the great utterances of man have to be judged not by the letter but by the spirit—the spirit which unfolds itself with the growth of life in history.

—Rabindranath Tagore, *Sadhana*

July 2012

The months following the trial were a strange limbo, as I awaited my sentencing. I tried to keep busy, spend quality time with my daughters and grandchildren, and avoid the pointless torment of replaying my trial and my decision not to testify.

I was also dealing with new feelings of betrayal. My friend and NSR partner Parag Saxena had initially been very supportive, assuring me that he never wanted to benefit from my misfortune. I had resigned from my chairmanship and offered to pay all additional costs incurred as a result of bringing on new senior advisors. The understanding was that my family would retain our ownership, but I would pay for the incremental costs. Now, right after the verdict, he appeared to turn on us, trying to push me out of the fund and offering me cents on the dollar for our ownership. Without so much as a conversation, he sent me a legal letter giving me twenty-four hours to respond or lose the shares altogether. I fought back and refused to accept such an unfair offer. I was grateful for the support of my childhood best friend, Anil Sood, who stepped up to join the NSR board and protect my interests.

Parag had no legal basis for taking away our ownership—it felt like a bullying tactic, a calculation that I would give in at my most vulnerable moment. He knew very well that the fund would not have existed without me, as I had raised almost all of its $1.4 billion. After he realized he could not simply take our ownership for nothing, he started a multi-pronged strategy to take control. He attempted to push out the director appointed by our family and used management funds to pay himself, against the partnership agreement and without the permission of the directors. I have unsuccessfully tried many times to settle the matter amicably, even offering him a larger portion of the overall gain. On a personal level, this was one of the most painful and unexpected chapters of the entire story. I could barely summon the emotional resources to deal with it after the ordeal of the trial, but I could not allow myself to just roll over and accept this further injustice.

Seeing me struggling with feelings of depression and helplessness, Sonu suggested one day that I come to Boston for a few weeks and help her build a new playroom for my three-year-old twin granddaughters, Meera and Nisa. I willingly threw myself into the project, happy that it gave me extra time with the children, who were a beacon of sanity in those dark days. But never far from my mind was the fact that I might never get to play with those little girls in that new playroom. If I were sentenced to a long prison term, they could be teenagers before I got out.

Those months were also a time for reflecting on my life through an unexpected lens. In corporate settings, we often conduct what's known as a 360-degree feedback process, where people get the chance to see themselves through the eyes of their peers, their subordinates, and their supervisors. At McKinsey, this was something every partner did regularly. Now, I found myself in the midst of an extraordinary

360-degree review of my own life and legacy, thanks to hundreds of letters that were written to the judge by my friends, family, and colleagues.

During the trial, thanks to Judge Rakoff's "Mother Teresa" ruling, very few mentions were made of my philanthropic work, and the jury was instructed not to be swayed by my reputation. When it came to sentencing, however, it was quite a different story. Rakoff was permitted to take into account the "history and characteristics of the defendant." So my lawyers encouraged me to solicit letters to the judge from my family, friends, and colleagues, attesting to my good character and contributions to society. I reached out to everyone I could think of, besides those in politics for whom it could be too sensitive. I could not possibly have anticipated the outpouring of response. Some volunteered before I had even asked, including Bill Gates and Miles White, CEO of Abbott, one of the leading pharma companies. Others, who felt unable to write for one reason or another, called me personally to explain and express their support, including President Clinton and Larry Summers.

One letter that particularly touched me came from Peter Dolan, former CEO of Bristol Myers-Squibb, who I'd served at McKinsey. When he abruptly exited the CEO role, he recalled in the letter, he could count on one hand the number of senior people in business who reached out to him, but I was one of them. All these years later, that gesture meant so much to him that he'd been one of the first to reach out to me when news of the case broke and I too found myself deserted by many former friends. Another letter that moved and humbled me was one of the longest—five full pages penned by an eighty-plus-year-old man, K.P. Singh, India's largest real estate developer, detailing our many humanitarian efforts together and the ways in which I had inspired him.

As I read these letters, I felt both embarrassed and reassured, and, above all, enormously grateful. Whatever fate had in store for me, I'd already had so many opportunities to do good in the world, and so many people were testifying that their lives were better as a result. Thanks to the work of organizations like the Global Fund, hundreds of thousands—perhaps even millions—of lives had been saved. Judge Rakoff had mocked me in the courtroom, joking that malaria still existed, so therefore my work could not have been successful. But the truth was, as I'd always said, if even one life was saved as a result of my work, I would feel I had lived a life worth living. This was what mattered—that I'd done my best. It was a poignant experience to review my life and legacy in this way, when so much of it had now been compromised, but I was grateful.

My family's letters, in particular, were bittersweet. My daughters shared favorite memories that brought a smile to my face. Early morning math coaching with Sonu, for which she rightly guessed I had gotten up even earlier than her in order to refresh my rusty memory on the rules of trigonometry. Endless card games with Kushy. Supervising their chores ("Yes, it is possible to have a Plan of Action for cleaning one's room," Megha joked, noting that my daughters' adulthood "has not diminished his belief that he is the best person to tackle any obstacle, major or minor, that comes our way."). Comforting Aditi and helping her to rearrange her apartment so it would feel like her own again after a boyfriend moved out.

I felt immense pride at their eloquence, even as I was embarrassed by their descriptions of my values and virtues, and the way in which I'd been a role model in their lives. They also saw, perhaps more clearly than anyone, that the very same character traits that had made me successful and respected were also the weaknesses that had left me vulnerable to my fate.

"He can seem at times to have a naïve belief in people," Sonu wrote, "which is why, I think, he has been so successful in his career and in his philanthropic work." What she did not write, but I knew she knew, is that it was that very same belief that had left me blind to the duplicity of the colleagues who had betrayed me. Anita spoke to this too. "He could never imagine that his friends or business associates could be involved in unlawful activities," she wrote. "Rajat has always trusted people and seen only the good in them. I am much more cynical or just more realistic about people and motives and have tried in vain to moderate his 'great guy' and 'good friend' descriptions."

She bemoaned my tendency to give money to "everybody with a hard luck story" and recalled our financial advisor's dismay at some of my well-meaning investments in friends' and family's businesses. Anita was also honest about my overcommitment: "I tried often to get him to slow down but there was always one more organization or one more group of people who needed help," she wrote. "Rajat Gupta never learned to say no." She was right. And though she didn't say it, I knew she knew that my inability to say no had left me stretched too thin, unable to deal with issues like the Voyager affair in a timely manner. Had I brought that to a head sooner, would any of this have happened? Or would Raj and I have parted ways before any of those calls took place? If I had taken Anita's advice and gracefully embraced retirement, never gotten into business with Raj, or stood firm in my resignation to Goldman, there's no doubt our lives would have taken a completely different course. "I try very hard, Your Honor, to emulate my husband," Anita had written, but I was left feeling that I should have been the one emulating her.

As each of my loved ones expressed to the judge their fear and sadness at the thought of losing me to imprisonment, my eyes overflowed with tears. I could not help but think back to the years of busyness and ask myself, over and over, had I missed precious opportunities to be with my family—the family I might now be parted from for years?

"Must Not One Judge the Man as a Whole?"

The day of the sentencing, October 24, fell just two days short of the anniversary of my arrest. Diwali was later that year, but it turned out that the hearing coincided with another Hindu festival, Dussehra, which celebrates the triumph of the god Rama over the ten-headed demon king Ravana, who abducted his wife. The symbolic meaning of the festival is the victory of good over evil. I don't know if Bharara had any role in scheduling, but I wondered if he found some satisfaction in it nonetheless.

Stepping into that all-too-familiar dark, wood-paneled courtroom, all the feelings of the trial flooded back—the frustration, the helplessness, the tormented indecision, the instant regret, the worry, the disbelief, the moments of hope, and the eventual despair. The past few months, it had begun to feel like a bad dream; now it became my reality once again. This room had been the page on which my story had been rewritten, and the law gave its stamp of approval to a false narrative. Now, Judge Rakoff would add another chapter to this tale, and I would be forced to live it. Was I to spend the next decade of my life behind bars, as the government was recommending, or would he set a "noncustodial sentence," as my lawyers had proposed, consisting of community service in some needy part of the world, such as Rwanda. My experience of Rakoff up to this point did not give me much hope that the saga would have a happy ending.

Judge Rakoff surprised me, however. Addressing the packed courtroom, he acknowledged that the volume and nature of correspondence he had received was unprecedented in his judicial experience. "The Court can say without exaggeration that it has never encountered a defendant whose prior history suggests such an extraordinary devotion, not only to humanity writ large, but also to individual human beings in their times of need," he declared.

It was incongruous to hear those words coming from the mouth of the same judge who had ruled against me, again and again, just a few months earlier. "On this day of judgment," he asked rhetorically, "must not one judge the man as a whole?" And yet that was precisely what he had refused to allow the jury to do at the trial. Yes, I understood that the rules governing sentencing were different than those governing evidence in a jury trial. But this change of tone seemed like more than that. Was Rakoff acknowledging, in some small way, the unfairness of the "cropped picture" to which I'd been reduced in his courtroom? Was he hinting that in his attempts to protect the impartiality of the process, he might have gone too far?

The letters certainly filled out that picture. The total number topped four hundred, and their authors ranged from luminaries like Bill Gates and Kofi Annan to ordinary people like my long-time barber, my personal trainer, and even my uncle's household servant in India, who had known me for four decades and took the time to pen a handwritten letter. Dozens of business colleagues and clients from every phase of my life had written, as well as classmates from every school I'd attended, extended family, friends, fellow humanitarians, school friends of my daughters, even Aman Kumar, son of my colleague-turned-government-collaborator Anil Kumar, who considered me an honorary "uncle." I was particularly touched by how many McKinsey partners wrote letters of support, despite the fact that (as I'd heard through the grapevine) the firm had discouraged people from doing so.

The attention given to my charitable works was not the only novelty in Rakoff's courtroom that day. After sitting in silence through the four weeks of the trial, the sentencing hearing was the first time my voice would be heard. My lawyers had advised me that I would have an opportunity to address the judge, and I had decided to take it. Preparing my statement had been a challenge, however, since I could not bring myself to express contrition or apologize for crimes I had not committed, no matter what the verdict said. It was important, however, that I not appear to be challenging the verdict, since that would hardly be likely to sway the judge in my favor. Draft after draft, I struggled to find an authentic expression. In the end, I made a list of all the things I did feel sorry for.

Most important was the impact on my family and friends. It took no pretense to express my regret and pain at the suffering I had caused them. Just thinking about Anita's helpless rage and my daughters' brave efforts to be strong for me brought tears to my eyes. Their happiness meant more to me than anything else, and the devastation they had endured cut the deepest. I felt that over the past few years I had failed in what I considered my most important mission in life: to be a source of strength for them. Aditi had spoken to this in her letter:

"When I find myself now worrying about what it would be like to lose my father to a prison sentence, the truth of the matter is that much of what I depended on I have lost already. When I see my father quiet or stressed the last thing I feel I can do is ask him for help or advice. Knowing that his greatest priority is for me to be happy, I hesitate to ever tell him that I'm not. These lies of omission have escalated over time, as I've waited for a 'better time' to burden him with my problems, and that 'better time' has not come." In closing, she acknowledged to the judge that many people were focused on the good work I could continue to do in the world, but her appeal was of a different nature. "I ask you for leniency for selfish reasons. I depend on my father. My relationship with him has already changed drastically, and I cannot bear the thought of losing any more of him." Recalling her words, I knew I could speak wholeheartedly to my pain and regret in that regard.

I could also say, unreservedly, that I felt terrible about the burden of negative attention that I had brought to the institutions that were dear to me, including McKinsey and the many nonprofits I advised. In particular, the organizations I'd founded—ISB, PHFI, and AIF—which were like children to me.

As for the verdict, I could not say that I accepted it, since I knew it to represent an untruth. But I believed in destiny, and I knew that in those moments when we cannot see the reasoning behind the whims of fate, acceptance is a virtue. The great sages of my Indian heritage had cultivated equanimity and detachment in the face of life's challenges, and I strove to emulate them by accepting what had happened to me with as much grace as I could muster.

It felt strange to speak aloud in that courtroom. I took a deep breath, looked the judge in the eye, and began: "The last eighteen months have been the most challenging period of my life since I lost my parents as a teenager."

This was no exaggeration. Since my parents' death, I would be the first to admit I had led a charmed life, facing few significant setbacks or obstacles. But now, I felt almost as destitute as the days on which I cremated my father and my mother. I expressed my authentic regrets with as much dignity as I could muster. I told the judge that I accepted what had happened, I was grateful to my family and friends, and I sought their forgiveness. That was my truth and it was all I could say at this juncture. It was too late for the testimony I could have given.

The matter of my sentencing was a complex one, since insider trading sentences are usually related to the financial gains (or avoided losses) of the defendant, which in my case were zero. In the end, Rakoff, who was well known for bypassing sentencing guidelines in favor of his own calculations, accepted neither the government's proposal nor my lawyers'.

"Human beings in their interactions with society are too complicated to be treated like commodities, and the attempt to do so can only lead to bizarre results. Nowhere is this more obvious than in this very case," he declared. Furthermore, he acknowledged, "Mr. Gupta's personal history and characteristics starkly contrast with the nature and circumstances of his crimes."

Again, I was surprised by the change in the judge's tone. I looked across at Gary, who was nodding, no doubt relieved that Judge Rakoff seemed to finally be showing the independent-mindedness and keen discernment for which he was so revered. However, the judge's apparent change of heart only went so far. The suggestion that I be sentenced to community service, he argued, would not act as sufficient deterrent. "While no defendant should be made a martyr to public passion," he reasoned, "meaningful punishment is still necessary to reaffirm society's deep-seated need to see justice triumphant."

In the end, Judge Rakoff sentenced me to only two years' imprisonment, followed by a year's supervised release. Compared to what it could have been, I guess it was a fairly lenient sentence, although it was considerably weighted down when he added enormous monetary fines. It simply made no sense to me that I should be financially penalized based on profits made by Galleon and losses Galleon avoided, when I never benefited in any way from those revenues. On top of this, the SEC would add its own even bigger fines, bringing the total to almost $20 million. I was ordered to surrender to prison on January 8, 2013, giving me only weeks to get my affairs in order.

Appeal

I was in a fighting mood after the sentencing. Yes, I felt I'd finally been seen and considered more fully. But this only served to heighten the injustice of the verdict. We had asked for bail pending appeal, but Rakoff denied this, so we appealed that ruling and won. With Sonu's help I exhaustively researched the best appeal lawyers, eventually hiring Seth Waxman, one of the top attorneys in the country. We filed the appeal immediately following the sentencing, arguing that the court in my trial had abused its discretion and requesting a new trial.

For the next two years, I swung between despair about what loomed in my future and gratitude to at least have this time with my loved ones. The appeal process was slow and cumbersome. Our case was heard in May 2013 by the Federal Appeals Court, and almost a year later, in March 2014, it was rejected. The appeals court insisted there was "ample evidence" of my involvement in a conspiracy and ruled that there had been no irregularity in the way the trial was conducted.

Anita and I were in Florida when I got the news. It was a beautiful day, and as I sat looking out over the blue-green Gulf waters, it was hard to fathom that before long I would be behind bars. How much time did I have? I called the lawyers, and they said that I could suggest a date and typically the judge would be accommodating. On the one hand, I saw no reason to wait long—the sooner it got started, the sooner it would be over. But on the other hand, there were some things I wanted to do: most importantly, spend time with my girls. I requested three months, and it was granted.

I decided that I would take each of my daughters on a father–daughter trip of their choosing. Sonu and I took the kids for a riotous week at Disneyland. Megha and I took a road trip to the beautiful Acadia National Park in Maine and ate lobster by the ocean. Aditi led me on a gastronomical tour of upstate New York, hiking during the days and fine dining at night. Kushy planned the most extensive trip. We flew to Vegas, saw a show, and then set out on a ten-day tour of the majestic landscapes of Arizona and Utah: the Grand Canyon, Zion, Bryce, and everything in between. We ended with a rafting adventure on the Colorado River, during which I foolishly insisted on keeping my phone in a pocket of my wet jacket and lost all the many photographs I'd taken to capture this special time. Nevertheless, it is imprinted in my memory as one of the happiest times of my life. Of all my daughters, Kushy had been most distressed by the trial, and it was such a relief to see her laughing and joyful again.

As spring gave way to summer, my imprisonment loomed. My IIT classmates were due to meet for a reunion in July, but I would be gone. Harbinder, one of my oldest friends, persuaded everyone to move the dates up, and we gathered at my house in early June. I had known these men for decades, and I was grateful that they came to offer me this sendoff, of sorts. On June 15, we celebrated Megha's birthday, once again a somber occasion, and two days later, on June 17, I surrendered to FMC Devens correctional facility in Massachusetts.

Part IV

Imprisonment and Freedom

When you move amidst the world of sense,
free from attachment and aversion alike,
there comes the peace in which all sorrows end . . .

—Bhagavad Gita, 2:64–65

17

The Anarchy of Destiny

The most important lesson that man can learn from his life
is not that there is pain in this world, but that it depends upon him
to turn it into good account, that it is possible for him
to transmute it into joy. . . .
Man's freedom is never in being saved troubles, but it is
the freedom to take trouble for his own good, to make the
trouble an element in his joy.

Rabindranath Tagore, *Sadhana*

Friday, June 20, 2016, FMC Devens correctional facility, Massachusetts

"You shouldn't trust anyone here."

I found it amusing how many people introduced themselves with variations on this phrase during my first week of incarceration, always with the implication that they were the only exception to the rule. Clearly, they couldn't all be right. But then again, I had rather a bad track record when it came to figuring out whom to trust. Maybe I should listen to the warnings and trust no one.

I had arrived at the minimum security facility, known as the "camp," a few days earlier, after spending several days in a solitary cell awaiting the results of a mandatory TB test. What a strange irony, I thought to myself, as I stared at the enclosing walls. I was being held here to ensure that I did not have TB; decades earlier, my father had been thrown into a similar cell in order to deliberately infect him with the disease.

The camp was a tin-roofed structure, two large buildings connected by a narrow section where all the administrative facilities were housed. One building contained the dorms and bathrooms, the other the visitors' room, which doubled as a TV room, and the kitchen and dining hall. It was not a large facility for the 130-odd inmates, and immediately I felt a sense of claustrophobia at the crowds and the noise. Thankfully, the grounds were spacious, with a walking track and playing fields, surrounded by the verdant New England landscape. There were no barbed wire fences or gates.

Upon arrival, I was introduced to the counselor, a clean-cut military type, who would assign me a bunk. I requested a lower bunk, since I sometimes suffer from back pain and was concerned about climbing ladders, but this request was summarily denied. I was shown to my new quarters. The dormitory was divided into small cubicles, each with two bunks, two closets, two footlockers, and two chairs. In my cubicle, the lower bunk was occupied by a large, muscular white guy with a shaved head and tattoos on every visible area of skin. I wondered what he was in for—he looked like he could kill a man with his bare hands. I said hello politely, but he didn't even acknowledge my arrival, let alone introduce himself. His first words to me were spoken the next morning, as I attempted to climb down the steel ladder as quietly as possible at 6:30 a.m. to be on time for breakfast.

"Why can't you be quiet? Can't you see I'm trying to sleep?!"

I'd soon learn that this guy liked his sleep—in fact, he would sleep till nine or ten every morning, at which time another prisoner would deliver his breakfast. He also liked to leave the small window open all night, which left me shivering. He was a man of few words, but he did soon inform me of his "rules" for our cell. I was not to leave anything on the floor or drag in any dirt from outside. He had already taken over both lockers and most of the hanging space but I wasn't about to argue with him. He was the only guy I met who didn't seem to have a prison "job." Later that day, I was ordering some things at the commissary (store) and he appeared and asked if I could order him a T-shirt.

"Okay," I said, assuming he must be out of credit for the month and would pay me back later. I soon realized, however, that he had no intention of paying me back—this was a kind of tax. After about a week, I was informed I would be moving to a new bunk, which I later learned he had requested. Having a bunk-mate didn't suit his lifestyle.

One of the first people I met at the camp was a short, stocky Puerto Rican guy named Mani. After introducing himself and assuring me that he was trustworthy and no one else was, he added, "I know how things work around here. I can protect you."

"Thank you," I replied, "but I don't need protection."

Mani was persistent, however, explaining that he knew the counselors and all the inmates and could help me navigate the quirks of the system. Eventually I decided I would take a chance on accepting his offer, and we worked out a form of compensation through me buying items for him at the commissary. Mani turned out to be as good as his word, helping me in many ways. In particular, he was a very resourceful microwave chef, who could create surprisingly good dishes with food from the commissary plus a few things gleaned from friends who worked in the kitchen. As a diabetic, I prefer to eat multiple small meals, so I relied on Mani to fill the gaps between the scheduled meals.

Mani had five daughters with five different women, and each of his daughters' faces was tattooed on his chest. As a father of four daughters myself, I found his obvious devotion to them touching, although I would not have chosen such a means of expression. He was in for relatively small drug-related crimes but had already served seventeen years in three different stints. Despite the severity of his sentence, he was happy and good-spirited. He was something of a leader in the prison, relied on by the staff to help new guys like me settle in.

To my surprise, I did indeed settle in to camp life, such as it was. I was the only Indian there, so I didn't naturally fit into any of the racially defined tribes that made up prison culture. The population was about one-third black, one-third white, and one-third Hispanic. I often hung out with the older guys who were in for white-collar crime, but I also made friends in the other groups. I found a surprising sense of community in prison, which made it bearable to be confined to a small space with one hundred and twenty-seven other adult men. Not that it was easy—prison life was full of small deprivations and jarring indignities—but I made the best of it. After my week in the SHU, I was careful to always be standing for the count and tried not to antagonize the guards.

Visits

On my first Friday behind bars, I was informed I had a visitor. Like all new arrivals, I was being held in the SHU at that point waiting for my medical clearance, so I was marched to the visitors' room in handcuffs. *Are they going to leave me cuffed in front of my family?* I wondered, a surge of shame flooding me. But thankfully the cuffs were removed before I was told to take a seat. The room was crowded and noisy—inmates talking with their families, children running around, guards occasionally barking out warnings when a rule was breached. Across the room were some vending machines and a coffee machine, and I immediately recognized the long, dark hair and quiet poise of the woman standing there with her back to me, methodically selecting snacks and making coffee. I stood there for a moment, watching her, tears of gratitude filling my eyes. I had not been allowed to call and tell my family whether they were allowed to visit, but my eldest daughter is enterprising and determined, so she had come anyway.

"Sonu," I shouted, but she could not hear me over the hubbub. Someone tapped her on the shoulder and she turned, setting down the coffee and rushing across the room to embrace me.

"Baba, your uniform is quite the neon orange," she said, stepping back with a tearful smile.

"Orange is the new black," I told her. Thank goodness we could laugh about it. I was glad she was the first to come—Sonu is strong and resilient, and she would prepare the others for the scene that awaited them. I was counting on her to be the rock for her mother and sisters during the year and a half ahead.

After that, my family came every weekend, except for a period when my visiting privileges were revoked as an arbitrary punishment. At first, I could see they were apprehensive and worried about me, but I did my best to be upbeat and let them know I was fine. Sonu would drive out every Friday after work, bringing my granddaughters Meera and Nisa. At five years old, they didn't really understand what this place was, but their parents had told them I was staying in a "camp." They accepted that I had to stay there, but often asked uncomfortable questions, like, why didn't I visit them in Boston any more? Why did I have to wear the same clothes as everyone else? I wondered when and how I would tell them the truth. My niece Arya, a couple of years older, figured it out for herself on the first visit and was quite upset, so Arvind stopped bringing her when he came to see me.

Before the twins' visits, I would make them special lollipops, using Jolly Rancher candies from the commissary that were melted down in the microwave and affixed to the stick of a Q-Tip. Seeing their delighted faces as I handed over these simple treats, I was reminded of my early childhood when we lived above a sweet shop in Kolkata, and my bedridden grandfather would pull two rupees out from under his mattress so my sisters and I could buy candies. Meera and Nisa were quite a hit with my fellow prisoners, as they would run over to the windows and wave to the men on the other side. Their visits every Friday, more than anything else, made my prison stay tolerable and even joyous at times. And in between visits, their joyful, loving faces framed with wild, unruly hair stared down at me from the bottom of the bunk above me, which I had carefully papered over with family photographs.

Anita visited every weekend as well and always did her best to appear strong, but I knew it was painful for her. Between visits, I worried about her being alone. My only comfort was knowing that her brother Arvind and his wife Lucy, who lived next door, was always there for her, as were her close friends Jill and Jody in Westport. Her oldest friend, Veena, and her husband, Shiv, had an apple orchard not far from the prison in Vermont, and I was always glad when Anita would go straight from her visits with me to spend time with them.

My other daughters took turns to visit with their mother, so I got to spend time one on one with each of them. They would buy me snacks from the vending machines, and I'd quiz them about their lives, their careers, their romances, and their breakups.

One day, during my time in the SHU, Anita came alone to see me. As we sat down in the visiting room, which was shared with the main prison, my eyes fell on a familiar face: the heavyset features, framed with dark, curly hair, of Raj Rajaratnam. There he was, just a few feet away, with his wife, Asha.

A flood of emotions coursed through me. He did not look very well. I knew he was on dialysis for kidney problems as a result of his diabetes, which is why he was at the Devens main prison, a special medical facility. I felt badly for him but also could not forget that he was the reason I was here. I pointed him out to Anita, who was sitting with her back to him. She, too, looked surprised, but then she said to me, "I have forgiven him and I feel bad for him and his family." This touched me—I knew how angry she had been at Raj's betrayal. It also made me wonder, was I, too, ready to forgive the man responsible for turning my life upside down? Or at least feel no anger toward him? I remembered how my father had harbored no animosity toward the British colonialists who detained and tortured him. I didn't know if I was capable of that degree of forgiveness and equanimity.

On the one hand, Rajaratnam had broken the law and betrayed my trust and that of many others. On the other hand, he had never said anything publicly against me and always maintained I was innocent and had done nothing wrong. I knew from an interview he had given to *Newsweek* that he had been offered significant incentives to do otherwise. "They want to get Rajat," he had told the reporter, claiming that federal agents had pressured him to wear a wire in return for a reduced sentence of less than five years. "I'm not going to do what people did to me."[1] He also told me that they had come to the prison and tried to persuade him to testify against me. Whatever Raj's many faults, I appreciated that he had not accepted their offer.

When our visits were interrupted for the 10 a.m. count, I found myself standing near him, and felt an unexpected surge of empathy and goodwill. I said hello and acknowledged him. He was clearly uncomfortable but acknowledged my greeting. I would not see him again until some months later when I was transferred to the main prison.

Passing Time

I passed much of my time at the camp playing board games and card games. I taught several people how to play bridge and we even had a tournament. My favorite Scrabble opponent was an erudite and well-educated Native American chief and casino boss, who had been jailed for inappropriate use of company resources, which had included using his company's limo service to take his dying mother to the hospital. I learned to play Spades, but never mastered the game. And I reacquainted myself with chess, a favorite high school game I hadn't played in fifty years.

My bridge partner was a guy who told me he had worked as a pilot and gotten caught smuggling marijuana. His wife had died of cancer, and he had a daughter who visited him regularly. I felt sorry for his loss, and I liked the guy. Later, after he was transferred to the main prison, I was shocked to learn that in fact he was in jail for insurance fraud, not drug smuggling, and his wife, who had been his accomplice, was not dead at all, but also in jail. I guess I still had a tendency to trust everyone.

Other camp activities included Toastmasters, and a book club that I started. We chose *The Sixth Extinction* by Elizabeth Kolbert as our first book, as I thought it would spark interesting discussions, but getting hold of enough copies was rather challenging. Eventually it became a discussion group, with topics including "the shared economy," "the US political landscape," and a particular favorite for that crowd: "criminal justice reform."

Every day, I walked on the outdoor track. I would often cover as much as ten miles a day. One day, I was joined by a fellow inmate who told me he'd been there ten years.

"You know, you remind me of another prisoner who was here a couple of years ago," he told me. "He looked different to you, but he did the same things—buying books for the library, helping people write legal briefs, teaching people about financial management, and helping them prepare for when they get out. What was his name?" My walking companion paused. "Greg! That was his name. Greg Earls."

I stopped in amazement. I recognized that name. Greg had called me, out of the blue, shortly before my sentence began. He'd gotten my name from the prison consultant and was calling just to reassure me that I'd be okay and give me tips on how to survive, which included many of these ways to help my fellow prisoners. I was touched to be compared to a man who had so inspired and comforted me as I prepared for incarceration.

Another walking companion was a man who soon became a dear friend, Dave. Almost seventy years old, he struck me as a gentleman, and at the camp he was a trusted advisor to many, with life-wisdom to share. We spent a lot of time together. Every Thursday, we would order a quart of ice cream to share from the commissary. Eating my fill, I would fondly remember the days when Anita and I were poor immigrants in Manhattan, sharing a single cone from Baskin-Robbins.

Without realizing it, I fell into a routine at the camp. Wake at 5:30, and report to the breakfast room at 5:45 for my "job," which was setting up for breakfast. Pranayama breathing exercises from 6:00 to 6:30. Breakfast, followed by cleaning the room. 7:30, out to the track for a walk, followed by an exercise group. 10:00 a.m. count. Lunch was early, at 10:30, followed by card games. Another count. A small meal prepared by Mani at 1:15. Reading, writing, or Scrabble in the afternoon. 4:00 p.m. count followed by dinner, followed by more walking. Volleyball or baseball and socializing from 6:00 to 8:00. Another snack from Mani and card games till the last count and lights out at 10:00.

As the leaves turned red and gold and the early mornings became chilly, I began to wonder how things would change in the winter months. I loved the several hours I spent walking out on the track but prison uniforms were thin. Another new friend came to my aid. One day in late fall, he presented me with an old coverall of the kind used by landscape workers in the winter. "I know you walk a lot," he said, as he handed me this generous gift that would allow me to brave the worst that the elements could throw at me. Two neck-warmers, two hats, a pair of gloves, and my leather sneakers completed the outfit. I felt ready for the Arctic, and Arctic it was that winter in Massachusetts. Many days, I was the only person out there, with my precious MP3 player tucked in my pocket and traditional *bhajans* accompanying my strides as the snow swirled around me. I supplemented my walking with a daily routine of pushups, supervised by my camp neighbor who'd been there twenty-five years and took it upon himself to be my personal trainer. I was soon in the best shape of my life. He was also the camp barber, who would cut hair for $3 in commissary goods.

He was a man of few words, but was easily the best handball player in prison, better than guys twenty-five years his junior.

Thanksgiving was fast approaching, and I could not think about the holiday without a heavy heart. Our family loved the American traditions and had been celebrating together for three decades. It was hard to imagine not being there this year. Anita felt the same; in fact, she told me that she was thinking of canceling the celebration altogether. I insisted that she go ahead, and we agreed that the whole family would visit me on the Friday and Saturday following.

My spirits lifted a little as the holiday atmosphere penetrated even the prison. Inmates bought food items from the commissary to contribute to a special dinner and dessert that the cooks would prepare. Although I wished I was at home surrounded by those I loved, I felt gratitude for my friends inside and for the effort everyone made to brighten the day. The next morning, the first half of my family arrived, since visitors were limited to six at a time: my brother Anjan, my sister Kumkum, my nephew Nikhil, and my nieces Nandita and Natasha. On Saturday, Anita and the girls followed.

On the legal front, I continued to fight. December brought an interesting development. My lawyers called to tell me about another case that could prove relevant to mine: *United States* v. *Newman* had overturned the convictions of two alleged insider traders, and in the process established a new standard for what could be considered "benefit" to a tipper. The case held that the benefit received by a tipper "must be of some consequence" and reflect a true quid pro quo.[2] It clearly established that mere friendship was not enough to constitute "benefit" in an insider trading case, and if that was the case, surely it should raise questions about my conviction, given that no substantive benefit had ever been demonstrated. My lawyers immediately requested that I be allowed to file a new appeal, based on this ruling. I did not hold out much hope for our Supreme Court appeal, which was pending, but this seemed more promising.

The Main Prison

For the last eight months of my sentence, I was transferred from the camp to the main prison. I had mixed feelings about this move. Given my status, I should not have been sent to this higher security facility, but the counselor had come up with some line about me having "poor living skills" to justify it. On the one hand, it was a better facility with more resources, private cells instead of dorms to sleep in, a large indoor space for walking when the weather was bad, air conditioning, and all-day television. I was given my own cell, with its own sink and toilet, and appreciated the greater privacy. On the other hand, there were greater risks, stabbings were common, movement was more restricted, and the food was awful. And I would leave many friends behind in the camp.

My new digs didn't turn out to be too bad. I got used to staring at barbed wire and soon didn't notice it. I developed a routine and made new friends. We even formed a "dinner club" for the nights when the cafeteria food was particularly bad. We'd purchase various items from the commissary and pay someone to prepare us a meal. One guy introduced himself to me on my first day as Manny, sparking a moment of sadness as I thought about his namesake, my friend Mani in the camp. This new Manny, a Haitian lawyer who was writing a regular column for a Haitian newspaper from the prison, would also become a friend. It was he who first told me, "You must write a book!" In fact, he insisted on helping me get started, listening to my story and making notes and outlines in notebooks from the commissary. We quickly got into the habit of eating meals together and kept up a running game of racquetball.

Besides Manny, I got to know many of my fellow inmates, and began to interview them and write down their stories. These surprising friendships gave me insights into lives that were vastly different than mine, as well as a glimpse of the underbelly of the criminal justice system and the so-called war on drugs.

My roommate for a period was a big Puerto Rican guy who was in on a drug charge. The first thing that struck me as I entered the cell we were to share was that he was already settled in the lower bunk. There was no ladder or even a chair from which to climb to the upper bunk, and I did not see how I could do it without injuring myself.

He must have seen my face, mortified at the situation, for he graciously got up and said, "Please take the lower bunk." I very much appreciated his kindness. Although he was twenty years younger than me, he was a heavy man and it certainly wasn't easy for him to get up there.

My roommate told me he was born in Puerto Rico in 1965 and came to the US at the age of seven. He never finished high school, married an older woman at sixteen, got divorced in his twenties, then remarried and had two children, a boy and a girl, whom he adored. He had a decent job as a truck driver, but a serious accident disrupted his life and rather than returning to the job, he turned to drug dealing. Within days he was busted by a trap: his very first sale was to an FBI informant.

The draconian drug laws took over. He felt forced to plead guilty and did not go to trial, even though it was a first-time offense and he was caught with a relatively small quantity. He was promised a shorter sentence, but the judge reneged and gave him fourteen years. He had been shuttled from prison to prison; this was his second stint at Devens. After several days of conversation, this proud man admitted to me with shame in his voice that he did not know if his wife wanted to be with him any more. She neither wrote, nor took his calls, or visited, and the same was true of his kids. He was worried that maybe she already had another man.

This sad story made me appreciate my own loving, loyal family and their commitment to visiting and writing to me. My roommate struck me as a good man, a gentle giant whose faith gave him strength. Without fail he prayed every morning and evening and before every meal. He ate healthy and worked out to stay extremely strong and fit.

His only goal was to get out of there as fast as possible and reconnect with his family. But fourteen years is a lifetime. I taught him card games and showed him some basic meditation techniques that I hoped would help him find equanimity through the inevitable trials ahead.

This story, I would soon learn, was typical of many inmates'. I got to know dozens of men like him during my time in prison. I often marveled that they were still alive, let alone cheerful and kind, after all that they'd been through. Yes, many of them had broken the law, but more often than not the punishment seemed to far outweigh the seriousness of the crime. Double-digit sentences seemed to be routine, and recidivism rates were high. I saw how the cycles of poverty, addiction, abuse, and mental illness feed into one another and set people up to fall on the wrong side of the law. It made me think a lot about destiny—where the cards fall for each of us, and how much control we have over our own fate in the face of circumstance. Could these men have lived different lives? Perhaps. But it would have been hard. Would I have done differently had I been born into a family or a community like theirs? What did it take to win true freedom from what Tagore called "the anarchy of destiny"?

What also struck me, over and over again, in the stories of my fellow inmates, were the terrible flaws in the justice system. So often, there was rampant prosecutorial overreach, and the misuse of plea-bargaining. "We're going to send you away for twenty years," was a common threat, even when the evidence was thin. "But give us the names of three other people, and we'll get it down to five." And so these guys gave out names, and more people went to jail, some deservedly, some not. America has the highest incarceration rate in the world, with almost 2.3 million people behind bars, one in five of them for drug-related offenses.[3] These men left behind families, children, often spiraling down into further cycles of poverty and crime in the absence of their breadwinner. Some of them would live out most of their able lives behind bars. Surely there was a better way.

These issues weighed heavily on my mind during my time in prison, and my feelings toward my adopted country were deeply conflicted. America is clearly a land of opportunity, a land where immigrants can succeed, meritocracy holds, and hard work pays off. It had afforded me an education and a career, and given me and my family a standard of living we could never have achieved at home. For all of this, I felt very much in America's debt. Yet the same country that had given me so much had taken away my freedom as punishment for a crime I did not commit. And now I was witnessing the incarceration crisis first-hand. How could this coexist with the America I had grown to love and respect? Before long, my consultant's mind was hard at work devising a new and better criminal justice system on the back of cafeteria napkins.

Cards with Raj

There were many more inmates in the main prison than there had been in the camp, but very soon my attention was drawn to one in particular: Raj Rajaratnam. Just like that day when I'd seen him in the visiting room, a strange mix of feelings passed through me at the sight of him. I could not help but hold him accountable, to a large degree, for getting me into this mess. Yet I did not feel bitterness or anger toward him. I also felt sorry for him—he did not look well at all.

We had not spoken since early 2009, but I figured if we were going to spend the next several months locked up together, we should talk some things through. So we took a walk around the prison. He seemed uncomfortable and was quick to defend himself when I brought up the Voyager affair. I had to remind him that he was the reason I was in here, for a crime I never committed. But I also thanked him for not fingering me to reduce his own sentence. I thought that this demonstrated character. It was clear I was not going to get an apology from him—he's just not the type. Anyway, I had forgiven him. From then on, we coexisted, even playing the occasional game of cards, chess, or Scrabble. We never discussed the case again.

On the whole, despite its dark moments, my time in prison is most memorable for the camaraderie, courage, and humanity of the people I came to know. Even though the authorities try to ensure that prison does not become a community, most of us look after each other and help whenever we can. This is remarkable given the stress everyone is under and the long sentences most inmates have to endure. As with anything in life, my incarceration had its ups and downs; its good, bad, and ugly; its harsh reality and its tender moments. I would not wish it on anyone, but it was one of the most interesting times of my life. And the most interesting part of all was the part that seemed the harshest and most unfair: a second stay in solitary confinement, midway through my sentence, lasting for seven full weeks.

18

The Gita and the SHU

Never be afraid of the moments—
thus sings the voice of the everlasting.

—Rabindranath Tagore, *Stray Birds,* 59

FMC Devens correctional facility, Massachusetts, April 16, 2015

"It's my Bible."

I used my most firm and authoritative voice, looking the prison guard steadily in the eye and daring him to question the validity of my religious text. On the table between us sat my copy of the Bhagavad Gita, the ancient Hindu holy book containing profound teachings on the nature of the self and the path to liberation, recounted through a conversation between Krishna and Arjuna on the battlefield. The guard held my stare for a moment, then dropped his gaze and pushed the book back across the table toward me. I gathered it to my chest, breathing a sigh of relief. I might be going back to solitary, but this time I would not be alone.

It was April, almost a year into my prison stay, and the day had started out with a feeling of hope. As I walked the track between breakfast and the morning count, enjoying the mild spring sunshine, I was feeling quite content—until I returned to find my bunk-mate anxiously waiting to tell me that the counselor was mad at me and coming to shake me down.

I had no idea what I'd done wrong, but I knew that if he wanted to find a reason to punish me, he would, no matter how carefully I'd been following the rules. Sure enough, he did, this time in the form of a pillow. On searching my bunk, his eyes lighted on the offending object, which a fellow inmate had helped me stitch together using towels purchased from the commissary, to support my back.

"What is this?" he demanded, brandishing the pillow. I tried to explain, but to no avail. Never mind that it had been sitting there in plain sight for months; he declared it to be "contraband"—an unauthorized object. He was writing me up, he told me, rather than simply confiscating the pillow. "I will report the incident to internal security and they will take whatever action is appropriate." My heart sank. I knew that was code for a trip to the SHU.

This time, I knew the drill, but I was still frozen with shock. Mani came by, full of concern, reminding me that he'd warned me some days earlier that the counselor was mad. I'd tried my best to play by the rules, but there were so many of them, and they were so inconsistently applied, that sooner or later I always seemed to trip up. I cursed myself for being careless. But this wasn't the moment for recriminations. I might only have minutes left, and I needed to call Anita.

It was a hard call to make: if the infraction seemed arbitrary to me, after ten months in this place, it was incomprehensible to my wife. I tried my best to assure her that I'd be okay, but I didn't know how long I would be gone or when I would next be able to call. "Tell my lawyers," I instructed her. "They'll be allowed to speak with me even in the SHU."

Back at my bunk I found my friends gathered to help me pack my stuff. My first priority was to take down the precious photographs that papered the underside of the bunk above my head. I'd spent hours carefully disassembling an album Sonu had sent and creating this collage of loving faces; now I had just minutes to take it down, trying not to tear the pictures. My handful of possessions went into plastic bags, my commissary food was divided among my friends, and my valuables went to Mani for safekeeping. Awad, another friend, came running in and offered me his radio, since MP3 players were not allowed in the SHU.

When the packing was done, Dave said, "Let's have our ice cream." It was Thursday, after all. "Don't worry," he tried to reassure me, "it'll just be a few days. You'll be back here for ice cream next week." But we both knew the system was unpredictable. As we sat in his cubicle, enjoying our sweet, cold treat in silence, we couldn't escape the possibility that we might not see each other for some time. Who knew when we'd be able to resume our weekly ritual. Mani, too, said goodbye as if this parting could be an extended one. We promised to keep in touch, no matter what happened.

The guards still hadn't showed up, so I decided to take one last walk. With each step, I reflected on the many peaceful hours I'd spent on the track—the sunrises and sunsets, the brilliance of the fall foliage, the bitter cold. Then my name rang out on the loudspeaker and it was time to go.

Four cops came to pick me up. When I told them the nature of my transgression, they laughed out loud. A pillow? I didn't think it was funny, since I had no opportunity to appeal this ludicrous charge. I gathered a few items I hoped to take with me: Awad's radio, a list of phone numbers, a book on Pranayama yoga, and the Bhagavad Gita. Not surprisingly, the guards objected, but I held firm, and while the radio was confiscated, I was allowed to keep my sacred texts. Clutching the two books in my cuffed hands, I followed the guards away from the facility that had come to feel like home.

Upon arrival at the SHU, I was issued an orange jumpsuit, underwear, and canvas shoes. Another attempt was made to take away my books, but I repeated my insistence that this was my Bible, and once again it seemed to work. I was taken to a cell just like the one I'd occupied before: twelve by eight feet, cold steel bunks, thin, lumpy, plastic-covered mattress, shower, basin, and toilet all exposed. How had I ended up here again? In a state of shock, I took the mattress from the upper bunk and laid it on top of the one on the lower bunk, and collapsed.

Sannyasin

Despite my exhaustion, I couldn't sleep. Hoping to banish the pointless self-recrimination that consumed me, I picked up the Gita. The version I'd brought contained the original Sanskrit text, an English translation, an English transliteration, and then commentary. Although I was familiar with many parts, I had never read the entire Gita from beginning to end in its original form. This was an opportunity, I told myself, to immerse myself in the scripture. I even managed to summon up a sense of gratitude: maybe the injustice of this confinement would be a catalyst for deeper spiritual growth, like a retreat. It struck me as strangely appropriate that the SHU uniforms were orange, since this was the color of the robes worn by renunciates, or *sannyasins*, in the Hindu tradition.

With no material possessions besides my Gita and one other book on the tradition of yoga, I felt a momentary kinship with generations of seekers who had given up their worldly life for a life of the spirit. I had not done so by choice, of course, but I could embrace the outcome nonetheless. When feelings of despair, rage, and helplessness closed in on me, I would return to my reading, determined to use this ancient wisdom to rise above the degradation and indignity of the SHU. Every day, I studied my Gita, immersing myself in the ideals that had inspired my country's great sages and heroes.

That first night, I began with the opening chapter, which contains a long and detailed description of the battlefield of Kurukshetra in the Mahabharata (the great war between good and evil). Although impatient to get to the spiritual heart of the book, I enjoyed the colorful scenes and the beautiful poetry. Keeping my voice low, I read aloud to myself, taking great pleasure in the powerful vibration of the Sanskrit diction. Soon, the cell walls faded, and I was transported into the chariot with Krishna, an incarnation of God, and Arjuna, the great warrior.

Chapter two opens with Arjuna declaring to Krishna, his charioteer, that he cannot take up arms against his cousins and other relatives who make up the opposing army. This begins one of the greatest sermons delivered in human history. Krishna explains to Arjuna the notion of the One everlasting soul (Atma). "Never is this One born, and never does It die; nor is it that having come to exist, It will again cease to be," he declares. "This One is birthless, eternal, undecaying, ancient; It is not killed when the body is killed."[1]

Lying in my cell, these familiar words took on a deeper meaning for me and provided great comfort. All the trials of my life began to seem less harsh when considered in light of the immortality of the soul. The idea that there is something within me that is beyond the physical, intellectual, or emotional ups and downs we all go through and that my life force is connected with some universal force and is immortal somehow made it so much easier to accept being in the SHU. My current incarceration was merely a passing shadow. Even the deaths of my parents appeared in a new context. The shedding of their bodies did not mean they ceased to exist. One verse described death as being like the Self taking off a set of worn-out clothes before putting on new ones. I meditated deeply on these ideas, until at some point in the night, I fell into a deep sleep with the open Gita resting on my chest.

I was awakened early by the sound of the food tray pushing against the slot in my door. Before I had time to even remember where I was, an instinctive reflex from my last SHU stay propelled me across the cell and I grabbed the tray before it fell. The food mostly tasted like cardboard, but thankfully there was some fresh fruit. As I chewed, slowly and deliberately, I reoriented myself. It was Friday. I was in solitary. I had no idea how long I'd be here.

In my brief conversation with Anita the night before, I'd asked her to call Sonu and tell her not to bring the twins when she visited today, but to come alone. I hoped she would come, and I'd be allowed to see her. The worst thing about being in the SHU is not the deprivation or the confinement, but the knowledge of the worry it is causing to loved ones. I was reminded of the saying that, as a parent, you are as happy as your unhappiest child. If I could see Sonu, at least I could reassure her that I was fine, and maybe she could communicate that to her mother and sisters.

Sonu was already in the visiting room when I arrived, after being paraded through most of the length of the prison in handcuffs. I was happy to see familiar faces among the other inmates sitting with their loved ones, but I was quickly ushered away to a special section in the visiting area for the people in orange jumpsuits. Seeing the pained expression on Sonu's face, tears welled up in my eyes. She gave me a long, reassuring hug, but as she pulled back, I could see tears rolling down her cheeks too. There was no joking this time. Sonu does not cry easily, so I knew how hard it must have been for her to see me dressed like this.

Soon we settled down to a long and wonderful father daughter chat, accompanied by snacks that Sonu would get me from the vending machines. We covered every topic under the sun, from her career to whether she wanted to have any more children; from her husband Meka's medical career to my financial affairs; from the political events of the day to my grandchildren's latest achievements. We focused on everything but my immediate plight, and for a few hours I could almost imagine that we were at home in Connecticut, sitting in the cozy library, catching up on an ordinary weekend.

Our conversation was rudely interrupted by the announcement that the visit was over. Although she had been there four hours, I knew it was not yet 3 p.m., the official end of visiting time. When I inquired about this, I was informed that the visits from the SHU had to end whenever our escorts arrived to handcuff us and take us back to our cells. Reluctantly, I said goodbye to Sonu and presented my wrists for the cuffs.

Back in my cell, I eagerly picked up the Gita and was soon immersed once more. The *shlokas* (verses) I was reading were familiar favorites—I have quoted these words in many speeches over the years and in every commencement speech I have given to a graduating class of students. But I heard them afresh as I read them aloud in my cell. The theme was *karma yoga*, the creed my father had always practiced. The literal translation is: "Your right is for action alone, never for the results."[2] Another way to think about this idea is that if you have done your best and you have worked with the best of intentions, then the results don't matter. This idea had always been extremely liberating for me.

The one question that troubled me, as I lay in my cell, was this: Had I done my best? My decision not to testify weighed heavy on my heart—I didn't feel I had lived courageously in that moment. Like Arjuna on the battlefield, I had been hesitant to fight. I had succumbed to fear and let the concerns of those around me about the possible outcomes of taking the stand sway me.

Now, I felt a renewed resolve. In my four-year fight against the injustice of my case, I had lost almost every battle. Every outcome had been an adverse one. Many times, I'd despaired about the futility of the fight. Why not simply give up? It would have been easy, at this stage, to feel that the war was already over. But several legal decisions were still pending in my case, including the Supreme Court ruling on my petition and a decision on whether to allow my new appeal based on the Newman case. I knew that all of these would test my resolve to stay the course, do my duty, and fight the injustice, especially if some of these decisions went against me.

I had always identified with the path of the karma yogi more than with the path of the sannyasin. I'd considered myself too worldly for the life of a monk—too driven and ambitious and eager to take action in the world. Living in the SHU, however, I felt more kinship with the ancient monks. I was reliant on the guards for basic sustenance and cut off from the world, with almost no material possessions. This was one of the great lessons of the prison experience: how little one really needs to be happy. One discovers joy in the smallest things that cost no money: sunshine, friendship, fall colors, movement. The unresolved question in my mind was: Will I still feel that way when I get out? Will results matter even less to me? I was attracted by the idea but also humbled by how difficult it might be to achieve.

Again and again, as I recited the words of the Gita, my father's image came to mind. A man of simple living and high thinking, he considered himself a karma yogi, but he also embodied many characteristics of a sannyasin. "He who does not hate and does not crave should be known as a man of constant renunciation,"[3] said the Gita. I never saw my father express either of those emotions. He wore his simple *dhoti* even when he was accompanying the prime minister on state visits around the world. That's not to say he was a saint—far from it. He'd actually been arrested as a young man for impersonating one of the students he was tutoring in order to help him cheat on an exam. The student was paying him handsomely for this ruse, and my father, who intended the money to go to his revolutionary cause, decided that the end justified the means.

He was generous to a fault with his time and money. He always gave whatever he possessed to anyone who needed it, often to my mother's frustration, and he was simply not attached to material things. While fully engaged in his profession and connected to his family, there was a definite sense of detachment from this world, a sense that only increased in his final years. On our long walks in the hospital grounds during his final months, he exuded tranquility and peace.

I was now older than he had been when he died, and I had lived such a different life, although his example was never far from my mind. Could I follow him into that deeper detachment as I entered the next phase of my life?

In Search of Equanimity

Early on Saturday morning, I was called for a visit. As I was walking past the other cells, handcuffed and escorted, I suddenly saw a familiar face through the glass window of one of the doors. It was a guy who had been my walking partner at the camp in the early days. He had left six months ago, supposed to be headed home! Could he have been here in the SHU for all that time? They clearly had taken away his home confinement time and possibly his "good time." All I knew was that he had argued with the case manager about his release date. I could not imagine what he must be going through, still here when he should have been home. What torment month after month of solitary confinement must be for someone I knew was accustomed to walking more than fifteen miles a day.

My friend's plight was momentarily pushed to the back of my mind when I saw Anita and Sonu across the room, waiting for me. I instinctively felt I should make the most of every moment with them, since I did not know when my visiting privileges might be suspended on the flimsiest pretext. I remembered a story my mother once told me, about the time when my father was jailed by the British, and because they were not married, she was unable to visit. Determined to find a way, she went to my father's brother and asked him to set up a visit for himself. She dressed in a nurse's uniform, and while my uncle engaged the guard in a long conversation, she was able to slip into the prison. After some time, the guard became suspicious that the nurse hadn't left, and my uncle was forced to confess, but luckily the guard took pity on the young lovers and allowed the visit to continue.

After I hugged my wife and daughter with a little extra appreciation, we all sat down. I could tell that Anita was very stressed by my situation, because her stress-relief mechanism was to feed me. She bought a mountain of snacks from the vending machine, and while they weren't exactly gourmet fare, compared to the food in the SHU they were quite good. It broke my heart to see the worry on my wife's face. I should have never given them an opportunity to send me to the SHU and make everyone who cares about me so unhappy. After they left, I felt sad and dejected, and turned to the Gita for comfort.

"The monk is called a man of steady wisdom when his mind is unperturbed in sorrow, he is free from longing for delights, and has gone beyond attachment, fear and anger."[4] I thought about this idea in the small hours of the morning, as I lay sleepless on my lumpy mattress, trying to calm my mind and emotions. Could I attain that kind of freedom here, in such emotionally and physically challenging circumstances? Another verse compared the way the wise man "withdraws the senses from the objects of the senses" to the way a tortoise draws in its legs.[5] I focused on drawing myself inward, away from the noise, the discomfort, the ache in my back, the worries about my family, the helpless frustration of my situation, the unanswerable questions.

The discipline of meditation is emphasized in the Gita. Some of my friends who are long-time practitioners swear by the profound influence meditation has had on their lives, but my own attempts, I had to admit, had been episodic and erratic. Whenever I visited my good friend Deepak Chopra, he would take the time to meditate with me, but alone I found it hard to be consistent. Now, the practice took on a new seriousness and urgency. I had no control over the fact of my confinement; no choice as to when I would eat, go outside, or even have the light on; no way to tell the time; but I could learn to control my inner experience. By "treating happiness and sorrow, gain and loss, and conquest and defeat with equanimity,"[6] as the Gita advised, I could win inner freedom, even in solitary confinement.

These ideas were both appealing and challenging to me. Could I treat honor and dishonor the same? Denunciation and praise? I had gone from being respected and even revered to being disrespected, insulted, and shamed. From the perspective the Gita taught, these experiences were equal. It was an attitude that is at the heart of the spiritual traditions of my ancestors, but one that I knew would make little sense to my American friends. Americans are so enamored with the drama of emotion—the highs and lows, the triumphs and the disasters, the trauma, the anger, and the healing. The idea of being free from it all doesn't even occur to most. "I don't understand how you can take all this and remain so calm!" was a common refrain. But for me, equanimity was liberation.

I resolved that I would not let the ups and downs of my prison existence affect me. What is the real difference whether I am in the camp or in the SHU? I asked myself. The fact that I was in the SHU did not have the power to make me unhappy. Life is a series of experiences, none of which is inherently good or bad. I was not going to give the people who were making decisions about my life the power to make me angry.

Soon, my resolve would be tested—by both positive and negative events. First, a wonderful visit from Anita and my third daughter, Aditi, who always cheers me up. For some reason, when I saw her, I remembered that she was the daughter we almost lost. Anita's first two births had been perfectly normal, so we had no concerns, and we headed to the birthing center as most pregnant women do in Denmark, where we lived at the time. Luckily, Ingrid, the wife of one of my partners, was a doctor, and she worked at the hospital next door. She came to check on Anita, and noticed that the midwife looked worried. Suddenly, she sprang into action, and had to use forceps, because Aditi was not getting enough oxygen with the cord choking her. We were very lucky she was there. Those precious few minutes flashed in front of my eyes, highlighting the fragility of life, and I touched Aditi's hand as if to reassure myself she was there. However deeply I might believe in the immortality of the soul, I was still deeply attached to my loved ones in their mortal bodies, for better or for worse.

Unaware of the thoughts going through my mind, my daughter proceeded to give me a full report of her recent dating experiences. Anita, once again, fed me as much as she could. Overall, it was an uplifting visit, but I reminded myself to practice equanimity even then.

Soon they would be gone and the feelings would change—could I remain poised in wisdom, as the Gita described? As I hugged them goodbye, I told them I was not sure when the next visit would be possible. Little did I know it would be two months before I would see them again, and every last reserve of my spiritual strength would be called on to remain steady.

The next three days brought one piece of bad news after another. On Monday, the guards came to fetch me for a call I had scheduled with my lawyers. By now I was used to pretty rough treatment, but this was extreme. They first attached a heavy chain around my waist, then handcuffed me in the front and double handcuffed that to the chain around my waist. I was taken to a small room with a desk and a phone and then the counselor connected the call. When I asked if my hands could be free to hold the receiver, he looked at me as if it was a completely unreasonable request. He told me to hold it between my chin and shoulder. I must have dropped the phone at least five times during the call, awkwardly retrieving it with my cuffed hands.

As I sat there, my neck stiffening painfully, my lawyer told me that the Supreme Court had refused to hear my appeal. This was a huge blow. As I was taken back to my cell, I kept telling myself: *Be detached. Do not let this pull you out of your inner peace.* I am doing my duty and fighting the injustice as best I could, I reminded myself. The outcome is not in my hands. I should not let it affect me. Don't get mad at the justices or the COs in the SHU. Don't be upset at the people who let you down. Forgive all and be at peace with yourself. And know that at the existential level, it does not really matter. I was roughly thrust back into my cell and the chains removed.

The next day, I was restless. It had now been four days and I did not know what they were going to do to me. Herb Henzler, my old McKinsey friend from Germany, and Pramath Sinha, the first dean of ISB, were both flying in to visit me. It would be really sad if they were turned away because of this stupid incident. I asked to use the phone and was told that one could only make a call after one month in the SHU. The only exception was for legal calls, so I requested one of those as soon as possible. Maybe my lawyers could get a message to my friends.

On Wednesday, my case manager came to meet with me. It was a stone cold meeting. She proceeded to read my rights, then told me my visits would be taken away for sixty days. I had been steeling myself for thirty days but this was much worse. My sisters were coming from India at the end of May—the only break during which they could make the trip. I explained this to her, but she did not even bother to reply. Surely she is also someone's sister, I thought. I would have appreciated at least some sympathy, even if she could not do anything. I asked her, "Now that my case is resolved, when am I going back to the camp?" She was evasive. What were they going to do to me? The meeting was over in less than five minutes.

Back in my cell, I started imagining the worst outcomes. I tried to meditate and steady my mind, but the racing thoughts, recriminations, frustrations, and questions would not leave me alone. So I picked up the book once again and began to read aloud, as Arjuna extolled the nature of the Divine. The rhythms of the beautiful poetry and the sounds of Sanskrit put me into a trance-like state.

"I am the taste of water, I am the effulgence of the moon and the sun . . . I am also the sweet fragrance in the earth, I am the brilliance in the fire, and the life in all beings, and I am the austerity of the ascetics . . . Know Me to be the eternal Seed of all beings. I am the intellect of the intelligent; I am the courage of the courageous. And of the strong I am the strength which is devoid of passion and attachment."[7]

Surrounded by concrete and steel, the glare of fluorescent lights and the clamor of suffering voices, I contemplated the Divine and found some peace. It was a different idea of God to the one my Christian friends prayed to; a God that was not waiting in a faraway heaven but permeating everything in this world, including my own self. Perhaps

I could not prove that such a Supreme Being exists, but the power that was carried in the Gita's words was enough for me to believe.

The Cage

Is this what a zoo animal feels like? I wondered. I was in a cage—thirty by ten feet with chain link fences on three sides and the ceiling, barbed wire above, and a cinder block wall at the end. Next to me was another identical cage, and five more lay beyond it. In each cage were anywhere between five and ten orange-suited SHU inmates, partaking of their daily "recreation outing."

I had been in the SHU a week before I discovered I could request this change of scene for ninety minutes a day. We were transferred like animals—handcuffed and escorted although it was all of ten steps from the cell area to the rec area. Once inside the cage, I politely greeted the other occupants and then began walking the longer side of the cage. Twenty steps one way; twenty steps back. The hard concrete floor was painful through the thin-soled orange canvas shoes we were required to wear, and the short back and forth was dizzying, but it felt so good to move. I missed my ten-mile-a-day walks.

I had been walking for a few minutes when suddenly I heard a crashing noise and saw an old man collapsing against the chain link fence, frantically trying to get a grip. There was a sudden flurry of activity and the emergency response personnel came. What was such an old man, certainly in his eighties, doing in prison at all? I wondered. And why on earth is he in the SHU? It was hard to watch the callous way they handled him, clearly showing that this human life did not have the same value as themselves in their eyes.

Soon, my maiden voyage to the so-called Rec-yard was over. It was one of the more humiliating experiences of my incarceration, but at least I had gotten some fresh air. I resolved to come out whenever I got a chance. Rec was also an opportunity to talk to other inmates—a welcome change from our solitary cells. The universal topic was the silly reasons people were in the SHU. Once we got past that, however, I had interesting conversations with many of my cage-mates, provided they were willing to keep pace with my walking. Other times, I just appreciated the feeling of the sun on my skin.

One day, there was a kid I'd never seen before in my cage. He had just self-surrendered a couple of days before and was headed to the camp. A very bright young man of Chinese ancestry, he was a Cornell graduate in computer science and a computer whiz. He'd worked for a hedge fund and was accused of being a Chinese spy and stealing secrets. He had really no option but to fight hard and was now in for a two-year sentence. While his case dragged on, he had started an online school to offer computer science courses to all ages, which was already taking off. His mother was going to run it while he was serving his time.

My new companion was an ambitious kid who wanted to change the world. I enjoyed talking to him. We walked back and forth in the small cage and ninety minutes went by fast. He would quiz me about how to build a business and how I was able to be effective in my philanthropic pursuits. He was intellectually curious and a fast learner. I started looking forward to the rec because I found talking to him very interesting and invigorating. One day, I told him I would like to learn something from him on topics I knew very little about. He was enthusiastic about the opportunity and turned out to be an excellent teacher. One day, as we paced the chain link fence, he gave me a ninety-minute lecture on cryptocurrency that explained the topic better than anything I'd ever read. I finally understood it. Another day we covered drones or quadcopters and all the technical as well as regulatory issues surrounding them.

I was now looking forward to my daily visit to the cage, but I learned that if you were not perfectly ready when they came for you, they might just skip you for the day. On other days, they would announce that the weather was not good enough, although I suspected this was just a way of minimizing their workload. I knew they didn't care that much if we got wet. Indeed, one day, when it was drizzling, many of us went out anyway. After thirty minutes, it started raining hard. The COs made no attempt to get us inside, and everyone just got soaked. When we finally came in, there were no extra clothes, so I had to stay in my wet clothes until they dried on my body.

Even when we were separated by steel doors, I was amazed at the sense of community that developed among the SHU inmates. People created "fishing lines" from the small plastic covers on the utensils we got for the meals, which could slide under the door and transport small gifts, such as extra coffee or newspapers, from room to room. I was impressed at the ingenuity of my cell neighbors.

I still needed to inform Herb, Pramath, and my sisters of my predicament and tell them not to come. I hated for them to make the long trip for nothing. Herb had been a true friend throughout this nightmare and had stood by me from the beginning. As for my sisters, they had made an enormous effort and planned quite a bit in advance to use their limited vacation time to visit. But as they say, "man proposes and God disposes." Reading the Gita so intensely all these days was teaching me to be even-tempered in the face of setbacks.

I wrote a letter to Sonu, but was not confident she would get it in time. I made requests and appeals. Again, the process seemed designed to humiliate: the only writing instruments they allowed were short pencils about three inches long with no sharpeners. I would chip at the wood with my nails, and sometimes try to file it against the metal edge of the bunk, but to little avail. I had to struggle to fill out the forms with my blunt pencils, and writing legible letters was tortuous. Eventually, the counselor came to inform me that all my appeals had been denied. I asked him to call Sonu. I also asked him when I was heading back to camp. Like the case manager, he was evasive.

In addition to these frustrations, day-to-day living in the SHU would have tested even the most accomplished yogi. The COs seemed to actively make life difficult for the inmates every step of the way. The process of getting clean clothes was another exercise in humiliation. They came around with a trolley stacked with clean jumpsuits and underwear, and you were expected to strip naked in front of the CO, slip your dirty clothes through the opening in the door, and then take the clean clothes in exchange.

Counselors, case managers, the unit manager, the warden, and others would randomly walk through the SHU at various points. The only way to have a conversation was to shout through the door and hope you could catch their attention. If for some reason you were reading or writing or resting, bad luck for you. It might be several days before you had another opportunity. At one point I was reminded of what they say about growing mushrooms: keep them in the dark and throw shit at them. That's how they treated us. I had done nothing to deserve this treatment and nor had most of the people in the SHU. But in a way I felt sorry for the staff at that prison. If your work, day after day, encourages you to treat human beings rudely and with indifference and contempt, what kind of person must you become? How does it affect your behavior toward other people, toward your family and friends? I tried to practice empathy and even forgiveness toward the prison staff. If I am part of the Universal Self, I told myself, the idea of helping others follows, as does the idea of forgiveness toward all, and the idea of joy in others' success becomes natural.

There is much discussion in the Gita about the virtues or divine attributes that we should aspire to. These include things like fearlessness, purity of mind, charity, sacrifice, truthfulness, absence of anger, renunciation, kindness to creatures, gentleness, modesty, freedom from restlessness, forgiveness, fortitude, freedom from malice, absence of haughtiness—the list goes on and on. I weighed up each quality and tried to honestly assess where I had expressed it and where I had come up short. I resolved to do better—to be unattached to my losses, to be kind toward the COs no matter how provocative their conduct was, to respect and be humble toward my fellow prisoners.

I'll admit I did not always live up to these lofty ideals. The counselor, in particular, was hard to forgive: he seemed particularly mean-spirited. Despite my spiritual aspirations, I could not resist taking a small measure of revenge. The only calls I was allowed to make were those with my lawyers, and for these calls the counselor had to come and get me from my cell, take me to the phone, and then stand and wait outside until I was finished. So I asked my lawyers to schedule legal calls every few days, not an unreasonable frequency given my new appeal. I took some satisfaction in making him stand there for an hour or more each time I took a call.

As the days turned into weeks, with no indication of when I would be allowed to leave the SHU, I was ever more grateful that I had insisted on keeping my Gita. Sometimes it was confusing, sometimes repetitive, and occasionally it seemed to contradict itself, but it lifted me out of the confinement of my cell and the inner prison of my anxious mind. I studied the timeless teachings on the impermanence of worldly attachments, the eternal nature of the soul, and the meaning of selfless service. When I was not reading, I worried incessantly about my family. I received occasional letters from them, but I was not confident that all my mail came through, or that my replies ever reached them.

Anita's letters, in particular, were painful to read—I could feel her loneliness and depression, although she tried hard to reassure me. She was struggling with some health issues, and I worried that she was not doing enough to take care of herself. She confessed that she had stopped answering the phone because she just could not bear to tell one more person the story of my current circumstances. The mail was piled high on her desk.

Anita also reported, to my great distress, that my devoted old dog, Rufus, was ailing and could barely move. "I think he is holding out for you to come home," she wrote. Tears filled my eyes reading her words: I had been hoping against hope that my dear friend and walking companion would still be around when I came home. But each letter brought more sad reports: she had taken Rufus to the vet, but it had been a struggle, as his hind legs and hips no longer worked at all. She didn't think she could put him through that again.

"He must be suffering a lot," I wrote to her. "For his sake, he should be put to sleep. Celebrate his life. He gave us a lot of joy. I am glad we had him. Death is part of life and he will always be with us." That night, as I lay on my hard bunk, my mind was filled with memories: walking with Rufus along the street near our home, the ocean breeze ruffling his golden coat; Kushy, as a teenager, playing with him on the beach; the soft noise of Rufus snoring as he slept at my feet in the study on a winter evening. I would miss him.

"You won't believe how empty the fridges are these days," Anita wrote in her next letter. "With just me here I hardly buy any groceries. The house feels terribly empty. I can't imagine how it will be without Rufus. He mostly sleeps these days but at least he is here."

Finally, I received a letter from Aditi informing me gently that my old friend had been put to sleep. She and Kushy had been there with Anita when the vet came to the house to give him the shot. I should have been there too. He'd been a faithful friend for so many years, accompanying me on daily walks. I mourned him alone in my cell, wishing I could at least call and talk to Anita about his final days. I worried about her, alone in the house. Only the mystical beauty of the Gita could banish the encroaching dark thoughts that night. I studied the now well-thumbed pages till dawn.

One morning, the CO came to my cell and told me to pack up my things. My solitary confinement had come to an end. I had been there seven long weeks—all because of a pillow. It was a cruel and unusual punishment, but strangely it was also a gift. I will never forget those weeks—not the humiliations or the draconian rules, nor the spiritual journey I took and the way it filled me with purpose and peace. As my father taught me, one cannot always control what happens in life, but one can always choose how one responds. I read the Gita three times, cover to cover, in Sanskrit and English, and I practiced meditation with more diligence than ever before in my life. I left that cell a stronger man, more resilient in spirit and more accepting of my fate.

Release

My father left prison with a long, deep scar on his back and a permanent limp—a lifelong reminder of what he had suffered, lost, and gained during his incarceration. On the day I became a free man, January 6, 2016, I bore no such reminders, besides a few more gray hairs. I was in the best shape of my life, thanks to my daily ten-mile walks and challenging pushup regime. I also felt spiritually stronger. As I finally stepped outside the prison gates, clutching a few plastic bags filled with my belongings, I realized that in a strange way I would miss the place—or at least I would miss the people I had gotten to know there.

I paused to look back for just a moment, and then turned toward my freedom. The coming weeks would test my equanimity and forgiveness, I knew. How would it feel to re-engage with old friends and colleagues, some of whom had turned their backs in my hour of need? How would I rebuild my life and envision my future, with so much of my legacy now tarnished by my conviction? What would I do with the time that remained to me?

Epilogue

When I stand before thee at the day's end
thou shalt see my scars and know that I had my wounds
and also my healing.

—Rabindranath Tagore, *Stray Birds,* 290

December 2, 2018

Today, I turn seventy, and it seems somehow fitting that I am writing these final pages of my book on this milestone day. A seventieth birthday is certainly a good moment for reflection, introspection, taking stock, and thinking about how best to use the limited time one has remaining.

In ancient Indian philosophy, it is said that there are four stages in life. *Brahmacharya*, the first stage, literally translates as "bachelorhood." It is a time to learn, influenced primarily by parents and teachers, and prepare oneself for playing a productive role in society. The second stage, *grihastha*, is family life, a time in which one builds a career and a family. Its objectives are to be a productive member of society, to acquire wealth, reputation, and influence, and fulfill responsibilities to family and friends. *Vanaprastha*, the third stage, literally means "forest life"—the time when one begins to detach oneself from worldly things. It is a time for giving back, as one's focus turns from oneself and one's family to the good of others and society at large. The final stage of life is *sanyas*, or renunciation. It is here that one lets go of material things and even relationships, preparing to leave this world. One's focus becomes self-realization and the achievement of a tranquil and serene state.

Looking back, I can see how these stages have unfolded in my own life, sometimes overlapping. My formal education was complete around my first quarter-century, and my next several decades were devoted to career and family. Somewhere during that period, my focus naturally began to shift toward giving back to society, something I continue to do to this day. I hope I will have a few more years with the energy and capacity to make a difference in the world. In prison, I was forced to practice detachment and given the opportunity, perhaps, to begin my *sanyas*.

Of course, no one's life moves smoothly through these stages. My life seemed blessed until that fateful day in 2009 when everything began to go wrong. Looking back at what happened to me, what I did, and what I could have done differently, there are no simple answers. From one perspective, I lost nine years. I fought so hard and for so long, yet I lost almost every battle. Should I have just given in and got it over much faster? From another perspective, those nine years were one of the most important periods of my life. After my indictment, I came to know who my real friends were. I learned how precious my family and friends are through their unwavering support. My journey through the criminal justice system taught me how flawed it can be. My time in prison was an extraordinary experience. I feel deep gratitude for what I learned there, for the friendships I made, and for the person I became.

At times, of course, I let myself imagine how things might have been different. Would this drama ever have unfolded if I had simply stuck to my decision to resign from the Goldman board in 2008? Would my case have had a different outcome had it occurred in a different time? Perhaps. There's no doubt that in the years following the financial crisis the deck was stacked against anyone accused of financial crimes. As a 2012 *Forbes* article mused, perhaps in those years we had "a tainted jury pool, an entire society that has a bias against anyone with a coat and tie." And understandably so, given the government's failure to prosecute those truly responsible for the economic meltdown. My case was just one among several that the author, Walter Pavlo, listed, in which circumstantial evidence was deemed enough to convict. "In each of these cases there was no absolute certainty that each of these men were involved in insider trading, yet juries found them guilty . . . and did so quickly." In my case, it took less than half a day. "Has that standard [of guilt beyond a reasonable doubt] been lowered by the economic times?" he asked.[1] I think there is little doubt that the answer is yes, and I paid a heavy price for it.

Above all, the choice not to testify continues to haunt me—not because I know the outcome would have been different, but because at least it would have allowed me to accept the outcome better, knowing I had done my best in every way. The fact is, I succumbed to fear in that moment, and that is something I find it hard to forgive myself for and to live with.

I find it painful that I could not continue on my journey of giving back to society in an impactful way. The loss of my reputation and my position of leadership—the hard-won fruit of those first two stages of my life—is also hard to bear. But the truth is, that was all lost long before my decision about taking the stand. The day the SEC charged me, the damage was done, and no matter what I'd done differently during the trial, I'd already paid that price.

In the end, however, I accept that perhaps this course of events was simply my destiny. It is not my job to understand why, it is just my job to make the best of it. Again, I remind myself, life is a series of experiences. None is inherently good or bad—it is what you make of it. I am thankful to have been reminded of what really matters in life.

In the last several months, as I've been completing this book, I have been saddened to read the press coverage on the organization that features most prominently in my story: McKinsey. I grew up in McKinsey and believed in the values it stood for: integrity, client interests first, partnership, and so forth. While I have no knowledge of the specific incidents in which the firm has been accused of wrongdoing, I do know that people on the inside feel that much has been unfairly portrayed and taken out of context. And I know all too well how that feels. I take no pleasure in seeing the organization I led go through its own reputational crisis, but I cannot help but wonder, if my case occurred now, would McKinsey still take such a "holier than thou" attitude and judge me without a fair hearing? I wish the firm well, and I hope that it finds its way back to its core values.

As for me, in the last few years, I have tried to reintegrate with society. Relearning some of the mundane tasks of life, getting reacquainted with the tools of modern living. Slowly, I have reconnected with old friends and I have spent a lot of time with my family, particularly my granddaughters.

On the personal front, my network of friends has shrunk considerably. I have become much more introverted and reflective. I am hesitant to make new contacts, uncertain how they will view my recent past. I wonder, should I reach out to people I knew before, but have not been in touch with these past nine years? What would be the purpose? While my friend circle is smaller, in many ways it is deeper. All you really need are a few good friends and a loving family.

I have also spent a considerable amount of time writing this book—a difficult, cathartic, and ultimately satisfying activity. Now that it is written, I have been asking myself, what's next? There is no question that my fall from grace and leadership positions has severely limited my options today. I no longer have the same opportunities to make my life purposeful. But then again, other opportunities to make a contribution in a quieter, more personal way continue to present themselves. In many ways the new doors that have opened are more appropriate for my stage of life.

It is yet to become clear what will motivate me, how I can make an impact and continue to improve the lives of others, while at the same time pursuing personal growth. I have re-engaged with some of the causes I cared about—and new ones, like addressing the issues with the criminal justice system. It has been gratifying to see how ISB and PHFI have prospered in this past decade, and I have gotten involved in an informal capacity with both of these institutions I helped found. I am also very excited about working with WHEELS and WIN, two not-for-profits that are committed to solving major societal problems through technological innovation. Our initial focus has been on maternal and child health, clean potable water, and sanitation. In the US, I aspire to make a contribution to criminal justice reform, specifically focusing on reducing recidivism and making prisoners productive members of society after they complete their terms.

At the same time, I want to try something completely different, to focus inwardly. Perhaps a greater emphasis on the spiritual dimension will offer avenues for personal growth? I am at peace with my past, and the question on my mind is: How should I complete this life with tranquility and with grace?

Notes

1. Solitary

1 "Occupy Wall Street Protestors Cheer Rajat Gupta's Arrest," NDTV, November 30, 2011, https://www.youtube.com/watch?v=1V29X_5oEtg, accessed January 2019.

2 Special Rapporteur on Torture Tells Third Committee Use of Prolonged Solitary Confinement on Rise, Calls for Global Ban on Practice, Sixty-sixth General Assembly, 18 October 2011, https://www.un.org/press/en/2011/gashc4014.doc.htm, accessed January 2019.

3. Reluctant Resignation

1 Susan Pulliam, "Goldman Director in Probe," *Wall Street Journal,* April 13, 2010, https://www.wsj.com/articles/SB10001424052702303348504575184261856306400, accessed January 2019.

2 Tara Trask and Linda Petersen, "Jurors' Perceptions in the Economic Decline," *The Jury Expert,* July 1, 2009, http://www.thejuryexpert.com/2009/07/jurors-perceptions-in-the-economic-decline/, accessed January 2019.

4. Elephant

1. Peter Lattman, "In Galleon Case, Spotlight on Rajat Gupta," *The New York Times Dealbook,* April 24, 2011, https://dealbook.nytimes.com/2011/04/24/in-galleon-case-spotlight-on-rajat-gupta/, accessed January 2019.
2. United States v. Rajaratnam, 09 Cr. 1184 (RJH), Memorandum and Order, August 16, 2011, http://www.law.du.edu/documents/corporate-governance/criminal/rajaratnam/Memorandum-and-Order-US-v-Rajaratnam-S1-09-CR-1184-SD-NY-August-16-2011.pdf, accessed January 2019.
3. Andrew Ross Sorkin, "Curious Accusations in SEC's Insider Case," *The New York Times Dealbook,* March 7, 2011, https://dealbook.nytimes.com/2011/03/07/curious-accusations-in-s-e-c-s-insider-case/, accessed January 2019.
4. Robert Kolker, "The Next Best Crooks," *New York Magazine,* April 10, 2011, http://nymag.com/news/business/wallstreet/preet-bharara-2011-4/, accessed January 2019.
5. Jesse Eisinger, *The Chickenshit Club: Why the Justice Department Fails to Prosecute Executives* (New York: Simon & Schuster, 2017), xiv.
6. "U.S. v. Raj Rajaratnam, et al.; U.S. v. Danielle Chiesi, et al. Hedge Fund Insider Trading Takedown," Prepared Remarks for US Attorney Preet Bharara, October 16, 2009, https://www.justice.gov/archive/usao/nys/pressreleases/October09/hedgefund/hedgefundinsidertradingremarks101609.pdf, accessed January 2019.
7. Jeffrey Toobin, "The Showman: How U.S. Attorney Preet Bharara Struck Fear into Wall Street and Albany," *New Yorker,* May 9, 2015, https://www.newyorker.com/magazine/2016/05/09/the-man-who-terrifies-wall-street, accessed January 2019.
8. United States of America v. Sheldon Silver, 15-CR-93 (VEC), Memorandum, Opinion & Order, April 10, 2015, https://

s3.amazonaws.com/pacer-documents/S.D.N.Y.%2015-cr-00093%20dckt%20000031_000%20filed%202015-04-10.pdf, accessed January 2019.

9 Richard Bradley, "The Power of Attorney," *Worth* magazine, October 1, 2014, http://www.worth.com/the-power-of-attorney/, accessed January 2019.

10 United States v. Rajaratnam, Memorandum and Order, 8 April 20, 20119 9:35, https://www.scribd.com/document/53801060/Closing-arguments-U-S-v-Raj-Rajaratnam

5. Guilty Until Proven Innocent

1 Peter J. Henning, "The S.E.C. Under Fire," *The New York Times Dealbook,* March 11, 2011, https://dealbook.nytimes.com/2011/03/11/the-s-e-c-under-fire/, accessed January 2019.

2 *Rajat K. Gupta* v. *Securities and Exchange Commission*, 11 Civ. 1900, Complaint for Declaratory and Injunctive Relief and Demand for Jury Trial.

3 Ibid., Opinion and Order, July 11, 2011

6. A Dark Diwali

1 '*Antyeshti* or Funeral Ceremony' from the *Manual of Brahmo Rituals and Devotions* by Sitanath Tattwabhushan, published at https://www.thebrahmosamaj.net/liturgy/funeral.html, accessed January 2019.

2 Robert Frost, *The Road Not Taken and Other Poems* (Penguin Classics, 2015).

8. The Firm

1 Rabindranath Tagore, *Gitanjali* (New York: Dover Publications, Inc., 2000), 25.

2 N.R. Kleinfeld, "When a Business Is Beheaded," *New York Times*, June 20, 1982, p. 003001.

9. Chicago

1 John A. Byrne, "The McKinsey Mystique," *BusinessWeek*, September 20, 1993.

10. Unity in Diversity

1 Ronald E. Yates, "The Firm Myths Not So Firm," *Chicago Tribune*, July 10, 1994.

13. Testimony

1 Press release: "Manhattan U.S. Attorney and FBI Assistant Director-In-Charge Announce Insider Trading Charges Against Former Corporate Chairman and Director Rajat K. Gupta," Wednesday, October 26, 2011, https://www.justice.gov/archive/usao/nys/pressreleases/October11/guptarajatindictmentpr.pdf, accessed January 2019.

2 Ben E. White, "Buffett Deal at Goldman Seen as a Sign of Confidence," *New York Times*, September 23, 2008, A1.

3 Richard Beales, "Has Warren Buffett Found a New 'Moat'?" *International Herald Tribune*, September 24, 2008.

4 Suzanne Craig, "Goldman to Cut 10% of Jobs as Downsizing Wave Grows," *Wall Street Journal*, October 23, 2008.

14. A Cropped Portrait

1 *Dirks* v. *S.E.C.*, 463 U.S. 646 (1983).

2 Kevin Roose, "Why the Rajat Gupta Trial Is a Big Deal," *New York* magazine, June 4, 2012.

15. Unsung

1 Eknath Easwaran (Trans.), *The Bhagavad Gita* (Nilgiri Press, 2007) 2:7, 89.

17. The Anarchy of Destiny

1 Suketu Mehta, "Exclusive: Raj Rajaratnam Reveals Why He Didn't Take a Plea," *Newsweek*, October 23, 2011, http://www.newsweek.com/exclusive-raj-rajaratnam-reveals-why-he-didnt-take-plea-68203, accessed January 2019.
2 *United States* v. *Newman*, 773 F.3d 438 (2d Cir. 2014).
3 Peter Wagner and Wendy Sawyer, "Mass Incarceration: The Whole Pie 2018," The Prison Policy Initiative press release, March 14, 2018, https://www.prisonpolicy.org/reports/pie2018.html, accessed January 2019.

18. The Gita and the SHU

1 Swami Gambhirananda (Trans.), *The Bhagavad Gita* (Advaita Ashrama, 2018), 2:20.
2 Ibid., 2:47.
3 Ibid., 5:3.
4 Ibid., 2:56.
5 Ibid., 2:58.
6 Ibid., 2:38.
7 Ibid., 7:8–11.

Epilogue

1 Walter Pavlo, "Can White Collar Defendants Get a Fair Trial?," *Forbes*, December 19, 2012, https://www.forbes.com/sites/walterpavlo/2012/12/19/can-white-collar-defendants-get-a-fair-trial/#5580214d590a, accessed January 2019.

Acknowledgments

If there is one thing I learned during the most difficult episode of my life, it is how much I value and appreciate my family, my friends, and my colleagues. The people who supported me through the events described in this book are too many to list here, but my deepest gratitude goes out to everyone who stood by me, reached out, wrote letters to the judge, testified at or attended my trial, visited me in jail, and welcomed me with open arms since my release.

When it came to telling my story, there are a few people in particular to whom I am indebted:

Ellen Daly—without whom this book would never have been completed. She was by my side throughout the process—patient, encouraging, disciplined, and creative, with an uncanny ability to be true to my voice. She would think nothing of traveling to our home, seamlessly integrating herself into the routine of the household but ensuring that I worked hard to fully engage in writing about the difficult parts of my story. She was always empathetic but true to the facts, always flexible but firm on the deadlines. She made it easy for me to open up to her, make myself vulnerable, and be able to put my real feelings in the book. She was always on the side of simple, honest, and authentic. I am truly grateful for all her help and support and in the process am privileged to have gained a true friend. I also want to thank all my friends and colleagues who reviewed the manuscript and made comments and suggestions.

Chiki Sarkar—without whom this book would never have been started. Chiki has been much more than my publisher, firmly planting the idea of the book in my mind and relentlessly pushing me to complete. She visited me in prison, followed up immediately on my release, and enabled me in every way possible. Her dedication to publishing on an accelerated timeline, ensuring an outstanding launch, while cheerfully having her second baby is truly inspiring. I am grateful for my long association with her family and the emotional connection with her that made this project a lot more personal and fun. I'd also like to extend my thanks to the amazing team at Juggernaut, Jaishree, Disha, Natasha, and Simran.

James Levine—without whom the book would not have seen the light of day in the West. Jim has been a true believer in me and this project. Despite many initial roadblocks, he crafted an innovative publishing strategy and put together an outstanding team to execute an effective launch, including my US publisher Arthur Klebanoff at Rosetta Books, my US publicist Lisa Linden, and legal reviewer Melissa Georges. Without Jim's unwavering support and exploring of every avenue open to us, this would never have happened. In the process I have come to admire his values and commitment to his clients, which goes well beyond the expected.

Appendix

Timeline of Key Events in Rajat Gupta's Life

Dec 2, 1948	Born, Kolkata, India
Fall 1954	Moved to Delhi
Nov 4, 1964	Father's death (on Diwali day)
Summer 1965	Mother diagnosed with terminal illness, aortic stenosis
Summer 1966	Graduates Modern School
Fall 1966	Begins engineering program at IIT Delhi
Feb 10, 1968	Mother's death
Fall 1968	Meets Anita Mattoo at IIT
Spring 1971	Offered job at India Tobacco Company, place at Harvard Business School
Summer 1971	Graduates IIT
Fall 1971	Moves to US, starts MBA at Harvard Business School

Spring 1973	McKinsey job offer, New York office
Summer 1973	Graduates Harvard
	Marries Anita
Fall 1973	Moves to New York, Anita starts at Columbia
Fall 1978	Daughter Geetanjali born
Summer 1981	Moves to Scandinavia
Summer 1982	Daughter Megha born
Spring 1983	Made head of McKinsey Scandinavia
Summer 1984	Elected senior partner
Summer 1985	Daughter Aditi born
Dec 1986	Elected to McKinsey board
	Moves back to US, settles in Chicago
Fall 1987	Nominated for McKinsey managing director
Spring 1989	Appointed Chicago office manager
Spring 1990	Daughter Deepali born
March 1994	Elected McKinsey managing director
Summer 1995	Indian School of Business project initiated
Spring 1997	Re-elected as McKinsey managing director
Summer 1999	Moves back to East Coast
Fall 1999	First encounter with Raj Rajaratnam as donor to ISB
Spring 2000	Re-elected as McKinsey managing director
Spring 2001	Formation of American India Foundation with Bill Clinton following Gujarat earthquake

July 2001	ISB opens
Fall 2002	Founding member, Global Fund to Fight AIDS, Tuberculosis and Malaria
Summer 2003	Finishes final term as McKinsey managing director
Fall 2005	Voyager Capital Partners founded. Gupta takes a 10% passive stake, with Rajaratnam taking 80% and Ravi Trehan 10% active stakes
Nov 2006	Announces intention to retire from McKinsey one year later
Nov 2006	Joins Goldman Sachs board of directors
Early 2007	Doubles investment in Voyager, unaware at the time that Rajaratnam has withdrawn a large sum of money from the fund
Mar 12, 2007	Participates in Goldman Sachs board conference call about first-quarter earnings from the NSR offices that were located in the Galleon building *In Count 2 of the charges against Gupta, the government alleged that Galleon traded on information related to Goldman earnings before they were made public. Gupta was found not guilty on this count.*
2007	Joins Procter & Gamble board of directors
Dec 2007	Retires from McKinsey
April 2008	Learns from Ravi Trehan that Rajaratnam has withdrawn \$23 million from Voyager, plus \$25 million in unagreed fees
May 2008	Participates in P&G board meeting during which the sale of coffee brand Folgers to the J.M. Smucker's Co. is discussed

June 3, 2008	Galleon Trader Michael Cardillo buys 17,800 shares of the J.M. Smucker's Co. *Gupta was not charged in relation to this incident, but it was mentioned in the indictment and given considerable attention at his trial. There was no record of a call from Gupta to Rajaratnam, only a call from an unassigned line at McKinsey to Rajaratnam's assistant. Call records show that Gupta was on another call at the time, on his private line.*
July 29, 2008	Wiretapped telephone call between Gupta and Rajaratnam in which Gupta mentions a discussion at a recent Goldman board meeting about the possibility of Goldman buying a commercial bank. Rajaratnam makes reference to his arrangement with McKinsey partner Anil Kumar. *Gupta was not charged in relation to this call, but the way it was made public was devastating to his reputation and his relationship with McKinsey. At trial, he never had the opportunity to explain the context for the call or to clarify that he did not know about or condone Rajaratnam's arrangement with Kumar.*
Summer 2008	Final closing of NSR fund
Sept 9, 2008	Resigns from the Goldman board with the intention of taking an advisory role at KKR
Sept 15, 2008	Lehman Bros bankruptcy announced. Gupta agrees to stay on the Goldman board to avoid destabilizing the bank's image
Sept 23, 2008	Participates in Goldman Sachs board conference call concerning Berkshire Hathaway's $5 billion investment

Following the board call, Gupta places a call to Rajaratnam about Voyager

Rajaratnam orders two of his Galleon traders to purchase a combined 350,000 Goldman shares

In Counts 3 and 4 of the charges against Gupta, the government alleged that he tipped Rajaratnam about the Buffett deal and Galleon profited. At trial, Gupta was not able to explain that his call to Rajaratnam was in pursuit of money that Rajaratnam owed to Gupta, and had nothing to do with the Buffett deal. Furthermore, the key witness he was planning to call to corroborate the actual reason for the call inexplicably backed out and refused to testify at the last minute.

Sept 24, 2008 Wiretapped phone call between Rajaratnam and Ian Horowitz, a Galleon trader, in which Rajaratnam claims to have heard from an unnamed source that "Something good might happen to Goldman."

Mid-Oct 2008 Learns that the Voyager fund has gone to zero and his $10 million investment is lost

Oct 23, 2008 The *Wall Street Journal* publishes an article based on leaked information claiming that Goldman is about to lay off 10 percent of its workforce

Participates in Goldman Sachs board conference call concerning the impending layoffs

Immediately after the board meeting, calls Rajaratnam about Voyager

In Count 5 of the charges against Gupta, the government alleged that he tipped Rajaratnam about Goldman's impending losses and as a result, Galleon avoided a loss

	of several million dollars. At trial, Gupta was not able to explain that, again, the actual reason for his call was related to the money he had lost in the Voyager fund. Earnings were not discussed at the board meeting.
Oct 24, 2008	Wiretapped conversation between Rajaratnam and a Galleon employee in which he claims to have heard from someone at Goldman that they were going to lose $2 per share (a figure that turned out to be incorrect)
Jan 29, 2009	Participates in P&G audit committee call discussing the company's earnings, to be released the next day
	Returns a call from Rajaratnam a few hours later
	In Count 6 of the charges against Gupta, the government alleged that Gupta tipped Rajaratnam about P&G earnings and as a result, Rajaratnam directed some Galleon funds to sell short approximately 180,000 shares of P&G common stock. Gupta was found not guilty on this count.
Oct 15, 2009	Rajaratnam, Kumar arrested and charged with securities fraud
Dec 2009	Gupta informed by Goldman's internal counsel that his name has come up in relation to the Rajaratnam case
Jan 2010	Kumar pleads guilty
Feb 9, 2010	Superseding indictment filed against Rajaratnam
Apr 13, 2010	The *Wall Street Journal* reports that prosecutors are investigating Gupta in relation to the Rajaratnam case

May 7, 2010	Gupta does not stand for re-election to the Goldman Sachs board
Nov 2010	Receives Wells Notice from SEC (notification of intent to charge)
Jan 2011	Danielle Chiesi pleads guilty
Jan 20, 2011	Second superseding indictment filed against Rajaratnam
Feb 25, 2011	Submits Wells Notice response to SEC
Mar 1, 2011	SEC files civil administrative proceeding against Gupta
	Resigns from remaining corporate and nonprofit board seats
Mar 2011	Rajaratnam trial begins
	Wiretapped call between Rajaratnam and Gupta of July 29, 2008 played in courtroom
April 2011	Gupta countersues SEC, claiming he was denied his constitutional right to a jury trial
May 11, 2011	Rajaratnam found guilty on 9 counts of securities fraud and 5 counts of conspiracy
	Judge Rakoff allows suit to proceed
Aug 5, 2011	SEC drops its civil administrative proceeding against Gupta, Gupta drops suit
Oct 13, 2011	Rajaratnam sentenced to 11 years in prison
Oct 26, 2011	Gupta indicted on five counts of securities fraud and one count of conspiracy to commit securities fraud, surrenders to FBI

	SEC brings new civil insider-trading suit against Gupta
May 22, 2012	*United States* v. *Gupta* trial begins
June 1, 2012	Anil Kumar testifies for the prosecution
June 4, 2012	Lloyd Blankfein testifies for the prosecution
June 8, 2012	Government rests its case
	Gupta makes the decision not to testify in his own defense
June 11, 2012	Geetanjali Gupta testifies for the defense
June 12, 2012	Defense rests its case
June 15, 2012	Convicted on three counts of securities fraud and one count of conspiracy. Acquitted of two counts of securities fraud
Oct 24, 2012	Sentenced by US District Judge Jed Rakoff to two years in federal prison. The judge also orders Gupta to pay a $5 million fine and $7 million in restitution. He is also fined $14 million by SEC.
Oct 2012	Gupta wins bail pending appeal from the appeals court
May 2013	Gupta's appeal heard by Federal Appeals Court
Mar 25, 2014	Gupta's appeal rejected by Federal Appeals Court on the grounds that there had been no irregularity in the way the trial was conducted
Jun 17, 2014	Gupta surrenders to FMC Devens correctional facility, Massachusetts
Dec 10, 2014	*United States* v. *Newman* overturns the convictions of two alleged insider traders, and in the process

	establishes a new standard for what could be considered "benefit" to a tipper. Since no tangible benefit was ever shown in Gupta's case nor any quid pro quo established, this is significant.
April 20, 2015	Supreme Court declines to hear Gupta's case
May 2015	Gupta files new appeal on the basis of *United States* v. *Newman*, arguing that under the standard of benefit defined by Newman, the judge in his trial improperly instructed the jury that benefit did not have to be tangible
July 2015	Judge Rakoff rejects Gupta's claim that his case is appealable based on the *Newman* ruling, ruling that his conviction still stands
Aug 25, 2015	Gupta files new appeal against Rakoff's ruling
Jan 5, 2016	Gupta released from jail
Feb 2016	Second Circuit Appeals Court agrees to hear Gupta's appeal on the basis of *Newman*
Nov 2016	Appeal heard in appellate court
Jan 2019	Appeal denied

Index

A Note on the Author

Rajat Kumar Gupta was the leader of McKinsey & Company, Inc., from 1994 to 2003. He was also a board member of major corporations including Goldman Sachs, Procter & Gamble, and American Airlines and advisor to the United Nations, the Rockefeller Foundation, and the World Economic Forum. He served as chairman of the Bill & Melinda Gates Foundation advisory board, the Global Fund to Fight AIDS, Tuberculosis and Malaria, and the International Chamber of Commerce, and was the founding chairman of the Indian School of Business, the American India Foundation, and the Public Health Foundation of India.

Born in Kolkata, West Bengal, in 1948, Gupta attended the prestigious Indian Institute of Technology Delhi and traveled to the United States to attend Harvard Business School in 1971. After graduating from Harvard, he joined McKinsey, where he would spend his entire thirty-seven-year consulting career, including his nine-year term as the firm's leader.

In 2011, Gupta was charged with insider trading and found guilty. He was sentenced to two years' imprisonment, which he served at FMC Devens in Massachusetts. Since his release in January 2016, Gupta has resumed his work in health and education, and added a new focus on criminal justice and prison reform. He lives in Connecticut with his wife, Anita, and is the proud father of four daughters and grandfather to four granddaughters.

AN EXTENSIVE LIBRARY

Including fresh, new, original Juggernaut books from the likes of Sunny Leone, Praveen Swami, Husain Haqqani, Umera Ahmed, Rujuta Diwekar and lots more. Plus, books from partner publishers and loads of free classics. Whichever genre you like, there's a book waiting for you.

juggernaut.in

DON'T JUST READ; INTERACT

We're changing the reading experience from passive to active.

juggernaut.in

Ask authors questions

Get all your answers from the horse's mouth. Juggernaut authors actually reply to every question they can.

Rate and review

Let everyone know of your favourite reads or critique the finer points of a book – you will be heard in a community of like-minded readers.

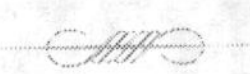

Gift books to friends

For a book-lover, there's no nicer gift than a book personally picked. You can even do it anonymously if you like.

Enjoy new book formats

Discover serials released in parts over time, picture books including comics, and story-bundles at discounted rates. And coming soon, audiobooks.

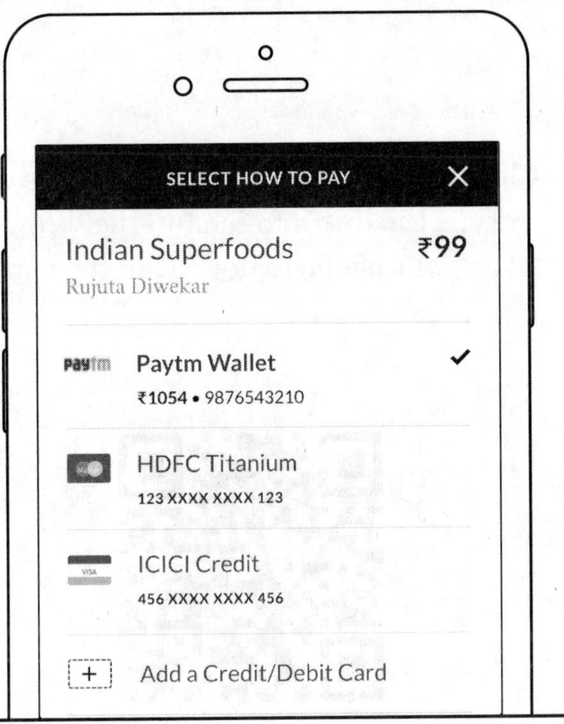

Paytm Wallet, Cards & Apple Payments

On Android, just add a Paytm Wallet once and buy any book with one tap. On iOS, pay with one tap with your iTunes-linked debit/credit card.

Click the QR Code with a QR scanner app
or type the link into the Internet browser
on your phone to download the app.

For our complete catalogue, visit www.juggernaut.in
To submit your book, send a synopsis and two
sample chapters to books@juggernaut.in
For all other queries, write to contact@juggernaut.in